SHANTIDEVA'S ENTERING THE CONDUCT OF A BODHISATVA

WITH AN INTERSPERSED COMMENTARY CALLED "A LAMP FOR THE MIDDLE WAY" BY DRUKCHEN PADMA KARPO

BY TONY DUFF
PADMA KARPO TRANSLATION COMMITTEE

Copyright © 2021 Tony Duff. All rights reserved. No portion of this book may be reproduced in any form or by any means, electronic or mechanical, including photography, recording, or by any information storage or retrieval system or technologies now known or later developed, without permission in writing from the publisher.

First edition, November 8th 2008
Second edition, October 11th 2021
ISBN paper book: 978-1-7923-7440-1
ISBN e-book: 978-9937-572-66-8

Garamond typeface with diacritical marks designed and created by Tony Duff

Produced, Printed, and Published by
Padma Karpo Translation Committee
Kathmandu
NEPAL

Committee members for this book: translation and composition, Lama Tony Duff; editorial Jason Watkins, cover design, Christopher Duff, editorial Robert G. Walker.

Web-site and e-mail contact through:
http://www.pktc.org/pktc
https://www.pktcshop.com
or search Padma Karpo Translation Committee on the web.

CONTENTS

INTRODUCTION v

PART ONE: ŚHĀNTIDEVA'S ENTERING THE CONDUCT OF A
    BODHISATVA 1
    Chapter 1: The Benefits of Enlightenment Mind 3
    Chapter 2: Laying Aside Evil Deeds 9
    Chapter 3: Fully Adopting the Enlightenment Mind 17
    Chapter 4: Heedfulness 21
    Chapter 5: Guarding Alertness 27
    Chapter 6: Patience 41
    Chapter 7: Perseverance 59
    Chapter 8: Meditative Concentration 69
    Chapter 9: Prajñā 91
    Chapter 10: Dedication 117

❀ ❀ ❀

PART TWO: ENTERING THE CONDUCT OF A BODHISATVA
    WITH AN INTERSPERSED COMMENTARY CALLED "A
    LAMP FOR THE PATH OF THE MIDDLE WAY" BY
    DRUKCHEN PADMA KARPO 125
    Preface: 127
    Chapter 1: The Benefits of Enlightenment Mind 131

Chapter 2: Laying Aside Evil Deeds 157
Chapter 3: Fully Adopting the Enlightenment Mind 177
Chapter 4: Heedfulness 191
Chapter 5: Guarding Alertness 203
Chapter 6: Patience 231
Chapter 7: Perseverance 263
Chapter 8: Meditative Concentration 281
Chapter 9: Prajñā 317
Chapter 10: Dedication 381

❋ ❋ ❋

GLOSSARY OF TERMS 391
INDEX 407

INTRODUCTION

This book is in two parts. The first part is the complete text of *Entering the Conduct of a Bodhisatva*, a very famous text composed by the Indian Buddhist master Shāntideva [8th century CE]. The second part is an excellent Tibetan commentary to Shāntideva's text entitled *Entering the Conduct of a Bodhisatva with an Interspersed Commentary Called "A Lamp for the Path of the Middle Way"*, composed by the Tibetan Buddhist master Padma Karpo [1527–1592 CE].

The first section of this book provides a plain English translation of Shāntideva's text without footnotes or other additions that would tend to obscure it, a version which is especially useful for reading and recitation. The second section of the book provides a version of the text with commentary included, a version which is necessary for studying the meaning of the text. Thus the book is a rich resource that provides both for those wanting simply to read and recite Shāntideva's text as well as for those wanting to study its meaning.

Entering the Conduct of a Bodhisatva by Shantideva

The *bodhisatvacharyāvatāra* in Sanskrit or *Entering the Conduct of a Bodhisatva* in English is a text that details the conduct to be followed by a person who wishes to attain true complete enlightenment. It was written by the very learned and highly accomplished Indian master Shāntideva during his stay at the famous Buddhist university of India called Nālandā. When he first recited the text to the masters and students of the university they were amazed by its beautiful composition and expert treatment of the topic. Since then it has only increased in fame and is now regarded as one of the essential texts to be studied by anyone who wishes to follow the path to unsurpassed, true complete enlightenment[1].

The title is sometimes shortened. For example, sometimes it is shortened to *Bodhicharyāvatāra* or *Entering Enlightenment Conduct*[2]. "Enlightenment conduct" is the standard term used in these teachings of the path to complete enlightenment to refer to the *conduct* that will be followed by a person wanting to attain the unsurpassed true complete *enlightenment*.

The title is also frequently abbreviated to *Charyāvatāra* or *Entering the Conduct*. "Conduct" in this case is understood to mean the "enlightenment conduct" described in the previous paragraph. For example, this abbreviation is seen in the title of Padma Karpo's commentary text, *Entering the Conduct with an Interspersed Commentary Called "A Lamp for the Path of the Middle Way"*.

Shāntideva's text, originally written in four-lined verse, is comprised of approximately one thousand verses divided into ten chapters. Briefly, the ten chapters are as follows.

---

[1] This is the correct terminology. It is explained further on in the introduction. This and many other details of buddhahood are fully explained in *Unending Auspiciousness, the Sutra of the Recollection of the Noble Three Jewels* published by Padma Karpo Translation Committee, 2010, authored by Tony Duff, ISBN: 978-9937-8386-1-0.

[2] The importance of the term "enlightenment conduct" cannot be overstated. A full explanation of it can be found in PKTC's publication *Samantabhadra's Prayer and Commentaries* by Tony Duff, ISBN 978-9937-572-60-6, a large treatise on Samantabhadra's Prayer which also provides explanations of the bodhisatva's conduct and is a good companion to Shāntideva's text.

The path to unsurpassed true complete enlightenment starts with understanding the great value of the enlightenment type of mind[3]. Accordingly, Śhāntideva started his text with a chapter on the benefits of that mind.

Having understood its great value, one decides to arouse that enlightenment mind and undertake the journey to complete enlightenment. Accordingly, Śhāntideva continued with a chapter on the preparations needed in order to fully commit oneself to developing that mind.

Next, one actually commits to that journey by taking the vows connected with developing the enlightenment mind. Thus the next chapter contains a complete rite for taking the vows.

Once the vows have been taken, one has to keep them well, so the next chapter contains advice on being heedful of one's conduct. That is followed by a chapter on how to stay alert, which is the essence of how to guard against corrupting the vows.

Next, one begins the actual training in the conduct of bodhisatva, a person who has accepted the vows of enlightenment mind. The training consists of perfecting what are known as the six paramitas or six types of transcendent activity. "Paramita" is a Sanskrit term that is sometimes translated as "perfection" but the literal meaning is "gone to the other shore", which refers to activities that, having crossed over samsaric styles of behaviour, are consistent with enlightenment.

The six paramitas are generosity, discipline, patience, perseverance, meditative concentration, and prajñā. The essence of the first two paramitas of generosity and discipline is covered in the first five chapters of the text, so Śhāntideva did not write separate chapters for them. The

---

[3] Bodhichitta correctly translated into is English is "enlightenment mind" or "enlightenment type of mind", which is explained at length later in this introduction.

text continues with chapters on each of the four remaining paramitas, chapters five through nine.

In the path to enlightenment, dedication of merit always concludes any main practice, so Śhāntideva adds a final, tenth chapter filled with dedications.

In sum, in the approach to enlightenment set out by Śhāntideva in those ten chapters, there is a preparatory phase of taking the vows of a bodhisatva, the first through fifth chapters. The preparatory phase is followed by the main practice, the practice of the six paramitas found in the sixth through ninth chapters. And the main practice is followed by a concluding phase in which appropriate dedications and prayers of aspiration are made in the tenth chapter. Those three phases are known in Buddhist scripture as the goodness of the beginning, middle, and end. They are the framework around which Śhāntideva has composed his text and consequently are the primary headings in Padma Karpo's commentary to the text.

The Commentary Called "A Lamp for the Path of the Middle Way" by Padma Karpo

Śhāntideva's text is both beautiful and expert in its treatment of the path of the bodhisatva, the heroic type of person who travels the path to unsurpassed true complete enlightenment. However, as he himself says, it was not intended to be an extensive presentation of the path to complete enlightenment, but a set of notes made for his own use that summarize teachings found in Buddhist scripture.

Śhāntideva wrote the text in summary form, so it is terse in places, especially in the ninth chapter, and sometimes so terse as to be incomprehensible. Assistance is required to understand what he wrote, therefore a number of commentaries to the text were written by Indian and Tibetan masters to provide that assistance. He also wrote the text in accordance with Buddhist scripture, but for the most part does not mention which scripture he is referencing. Commentaries such as the one by Padma Karpo are useful in that they name and even quote the scripture referenced by Śhāntideva.

There are many types of commentary in the Buddhist tradition. For example, there are "complete commentaries" that provide extensive information about a text, "annotated commentaries" that quote the original text and then clarify it by adding footnotes, "word by word commentaries" that take every single word of the original and explain it, and so on. Padma Karpo's commentary to Śhāntideva's text is what is called an "interspersed commentary". Such a commentary starts with the complete, original text and then has new text inserted into the original anywhere that some explanation is needed. The result is an amplified version of the original text which is easier to read and understand than the original.

The Ninth Chapter of Shantideva's Text

The ninth chapter of Śhāntideva's text, which is the chapter on the sixth paramita, Prajñāparamita, is regarded by learned Buddhists of the Tibetan tradition, among others, to be very special. Therefore the ninth chapter is specifically mentioned here as being a particularly important part of the book.

Prajñā is a most important topic in the bodhisatva teachings. As Padma Karpo makes clear in part of his commentary to the ninth chapter, Prajñāparamita is the basis for the other paramitas to become paramitas and at the same time is the culmination of the first five paramitas.

The Sanskrit term "prajñā" literally means a *better* type of *knowing*. There are several types of this "better knowing", but all of them have the shared characteristic of being a type of mind that sees correctly. One way to categorize prajñā is to point out that there are worldly and transcendent types of prajñā. Worldly prajñā can be as simple as a mind that correctly knows which dish detergent of the many dish detergents on the shelf at the grocery store is the one that will suit your needs. Transcendent prajñā can refer to the various types of prajñā both dualistic and non-dualistic that are needed as part of a spiritual journey or can refer only to prajñā that is directly seeing reality as it is.

Śhāntideva's explanations of prajñā throughout his text are only concerned with transcendent prajñā. In the ninth chapter, the reader is led into the cultivation of both dualistic and non-dualistic prajñās. The first is used to reach a correct understanding of view, which then leads to the second, the development of prajñā that is directly seeing reality as it is. These are large topics that require considerable explanation, so it is no surprise that the ninth chapter is by far the longest chapter in the text. It is also the most difficult to understand.

It was mentioned earlier that Śhāntideva's text is terse in places. This is especially true in chapter nine. There are places in it where the text when literally translated into English would be incomprehensible to most readers. Therefore, having a commentary is particularly important to being able to understand chapter nine.

Most of chapter nine is presented as a dialogue between Śhāntideva, who upholds the view of the Madhyamaka or Middle Way, and other non-Buddhist and Buddhist schools of philosophy. In ancient India there were six main Hindu schools and four main Buddhist schools of philosophy. Two of the six Hindu schools and all four of the Buddhist schools of philosophy are included in the dialogues of chapter nine. However, Śhāntideva did not provide a thorough tutorial on these various views in chapter nine, leaving Westerners and others who do not know the details of these views in a difficult position. Padma Karpo's commentary is helpful to the point of being essential to being able to understand the dialogues between Śhāntideva, representing the Madhyamaka or Middle Way Buddhist school, and the various other schools.

Even with Padma Karpo's commentary, I am sure that some people will feel bewildered as they read the dialogues of chapter nine. Nonetheless, by carefully considering the words of the text and commentary, a better understanding of the Middle Way Buddhist view can and does emerge. That appearance of that better understanding corresponds exactly to the emergence of a dualistic type of prajñā, which is one of the two intended functions of chapter nine. It might happen that, as you figuratively bang your head against the wall, trying to understand what the dialogues are about, you suddenly notice that a little prajñā has indeed emerged. At that point, the struggles of trying to understand the dialogues of the ninth chapter have had the desired effect and you could and should rejoice at that. The second intended function of chapter nine is, of course, that the dualistic prajñā that you develop through studying chapter nine will lead you to the non-dualistic prajñā that sees reality as it is, releasing you from samsaric existence.

How to Use the Two Main Texts for Study and Recitation Practice

How to use "Entering the Conduct of a Bodhisatva" by Shantideva

Śhāntideva's text was composed using one of the standard poetic forms of the Sanskrit language called "gatha". It consists of four line verses grouped into two, two-line couplets. Moreover, each of the four lines has a fixed number of syllables. The content of a verse can then be constructed in several ways, for example, you could have four sentences, one to each line; or you could have two sentences, one to each couplet; or you could have one sentence filling the entire verse; or you could have two clauses, each one occupying a couplet; and so on. Other combinations also are possible.

The gatha form gives articulate authors enormous freedom to make elegant compositions. Although English-speaking people might refer to compositions made with this form as poetic verse, such compositions are, in fact, more like English prose. Therefore, and as with some other translators, we chose to present Śhāntideva's text as prose, not as four-line verses.

Neither the Sanskrit original nor the Tibetan translation of Śhāntideva's text have verse numbering in them. The addition of verse numbering in English translations up till now seems to have been done to satisfy the desires of academics. Moreover, there are Sanskrit and Tibetan editions of Śhāntideva's text in which lines and sometimes whole verses have been added or omitted, causing the verse numbering of the respective English translations to be incompatible, which becomes a source of confusion. Therefore, seeing no need to perpetuate this artifice, we did not provide it.

The value of rendering Śhāntideva's text as prose was noticed in group recitations of the prose text with myself and others. We found that reading aloud the entire text as a teaching session in itself or a portion of it as the preparation for a teaching session worked very well. In the latter case, we found that reading the first four or five chapters of the text and chapter three in particular was an effective substitute for doing the liturgies of taking refuge, arousing enlightenment mind, and so on usually done prior to a teaching session. We have envisaged all-morning or afternoon sessions where the entirety of Śhāntideva's text is recited aloud, as has been done in recent years in the first three months of three year retreats for Westerners. It is arduous to read Śhāntideva's text from morning till night every day for months at a time, but it is very effective for training the intellect in the thoughts and ways of a bodhisatva.

Thus, the style of presentation of Śhāntideva's text in this book as prose rather than poetry not only works for study purposes, but works equally well for recitation practise. I have the sincere and strong wish that others will use our presentation of Śhāntideva's text as a resource for reading, reciting, and studying.

How to Use "A Lamp for the Path of the Middle Way" by Padma Karpo

As explained earlier, Padma Karpo's commentary does not attempt to keep Śhāntideva's text in its gatha-style verse form, but writes it out as prose, then intersperses it with commentary.

Padma Karpo's commentary has the words of Śhāntideva's text marked off so that his words and the words of the commentary can be readily distinguished from one another. The Tibetan technique for marking off text is not applicable to English text, so we used a different method. In the e-book version, we bolded Śhāntideva's text and changed its colour to a deep blue while leaving the commentary's wording in black and un-bolded. In the paper version, we simply bolded Śhāntideva's text, leaving the commentary's wording plain and in black.

For study purposes, it is best to read Padma Karpo's *Lamp for the Middle Way*, a text which presents Śhāntideva's text with commentary interspersed, and study the meaning. For recitation purposes, it is best to recite Śhāntideva's text itself aloud without use of the commentary. In order to facilitate this, we have put the complete plain text of *Entering the Conduct* as the first part of this book and the complete text of *Lamp for the Middle Way* as the second part of this book. Thus, use part one for reading and recitation and part two for study.

Note that Śhāntideva's text as it appears in the first part is not a separate translation from what appears in the second part. First, the entirety of Padma Karpo's text with Śhāntideva's text included was translated and placed as part two of this book. Then Śhāntideva's text was extracted from that and placed as part one of the book. Thus part one of this book presents Śhāntideva's text with nothing added or removed.

About the Authors

Shantideva

The story of Śhāntideva has been told many times and is available in many languages. Andreas Kretschmar gives an excellent exposition of Śhāntideva's life in the first volume of his translations of Khenpo Kunpal's commentary on Śhāntideva's text.[4]

---

[4] Andreas Kretchmar's work contains translations of Śhāntideva's text and
(continued ...)

All-knowing Drukchen Padma Karpo

Padma Karpo was the fourth of the Drukchens, or heads of the Drukpa Kagyu school of Tibetan Buddhism. The Drukchens in general are regarded as the emanations of Tsangpa Gyare, the founder of the Drukpa Kagyu school and one of the great disciples of Phagmo Drupa, who was in turn one of the great disciples of Lord Gampopa of the Kagyu school.

As with all of the Drukchens, Padma Karpo is considered to have been very highly realized. He was also known for his extraordinary knowledge; he was one of the two or three persons who appeared in each century in Tibet and who was so knowledgeable that he received the title "kun mkhyen" in Tibetan, meaning "All-Knowing". This title has often been translated as "omniscient" in English, but it means "a person who knows it all". Padma Karpo was also very expert at composition and a prolific writer, his collected works totalling twenty-four or more full Tibetan volumes of over three hundred folios each.

Figure 5. All-knowing Padma Karpo, the fourth Drukchen

---

[4] (... continued)
of one of the most famous Nyingma commentaries to it, the treatise by Khenpo Kunpal. His work and the commentary presented in this book complement each other very well. Andreas has allowed us to make all of his works on Śhāntideva's text free. They are available on our PKTC website.

Padma Karpo was uniquely skilled at weaving many complex ideas together into a minimum of space. Learned Tibetan scholars and teachers regard him as one of the most rewarding yet difficult writers to read; rewarding because of the depth of his knowledge and realization and difficult to read because he weaves so many threads of information into his compositions. Nonetheless he is one of the most widely read of the early Tibetan authors and is frequently read by people of Tibetan Buddhist traditions other than the Kagyu tradition simply because his works are so illuminating.

Explanations of Essential Terminology

Bodhi, buddha, bodhichitta, and bodhisatva

The teachings which show the path to unsurpassed, true complete enlightenment contain several terms that are fundamental to the teaching. In Sanskrit, these terms are: bodhi, buddha, bodhichitta, and bodhisatva. All of these terms are derived from the one Sanskrit root "budh" which has the straightforward meaning of "an illumined or enlightened condition".

What is the primary connotation of "budh"? It is "being filled with knowledge". And what is the flavour of that "being filled with knowledge"? It is "brightness" or "illumination" . When these meanings are put together, we find that the English term "enlightened" is a very close match to the original Sanskrit term. As further support for this understanding, it is important to note that Indian scholars of Sanskrit have said that the next best word in Sanskrit to explain the root "budh" is "avagamana", which means "to have a mind filled with knowledge".

It is very important to understand that "budh" *does not* have the meaning or connotation of "awakened". It is a complete mistake to say that it does. It is also very wrong to say, "Perhaps 'budh' means 'enlightened', but who cares? No harm is done if we substitute 'awakened' for 'enlightened'!" In fact, a lot of harm is done. Simply stated, when "awakened" is used for the translation of "budh", the audience is being given the wrong meaning. Because of it, the audience loses a lot of crucial meaning on the one hand and gains a lot of misunderstanding on the other.

Where did this grossly mistaken translation of "budh" come from? The source of this mistake can be traced to a misunderstanding of the Tibetan word "sangs rgyas" for the Sanskrit word "buddha". The Tibetan term is made up of two terms "sangs" and "rgyas". The first of the two has a primary meaning and a secondary meaning. The primary meaning is exactly "to be cleared out". The secondary sense is "to wake up", but note that the secondary sense actually means "to clear away the fogginess of sleep (and so to wake up)".

Translators who had not understood the Tibetan word "sangs" thought that the meaning of "sangs" was only "to wake up", so they translated "buddha" as "the awakened one", "bodhi" as "awakening", and so on. Doing so was a mistake from beginning to end. The correct way to understand "sangs" in the Tibetan word for "buddha" is "cleared off" or "cleaned out", meaning that all of the ignorance that pollutes the samsaric mind has been cleared off so that an enlightened condition prevails. An in-depth treatment of this matter can be found in *Unending Auspiciousness, the Sutra of the Recollection of the Noble Three Jewels* cited earlier.

In short, bodhi, buddha, bodhichitta, and bodhisatva do not respectively mean awakening, awakened one, awakening mind, or awakening hero as is often seen. They respectively mean enlightenment, enlightened one, enlightenment mind, and enlightenment hero and that is how they appear in this book.

This is how these four, crucial terms are used in the bodhisatva teachings of the Great Vehicle. First, a person decides that the type of existence he has at present, one based on a fundamental ignorance of reality, is unsatisfactory. He decides to travel the path to a totally satisfactory type of existence in which there is no ignorance of reality. That type of existence is the state of *bodhi* or enlightenment. In order to achieve that he starts by arousing in himself the *bodhichitta* or enlightenment mind. Once he has accepted the need for and aroused in himself that enlightenment mind, he is known as a *bodhisatva* or an enlightenment hero, a person who is heroic because of undertaking the long and difficult path to enlightenment. When he has completed the path to enlightenment, he is no longer a bodhisatva on the path to enlightenment but a *buddha* or enlightened one.

Bodhi and buddha or enlightenment and enlightened one

This book is about the journey to enlightenment. Buddhism speaks of two kinds of bodhi or enlightenment and, correspondingly, two kinds of buddha or enlightened ones.

Arhats or "foe destroyers" have attained a degree of enlightenment, hence are also known as arhat buddhas, but theirs is not the highest degree of enlightenment. Tathāgatas, or "ones gone to suchness", are also known as "buddhas", with theirs being the highest degree of enlightenment. In order to distinguish the highest degree of enlightenment from both lesser and false types of enlightenment, it is called "unsurpassed, true complete enlightenment" and in order to distinguish the highest type of buddha from both lesser and false types of buddha, it is called an "unsurpassed, true complete buddha".

In those names, "unsurpassed" simply means that there is no other, higher form of enlightenment or buddha. "True" means an authentic enlightenment or buddha; it is put there to eliminate all types of being who claim to be a buddha but are fakes. "Complete" means that this enlightenment or buddha is a complete one, not a partial one. Note that "true complete" is correct; it does not, as can be understood from the explanation just given, mean "truly complete".

Bodhichitta or enlightenment mind

The Sanskrit term "bodhichitta" is translated into Tibetan with "byang chub sems" in which "byang chub" is the Tibetan equivalent of "bodhi" and "sems" is the Tibetan equivalent of "chitta". Several translations of the term into English have appeared but most of them are not exact or are wrong for various reasons. Firstly the term "bodhi" does not mean "awakening" but very closely matches the English term "enlightenment". The Sanskrit term "chitta" corresponds to the English "mind", though there is the problem that chitta is a specific term for a specific type of mind and since there is not a specific term corresponding to that in English we have to use the generic word "mind".

How should the two terms contained in "bodhichitta"—enlightenment and mind—be joined? The Sanskrit bodhichitta has the two terms placed together in such a way that bodhi describes the type of chitta. The Tibetan translates that juxtaposition and meaning exactly either by putting the terms one after the other as in "byang chub sems" or by joining the two terms with a "kyi" to make "byang chub kyi sems". When a "kyi" is used, it does not add meaning but explicitly shows the appositional connection between the two terms which is present in the original Sanskrit. In other words bodhichitta is a mind and, in particular, an enlightenment kind of mind. In English, the correct way to join the terms so as to give the meaning required is to write enlightenment followed by mind and with no more grammatical apparatus included—"enlightenment mind".

It would be very wrong to translate "bodhichitta" with "mind for enlightenment". This can be known through the correct grammatical analysis given above and also through Indian and Tibetan commentaries which unanimously point out that the term "enlightenment mind" applies to a whole range of minds, starting from its form in its very first arousal in a samsaric person all the way through to its final and most complete form in a true complete buddha. The *Ornament of Manifested Realizations*[5] of Maitreya and Asaṅga divides enlightenment mind into twenty-two types corresponding to twenty-two levels of development of that mind up to and including that of a buddha. There are various

---

[5] Skt. *Abhisamayālaṇkara*.

other teachings within the Buddhist scriptures that establish the same point.

The English translation "mind for enlightenment" is not only incorrect grammatically but excludes the enlightenment mind of a buddha or enlightened one. Thus, use of the term has caused and continues to cause a wrong understanding to arise in the minds of English-speaking people. On the other hand, the translation "enlightenment mind" is not only correct grammatically but is also correct from the standpoint that it includes all possibilities of the enlightenment type of mind. Its use causes a correct understanding of the term "bodhichitta" to arise in the minds of English-speaking people, therefore, it is used in all of our translations including in this book.

Note that there is a less-used term, "mind for enlightenment". "Mind for enlightenment is not the same as "enlightenment mind". The former is the general term for all levels of the enlightenment mind, from someone who has first engendered that mind all the way up to someone who has, in becoming a buddha, perfected it. However, at the time when one is on the path and is arousing a mind which has the thought that it will turn towards enlightenment, that mind is enlightenment mind, of course, but is also described as "mind for enlightenment", meaning a *mind* that has consciously oriented itself towards or *for enlightenment*. This distinction is used in the commentary and I have maintained it correctly in the translation, so be careful not to confuse the two.

Bodhisatva or enlightenment hero

Following on from that, there is the Sanskrit term "bodhisatva" which is the name given to a person who has aroused the enlightenment mind. In it, "bodhi" is equivalent to "enlightenment" as mentioned earlier and "satva" refers to a person who is an heroic type of person, a true warrior. "Satva" was translated precisely into Tibetan with "dpa' bo" which means an heroic person, one who is not overcome easily but heads toward his goal in a strong, courageous, and determined way.

Note that "satva" and "sattva" are two different terms. The former means "hero" as just described. The latter simply means "a being"; it is the term in Sanskrit that Tibetans translated as "sems chan" and which we translate into English as "sentient being".

Thus the term "bodhisatva" should be translated into English as "enlightenment hero" or something very similar. However, the terminology for the translation of "bodhisatva" has not been settled in English and the term "bodhisatva" has become part of dharma jargon in English, so I have left it as bodhisatva throughout this book. Still, I think you would find it very helpful to read it as "enlightenment hero".

Enlightenment conduct

The bodhisatva arouses the enlightenment mind, then takes the vows of a bodhisatva, and then follows the conduct of a bodhisatva from the beginning of his journey all the way up until the time that he achieves bodhi and becomes a buddha. Thus the issue of a bodhisatva's conduct, also known as enlightenment conduct, is singularly important to a person wanting to have the unsurpassed enlightenment of a true complete enlightened one.

The great Indian Buddhist master Śhāntideva put a lot of effort into reading the sutras of the Buddha and the Indian treatises on them that deal with this topic and then wrote the text *Entering the Conduct of a Bodhisatva* which forms the basis for this book. Śhāntideva points out at the beginning of his text that he wrote it not to prove that he was expert in these matters or very capable at composition but as a set of notes which distilled these teachings into a form that he could easily remember.

Related Matters

Source

The Tibetan text for this translation was the electronic edition produced by the Drukpa Kagyu Heritage Project which was input from the original in Padma Karpo's Collected Works⁶. The electronic text is available on PKTC's web-site.

Resources

Andreas Kretschmar is a long-time translator of excellent abilities. He has translated many chapters of Śhāntideva's text together with the very famous Tibetan commentary to them by the Nyingma Khenchen Kunpal. Andreas' work consisting of several chapters of Śhāntideva's text and Khenchen KunPal's commentary translated into English and also into his native German is a remarkable achievement.

We mentioned earlier that Andreas' presentation of Śhāntideva's biography is an excellent resource for learning more about that. He also gives in volume one of his English translation a thorough presentation of the various Sanskrit texts and Tibetan texts connected with Śhāntideva's text. Therefore, rather than provide a bibliography of those texts here, you are referred to the bibliography in Andreas' work. Still, there is a short account of such texts in this book at the beginning of Padma Karpo's preface to his commentary.

Note that all of Andreas' work is entirely free. It can be downloaded from our PKTC web-site and from other web-sites, too.

Translation issues

One of the features of Śhāntideva's text is beauty of poetry. I have tried to retain a sense of that, but have aimed for accuracy of meaning first and beauty of composition second. In particular, I have tried not to lose the meaning of the words for the sake of a pleasant-sounding result. As an example, one translator continually took the term "migrator", a term which has a strong significance in the Buddhist way of speaking, and turned it into "all the world". "All the world" might sound nice to some ears, but it is a major mistake and detracts from the meaning.

---

⁶ Tib. padma dkar po'i bka' 'bum

This is one of many such examples. See the glossary for the meaning of migrator.

Over the many centuries since Śhāntideva's work was composed, several versions of his text have appeared both in the original Sanskrit and in the Tibetan translations of it. There are, as is to be expected, differences between the versions. Many of the differences have no effect on the translation into English, but there are places where they do have an effect, hence you will find that the meaning of Śhāntideva's text as presented in the currently-existing translations into English will differ from one translation to another. As an obvious example, there is a place in chapter nine where some Tibetan editions include three verses that are not present in either Sanskrit or other Tibetan editions.

Thus it is important to understand that nowadays there is no "perfect" version of Śhāntideva's text, whether in Sanskrit, Tibetan, or English. However, that does not mean that these various versions should be rejected. The versions that do exist are sufficiently intact that one can accept them as Śhāntideva's text and use and appreciate them for the brilliant exposition of enlightenment conduct that they are.

Gender considerations

There has been an undercurrent of criticism of Śhāntideva since his text was translated into English. It has generally come from feminists who object strongly to what they see as misogynistic treatment of women in *Entering the Conduct of a Bodhisatva*.

Śhāntideva was a fully-ordained Buddhist monk living in the largest all-male monk assembly of his time. What he wrote was exactly what was taught by the Buddha to his monk disciples as a means for not being seduced into sexual activity that would break their vows. This is the proper context for providing a correct understanding of these teachings.

I will say this. As a translator, it is not my job to modify the texts I am translating to suit my ideas or the ideas present in the culture of my time. Śhāntideva was writing as a monk, in a monastic setting, and moreover was echoing the words of the Buddha as preserved in Buddhist scripture. It is not my job to re-write the details of him, his culture, or for that matter, the teachings of the Buddha.

Therefore, no attempt has been made in this book to change the terminology or gender of terminology used by Śhāntideva. His is a text from a certain time and place and the wording of the text reflects that. If the culture in which it was written was "gender biased", well, so be it! It is not up to me or any other translator, male or female, to change the wording of ancient texts to suit our needs. That would be an incredibly arrogant thing to do!

Sanskrit and diacriticals

Sanskrit terms are an important aspect of the explanations found in the texts in this book. They are properly rendered into English with diacritical marks. Therefore, for the sake of precision, diacritical marks have been used with these terms throughout this book. However, some Sanskrit words used in Buddhism have become so much part of English that they are now written without diacritical marks, for example, sutra, samsara, nirvana, paramita, and others.

The IATS system for the transliteration of Sanskrit into Western languages is the system generally used in Western academic circles. However, it is hard for non-scholars to read, so we have modified the system slightly to make it more readable. This approach seems to be commonplace amongst translators of Tibetan Buddhism. In it:

śʹ is written the way it sounds, as śh ;
ṣ is written similarly as ṣh ; and
ṛ is written similarly as ṛi ;
ca is written as cha; and
cha is written as chha.

The other letters for transliteration are used in the same way as they are used in the IATS scheme. In general, if you do not understand the system, simply read the letters as though they did not have the diacritical marks and, with our modified system, you will have a good approximation to the actual pronunciation.

With my very best wishes,
Lama Tony Duff,
Swayambunath,
Nepal

PART ONE

Shantideva's
Entering the Conduct of a Bodhisatva

CHAPTER ONE

The Benefits of Enlightenment Mind

In Indian Sanskrit language, "bodhisatvacharyāvatāra"
In Tibetan language, "byang chub sems dpa'i spyod pa la 'jug pa"
In English language, "Entering the Conduct of a Bodhisatva"

Prostration to all of the buddhas and bodhisatvas.

I respectfully prostrate to the ones gone to bliss who have the dharmakāya, together with their sons, and to all the worthy ones as well. I will present the topic of engaging in the vows of the sugatas' sons in accordance with scripture and in summary form.

Nothing will be expressed here which has not already been said before and I have no skill in the art of composition, therefore, without thought of benefit for others, I compose it in order to cultivate my own mind.

Because it is a cultivation of virtue, doing it will increase the force of my faith for a while and if others whose circumstances are similar to mine see it, it will be meaningful for them, too.

This leisure and endowment is extremely difficult to gain and with it what is meaningful for mankind can be obtained, so if the benefit it offers is not accomplished, when in the future could such a support be truly received again?

Just as in the gloom of a dark night a flash of lightning inside clouds for an instant illuminates all around, similarly, in the worlds by the power of the buddhas for a minute fraction of the time, intelligent minds seeking what is meritorious sometimes arise.

Thus, virtue is perpetually feeble and evil is overwhelmingly strong, so what virtue other than the mind of complete enlightenment could overpower it?

The leaders among Capable Ones, who have given the matter their utmost consideration for many aeons, have seen exactly this to be beneficial; by it, the immeasurable mass of beings easily attain the supreme bliss.

Someone who wants to defeat his own abundant sufferings of becoming and wants to dispel the unhappiness of sentient beings, and who wishes that all others will live in abundant happiness will never let go of the enlightenment mind.

When the enlightenment mind has been produced, instantly those who had been wretches bound in the prison of samsara will be described as "sons of the sugatas" and will become objects of prostration in the worlds of gods and men.

Like the alchemist's liquid that transforms iron into the supreme form of gold, it transforms this impure body that has been taken up into the priceless jewel of a conqueror's body, therefore this "enlightenment mind" should be most firmly adopted.

If the sole captains of migrators have thoroughly examined it with their measureless intellects and seen it to be a thing of great value, then those wanting to be free of the abodes of migrators should properly and firmly adopt the precious enlightenment mind.

All other virtues are like the Plantain tree in that, having produced their fruit they are exhausted, but the living tree of the enlightenment mind perpetually bears fruit without being exhausted by doing so and grows ever larger.

Like someone who has done unbearable evil but relies on a strong man will be freed from very great fears, a person who relies on the enlightenment mind will for a while be freed, so why do small-minded people not rely on it?

Like the fire of the end of time, it definitely incinerates great evils in an instant. Its fathomless benefits were explained by the very intelligent Guardian Maitreya to Good Wealth.

That enlightenment mind when summarized is understood to be of two types: a mind that aspires to enlightenment and one that engages in enlightenment.

Like the way that wanting to go somewhere and actually going there are understood, intelligent people will understand that there is a sequence to these two.

The mind that aspires to enlightenment gives rise to greater results while in samsara, but unlike the mind of engagement does not give rise to a continuous stream of merit.

From the time that the mind of engagement has with an irreversible attitude genuinely been adopted, from that time on, even if asleep or not paying attention, there will be a force of merit that is continuous and equal to space.

This explanation can be accepted because of what the Tathāgata himself said in the *Sutra Petitioned by Subāhu* for the sake of sentient beings who are inclined towards the lesser vehicles.

If someone in thinking, "I will remove just the headaches of sentient beings", is having a beneficial thought that will result in gaining an unfathomable amount of merit, what need is there to mention the result of wishing to dispel the unfathomable unsatisfactoriness of each sentient being and of wishing to produce unfathomable good qualities in each one of them?

Who of your father or mother, either one, has this kind of beneficial mind? Do gods and ṛiṣhis either one or Brahmā even, have this?

Those sentient beings up till now have not even dreamt of this kind of mind for their own sake, so how could they have given birth to it for others' sakes?

This special, precious mind that in thinking of sentient beings' sakes thinks of others without thoughts of one's own sake arising, a wonder that has not previously existed in this world, has been born!

How could the merit of the precious mind that is the cause of gladness in all migrators, that is a salve for the suffering of sentient beings, be measured?

If even just the thought to be of benefit is more special than offering to the buddhas, then what need is there to mention the mind that is striving for the sake of the happiness of every one of the sentient beings without exception?

They have a mind that wants to get rid of suffering, but they rush to manifest suffering. They want happiness, but their delusion defeats their own happiness as though it were an enemy.

This is someone who will satisfy with every happiness those having little happiness and will eliminate all of the sufferings of those having many sufferings, and who will even dispel their delusion. Where is there virtue equal to this? Where is there a spiritual friend like this? Where is there something as meritorious as this?

If any beneficial response is deemed worthy of a little commendation, what need is there to mention the praiseworthiness of the bodhisatva who unconditionally does good?

If someone provides a few migrators with food on a regular basis or gives just food for the moment or gives in an abusive way enough to last for half a day, even then beings will honour it, saying, "This is virtuous activity". What need then to mention someone who perpetually gives to sentient beings beyond count for a long time the unsurpassed bliss of the sugatas and the fulfilment of all yearnings?

The Capable One said that someone who gives rise to a negative mind towards a son of the conquerors who acts as a donor like that will dwell in hell for as many aeons as the negative mind was produced.

However, anyone who develops great admiration for him will have a result that will be even greater than that. Even when someone creates a major problem for the conquerors' sons, evil does not arise in them and their virtue naturally increases.

I prostrate to the bodies of those in whom the precious jewel of that holy mind has been produced and I take refuge in those who are sources of happiness because of uniting even those who have harmed them with happiness.

That was the first chapter of *Entering the Conduct of a Bodhisatva*, called "Explaining the Benefits of Enlightenment Mind".

CHAPTER TWO

Laying Aside Evil Deeds

In order to adopt the precious mind I nicely make offerings to the tathāgatas, to the stainless Jewel the holy dharma, and to those oceans of good qualities, the buddha sons.

As many flowers and fruits as there are; whatever types of medicine there are; as many precious things of the world as there are; whichever delightful pure waters there are; precious mountains and likewise forests and other solitary and pleasing places; trees decorated with ornaments of flowers; and trees whose branches are bowed with excellent fruits,

And as well as that, in the worlds of the gods and others like them, fragrances, incense, wish-fulfilling trees, jewel trees, crops that grow without cultivation,

And furthermore, ornaments that are suitable to be offered such as lakes and ponds ornamented with lotuses and dotted with wild geese of extremely sweet cry and delightful plumage—

If I mentally imagine all of those un-owned things existing through to the limit of all-encompassing space then nicely offer them to all the Capable Ones supreme among beings together with their sons, then you superior places of offering, you of great compassionate activity, considering me with love accept those things I have offered!

Having no merit I am destitute and have nothing of value to offer at all. Therefore you guardians who are concerned with others' sakes, accept this by means of doing it for my sake!

I forever offer all of my body to the conquerors and their sons. You supreme heroes accept me completely! I will respectfully be your servant.

Now that I have been taken into your care, I am not afraid to be in becoming, and because of that I will benefit sentient beings; I will truly go beyond my earlier evil deeds and henceforth shall do no more.

In very sweetly-scented bathing chambers with brilliant crystal floors, with delightful pillars ablaze with jewels, with pearl hangings glowing with light, and canopies overhead, I bathe the bodies of the tathāgatas and their sons using many jewelled vases filled with delightful waters made pure with aromatics to the accompaniment of much song and music.

I dry their bodies with incomparable cloth clean and well-moistened with fine scent. Then, I offer them nicely dyed garments that have been made fragrant with the finest scents.

I will adorn the noble ones Samantabhadra, Mañjughosha, Lokeshvara, and the others with various raiments excellent, fine, and smooth and with jewellery possessing hundreds of supreme qualities.

I anoint the bodies of the leaders among Capable Ones, bodies that blaze with a lustre like that of polished refined gold, with supreme perfumes whose fragrances waft throughout all of the third-order world.

And to those leaders among Capable Ones, a supreme place for making offerings, I offer all the sweet-smelling flowers—the delightful Mandāravā, Lotus, Utpala, and others—and delightful well-designed garlands, and all-pervading cloudbanks of the fragrant smoke of the best incense whose scent steals away the mind.

I also offer them foods of the gods that include a variety of foods and drinks. I also offer them rows of jewelled lamps mounted in lotuses of gold. On the land over which incense water has been spread, I scatter the petals of delightful flowers.

I offer to those who have a nature of compassionate activity immeasurable palaces filled with praises expressed in delightful melodies, ablaze with the beauty of hangings made of pearls and precious ornaments, and which have become ornaments of unfathomable space.

And I perpetually offer to the Capable Ones beautiful umbrellas of precious substances which are delightful in appearance with their golden handles and ornamentation around the rims and whose nice shape when held erect is lovely to behold.

As well as that, may a mass of offerings resounding with delightful music and pleasing melodies, like thunder-bearing rain clouds that relieve the sufferings of sentient beings, be present.

May a continuous rain of precious substances, flowers, and so on descend upon all the volumes of the holy dharma Jewel and upon the stupas and statues.

Just as Mañjughoṣa and the others made offerings to the conquerors, so I too will make offerings to the guardian tathāgatas together with their sons.

I will praise those oceans of good qualities with oceans of types of melodious praise. May those clouds that broadcast pleasant-to-hear melodious praises certainly always arise for them.

I prostrate with bodies as numerous as all the atoms within the fields, bodies bowed down to all the buddhas gone in the three times, to the dharma Jewel, and to the supreme assembly.

I prostrate also to the bases of enlightenment mind and the stupas. I prostrate to the preceptors, likewise to the masters, and to those of supreme yogic activity.

Until the heart of enlightenment has been reached I take refuge in the buddhas. I likewise also take refuge in the dharma and in the bodhisatva assembly.

I mentally invite before me the complete buddhas and the bodhisatvas seated in all ten directions, the ones who have great compassionate activity, then supplicate them with palms joined.

In samsara having no beginning, in this lifetime and in others, I, due to not knowing, have done evil deeds and have ordered them done and I, taken over by the confusion of delusion, have rejoiced in what was done. Having seen those mistakes as mistakes, from my heart I lay them aside before the guardians.

Before this I have done wrongs in relation to the Three Jewels and parents, gurus, and others through the afflictions by way of body, speech, and mind and I, a person whose many wrongdoings have produced faults in me, a person of evil deeds, have done evil deeds that are utterly intolerable. In the presence of the guides I lay all of it aside.

I may well perish before the evil deeds have been cleaned away, so the way to do it as above is to please protect me in a way that will swiftly and certainly free me from them.

The untrustworthy lord of death does not wait for this and that to be done or not done; in every case whether I am sick or healthy this fleeting life cannot be relied on.

Leaving everyone behind I must depart alone, but not having understood that, I have done various kinds of evil deeds for the sake of my friends and foes.

My foes will become nothing, my friends too will become nothing, I will become nothing and likewise all will become nothing.

Like experiencing a dream, the things I have had for my use will become memories and, having passed, all of it will not be seen again. The many friends and foes of this brief life will have passed, but the unbearable evil which I did for their sakes remains ahead of me.

Not having realised in that way that "I am but a fleeting event", motivated by delusion, desire, and anger I have done many types of evil deeds. Day and night by turns, this life which cannot stay is always slipping away and if it cannot be extended, why would death not come to one like me?

While lying in bed I may be surrounded by my friends and relatives, but the feelings of this life ending will be experienced by me alone. When seized by the messengers of death what help will relatives be, what help will friends provide? At that time merit alone would protect me, but then I never did attend to that!

O guardians! Careless me who goes unaware of a fear like this has gone about producing many evil deeds for the sake of this transient life. Petrified is the person who is today being led to the place of execution. If with dry mouth, bloodshot eyes, and so on his appearance has changed from how it was before, what need to mention someone being clasped by the frightening-to-see physical forms of the frightful ones, the messengers of death, and having the total weakness that comes with being stricken with the disease of great fear?

"Who will give me good protection from these very great fears?" With terrified, wide-open, and bulging eyes I search the four directions for a refuge, but seeing no refuge in the four directions I will become enveloped in gloom. If there is no protection there, then at that point what should I do?

Due to that, from today I go for refuge to the conquerors, the guardians of migrators, the ones who strive to provide a refuge for migrators, the ones of great strength who dispel all strong fears.

Likewise I truly go for refuge to the dharma they have mastered that dispels all the fears of samsara and also to the assembly of bodhisatvas.

Completely afraid, I shall offer myself to Samantabhadra. To Mañjughosha also I shall offer this body of mine.

Also to the guardian noble Avalokiteśhvara whose compassionate activity is not confused, I cry out weakly asking him to be a refuge for this evil doer.

In my search for refuge I cry out from my heart to the noble ones Ākāśhagarbha and Kṣhitigarbha, and to all the guardians who have greater compassionate activity, seeking refuge in them.

And I also go for refuge to Vajrapāṇi, the possessor of the vajra who upon being seen makes beings who arouse aversion in us, such as the messengers of death, flee with fear in the four directions.

Before this I have transgressed your command. Now that I have seen the great fear that results from doing so, I take refuge in you; by doing so please quickly remove the fear.

If I need to comply with a physician's words when frightened by an ordinary illness, what need is there to mention being perpetually struck by the illness of hundreds of wrongdoings of desire, and so on? And if just one of them could destroy all the humans present on this earth and no other medicine to cure them could be found, then thinking not to act in accordance with the word of the all-knowing physicians regarding that which would uproot every pain would be extremely deluded and worthy of denigration.

If there is a need to stay attentive near even a small cliff, what need is there to mention being concerned about the precipice that drops for a thousand leagues to a place where one remains for a long time?

It is not all right to sit here happily thinking that for today at least I shall not die. The time when I will become nothing will arrive, there is no doubt.

Who will provide me with no fear? How will I definitely be freed from this? When there is no doubt that I will be nothing, how can I remain at ease?

What remains with me of the experiences now ended of the past? Through my strong clinging to them I have gone against the words of my guru.

Having discarded this occasion of being alive and similarly its relatives and friends, if I must go on all alone to places unknown, what is the use of having all the so-called friends and foes?

"Non-virtue is the source of unsatisfactoriness; how can I definitely be freed from that?" It is right for me to consider only this at all times, day and night. Whatever evil deeds I have done by unknowing delusion of the natural unmentionable acts and those associated with a vow, within the actual sight of the guardians with palms joined and with a mind fearful of unsatisfactoriness, prostrating again and again, I lay all of them aside. I ask the guides to accept the evil deeds I have done as mistakes.

This is not good, therefore henceforth I will do it no more.

That was the second chapter of *Entering the Conduct of a Bodhisatva*, called "Laying Aside Evil".

CHAPTER THREE

Fully Adopting the Enlightenment Mind

With gladness I rejoice in the virtue that gives relief from the suffering of all sentient beings' bad migrations and in the virtue which places those having suffering in happiness.

I rejoice in the accumulated virtue that has become a cause of enlightenment. I rejoice in bodied beings' definite emancipation from the suffering of samsara.

I rejoice in the enlightenment of the protectors and also in the conquerors' sons. With gladness I rejoice in the ocean of virtue of arousing the mind that makes happiness for all sentient beings and in its works to benefit sentient beings.

With palms joined I supplicate the buddhas of all directions to please light the lamp of dharma for sentient beings suffering and bewildered in darkness.

With palms joined I supplicate the conquerors who have asserted that they will pass into nirvana please not to leave these migrators blind and to remain for countless aeons.

Having done all of these, may the virtue that I have accumulated dispel all the unsatisfactoriness of every sentient being.

For as long there are sick migrators and until their sicknesses are cured, may I be their medicines and physicians and their nurses as well.

May a rain of food and drink descend that will remove their pangs of hunger and thirst.

At the time of the intermediate aeon of famine may I become food and drink.

May I stay before those sentient beings who are poor and destitute as all the various requisites they might need.

Without any sense of loss I give up my body and likewise resources and all my virtue of the three times as well in order to accomplish the aims of all sentient beings.

By giving up everything one goes to nirvana and I have a mind to accomplish nirvana. Giving up everything all at once is best done now, giving it all to sentient beings.

Because I have already given this body to all bodied beings to do with as they please they have it forever to kill, revile and beat, and so on, whatever makes them glad.

Let them toy with my body or mock it or ridicule it, but because this body of mine has already been given to them why should I treat it as something for my own use?

Let them do anything with it that will not bring them harm or an evil deed. Whenever others come into contact with me, may it never be meaningless for them.

Having come into contact with me, may minds of anger or faith that are aroused in them always be a cause for the fulfilment of all their aims.

May those who speak badly of me or harm me in other ways and likewise who insult me all have the fortune to be enlightened.

May I become a guardian for those without a guardian, a guide for travellers on the way, and a boat, ship, and bridge for those wanting to cross the waters.

May I become an island for those seeking an island, a bed for those wanting a bed, and a servant for all bodied beings wanting a servant.

May I become a wish-fulfilling jewel, an excellent vase, a powerful vidyamantra, great medicine, a wish-fulfilling tree, and a cow that provides the wishes of bodied beings.

May I in the same way as do the great elements—earth and the others and space—forever be a basis for the many types of necessities of life of the fathomless sentient beings. Likewise, may I be a cause of the necessities of life in all circumstances in the realms of sentient beings reaching to the end of space until all have reached nirvana.

Just as the sugatas of former times aroused the mind for enlightenment and progressively stayed in the stages of the bodhisatva trainings, just so, for the benefit of migrators I arouse the mind for enlightenment and likewise will progressively train in the trainings.

Those who with intelligence have like that taken up the most admirable enlightenment mind will also at the end in order to increase it give lofty praise for this sort of mind.

Today my life has become fruitful for I have gained a good human existence; today I have been born into the family of buddhas and have become a son of the buddhas.

Now whatever happens, I will only perform actions befitting the family; I will not put a stain on this faultless well-disciplined family.

Just like a blind man finding something valuable in a heap of dust, by some coincidence this enlightenment mind has been born in me.

This is the supreme nectar that overcomes the lord of death of migrators. This also is the inexhaustible treasure which eliminates the poverty of migrators.

This also is the supreme medicine which completely alleviates the diseases of migrators. It is the living tree that provides rest to migrators wandering and tired on the path of becoming.

It is the palanquin which liberates all migrators from the bad migrations. It is the rising moon of mind that dispels the torment of migrators' afflictions.

It is the great sun that utterly removes the distorted vision of migrators' unknowing state. It is the buttery essence that comes from churning the milk of the holy dharma.

For the migrator guests travelling the paths of becoming and wanting to live in the enjoyment of happiness, this places them in the supreme happiness; it satisfies these sentient beings who are its great guests.

Today in sight of all the protectors I have called on migrators to be guests in happiness until sugata-hood; gods, demi-gods, and others be glad!

That was the third chapter of *Entering the Conduct of a Bodhisatva*, called "Fully Adopting the Enlightenment Mind".

CHAPTER FOUR

Heedfulness

A conquerors' son having in that way most firmly taken up the enlightenment mind shall, without wavering from it, always exert himself at not straying from the trainings.

For something undertaken rashly or not considered well, although a commitment to complete it may have been made, it is right to examine whether it should be done or given up. Having been examined by the great prajñā of the buddhas and their sons and examined repeatedly by myself as well, what could there be in this that should be deferred? If having committed myself like that I were not to act to accomplish it, I would have cheated all sentient beings.

And what sort of migrator would I become in future? If the Buddha has said that a person who, having made up his mind to give a small, ordinary thing, does not give it will become a hungry ghost, then if I have made a strong intention to invite all migrators as guests to unsurpassed happiness then cheat them all, how could I go to a happy migration?

That people who have let go of the mind of enlightenment even then achieve emancipation is due to the inconceivable modes of karma known only by the all-knowing one.

That is the heaviest of downfalls for a bodhisatva; it is such that if it happens, it diminishes the welfare of all sentient beings.

Someone else who for even just an instant hinders or obstructs a bodhisatva's merit will, because he has diminished the welfare of sentient beings, have endless bad migrations.

If in destroying even one sentient being's happiness I become a degraded person, then what need is there to mention destroying the happiness of bodied beings infinite as the entirety of space?

Those who go around in samsara mixing the force of such downfalls and the force of enlightenment mind will be hindered from attaining the bodhisatva levels for a long time.

In view of that, I shall respectfully practice just as I have committed to doing. If I am not diligent from today on, I will go lower and lower.

Countless buddhas who worked to benefit all sentient beings have gone by, but because of my own faults I did not come under their curative care.

If I continue to do the same, the same thing will happen again and again and in bad migrations I will experience sickness, bondage, being killed, being sliced apart, and so on.

If such things as the occurrence of a tathāgata, faith, obtaining a human body, and the chance to become familiar with virtue are rare, when will they be obtained?

Just now I am not sick, have food, and am free of troubles, but life can be cheated in a moment; the body is like something on loan for a while. This sort of behaviour of mine will not gain me even a human body! And if a human body is not gained, there will only be evil, no virtue.

Now, when I have the fortune needed to be virtuous but do not act virtuously, what will I be able to do when stupefied by all the sufferings of the bad destinies?

If I do not act virtuously but instead regularly accumulate evil deeds, then even in a thousand million aeons I will not hear even the words "good migration".

Because of that the Bhagavat said that it is extremely difficult to gain a human existence, as difficult as it is for a turtle to insert its neck into the hole on a wooden ox-yoke floating about upon a great ocean.

If even the evil done in an instant can result in an aeon spent in the hell of Unremitting Torment, then what need to mention that the evils accumulated in beginningless samsara will not result in going to the good migrations?

Having experienced just that alone does not bring complete emancipation; while that was being experienced, other evil deeds were being incessantly produced.

Having found such leisure as this, if I do not familiarize myself with virtue, there could be no cheating myself greater than this, there could be no stupidity greater than this.

If I realize that but through stupidity continue to procrastinate, when the time to die comes, a tremendous misery will arise. If my body is burned for a long time by the hell fires so difficult to bear, there is no doubt that my mind will be tormented by the blazing fire of unbearable regret.

Having found by some coincidence this beneficial state that is so extremely difficult to find, if while having knowledge of that[7] I in later lives lead myself back to the hells again, it ends up that, as though stupefied by a mantric spell, I have been mindlessly here in this world. I do not know what is causing the stupidity; what is there inside of me?

Anger, craving, and so on are enemies who do not have arms, legs, and so on, and they are not courageous or clever. How have they made me like their slave?

While present in my mind they harm me for their enjoyment and I even tolerate it without anger, but that is inappropriate patience that will bring me down.

Even if all the gods and demi-gods were to rise up against me as enemies, they would not be able to lead me to and put me into the fires of the hell of Unremitting Torment. Yet this enemy of the mighty afflictions casts me in an instant into those fires which burn up everything they meet, even Meru, not leaving even ashes behind. My enemy the afflictions being without beginning or end lasts for a long time; no other enemy is capable of lasting for a long time like that.

If in order to have harmony with those other enemies I serve them with respect, they will become allies who will give all aid and comfort, whereas if I serve the afflictions, they will come again later and harm me with suffering.

---

[7] Padma Karpo explains "while having knowledge of that" as having knowledge of karmic cause and effects, which then connects this verse with what was explained in the previous few verses. However, those words can also mean that one is aware of having this very difficult to find leisure and endowment which then fits with the previous verses and the rest of this verse.

Thus the afflictions are a lasting and ongoing enemy, the sole cause for the increase of all that harms me; if I make a definite place for them in my heart, how could I be glad without fear in samsara?

If these guards of the prison of samsara who are my killers and butchers in hell, and so on, live in a web of attachment within my mind, how could I be happy?

Thus, for as long as I have not with certainty directly seen that this enemy has been defeated, I will not put aside striving to defeat the enemy. Proud people who have been angered by a slight harm done to them cannot sleep until their enemy has been destroyed.

On the battlefield, a warrior facing afflicted ones whose nature is to cause suffering by death is so focussed on wanting to destroy them that, disregarding the suffering of being struck by the weapons of spears and arrows, he does not withdraw until his purpose has been achieved. If that is so, what need is there to mention that my strivings to definitely destroy the enemy whose nature is only ever the cause of all suffering might cause me hundreds of sufferings today but will not deter me or make me faint of heart.

If without real meaning the scars of wounds inflicted by enemies are worn on the body like ornaments, then why when then why when I am genuinely striving in order to accomplish a great meaning should I allow myself to be affected by the suffering entailed?

If fishermen, outcastes, farmers, and so on thinking just of their own sustenance tolerate the harms of heat and cold, and so on, then why am I not patient for the sake of migrators' happiness?

I committed myself to liberating migrators of the ten directions reaching to the end of space from their afflictions, but at that time was not liberated from the afflictions myself. Declaring that without knowing my own capability was madness, was it not? Thus, I will forever defeat the afflictions without turning back.

Clinging to and holding a grudge against the afflictions, I will wage war against them except for the type of affliction used as a destroyer of affliction.

For me to be chopped up then killed or have my head cut off would be relatively easy; under no circumstances will I ever bow down to the enemy of the afflictions.

Ordinary enemies might be expelled from one country but stay in other countries where they settle and recoup their capacities then return again. But the way of the affliction enemy is not like that.

All afflictions are to be abandoned by prajñā. When the afflictions are removed from my mind where do they go? Where do they stay in order to return to harm me? Weak-minded, I have ended up without the diligence needed to tame them.

If the afflictions are not present in the object, not present in the sense faculties, and not in between nor somewhere other than that, then where do they reside, these ones that harm all migrators? They are similar to an illusion because of which I must get rid of the fear in my heart then attend to striving in order to take hold of prajñā! Why without any meaning at all would I inflict on myself the harms of being in the hells, and so on?

Having thoroughly contemplated this topic that way, I will exert myself at accomplishing the trainings as they have been explained; if I do not listen to a physician's words, how could I be cured of a sickness which must be cured with medicines?

That was the fourth chapter of *Entering the Conduct of a Bodhisatva*, called "Heedfulness".

CHAPTER FIVE

Guarding Alertness

Those wanting to guard the training will closely guard the mind, for if they do not guard the mind, they will not be able to guard the training.

The elephant of mind when unleashed can create the harms of the hell of Unremitting Torment, whereas a drunken wild elephant in this world cannot create such a level of harm. If the elephant of mind is firmly bound with the rope of total mindfulness, all feared things will become non-existent and all virtues will come to hand.

All tigers, lions, elephants, bears, snakes, enemies, the sentient beings who guard those in hell, black magic, and likewise rākṣhasas will be bound by binding this mind alone.

The one who speaks authentically taught that, "All of them will be tamed by taming this mind alone, for all feared things as well as the unfathomable sufferings come from mind".

Who intentionally made the weapons of the beings in hell? Who made the burning iron ground? From whom do those groups of females come?

The Capable One said that all such things arise from the mind of evil. In that way, in the whole three worlds there is nothing to be feared other than mind.

The Buddha said, "If the paramita of giving is the removal of the poverty of migrators, because there still are starving migrators the previous protectors did not complete the paramita, but how could that be? The paramita of generosity is completed by having a mind to give all beings everything that one has together with the virtue accumulated as a result.

The paramita of discipline is not about fish, and so on being removed to a place where they will not be killed; it is explained in terms of achieving a mind of abandoning.

Unruly sentient beings are as infinite as space, so they can never be entirely defeated. However, if this mind of anger alone is defeated, it will be the same as defeating all those enemies.

How could I get the leather needed to cover the surface of the earth? However, wearing leather the size of my shoe soles will be the same as covering the entire surface of the earth with it.

Likewise, I cannot change the course of external things, but I can change the course of my mind, so what need is there for me to take the approach that everything else is to be changed?

Meditation produces a clarity of mind that results in birth in the worlds of Brahma, and so on, but even when body or speech is involved, if mind's operation is weak, that sort of result does not come.

It has been said by the one who knows of such things that all recitations and austerities, even though done for a long time, are meaningless when done with a mind distracted elsewhere. Those who do not know the supreme chief of dharmas, the secret of mind that is free of the extremes of existing and not existing, might want happiness and the destruction of suffering, but will just wander about in an ordinary, meaningless way.

That being so, I should hold this mind of mine well and guard it well. Except for the yogic activity of guarding the mind, what would be the use of many yogic activities?

Just as I would be very protective of a wound when in a jostling uncontrolled crowd, so I should always guard this wound of a mind when staying amongst bad people.

If I am careful of a wound for fear of the small suffering that goes with it, why would I not guard the wound of mind for fear of being crushed by the mountains of Crushing Hell?

If I stay within this sort of behaviour, then whether I stay amongst bad people or amongst women, the steady effort to keep my vows will not deteriorate. It would be better for my gains and honours, my body and sustenance of life, and my other virtues also to deteriorate than ever to let the virtues of mind deteriorate!

With palms pressed together I say to those wanting to guard the mind, "Guard it with mindfulness and alertness with all your might!"

The bodies of people who are disturbed by sickness have no strength to do anything. Similarly minds disturbed by stupidity have no power to do any virtuous activities.

With a mind lacking alertness, any hearing, contemplating, and meditating that is done will, like water leaking out of a cracked vase, not stay in memory.

There are those of much hearing, faith, and diligence, but if they develop the fault of not having alertness, they will come to have the muck of downfalls.

The thieves and robbers that come with not having alertness follow along from the deterioration of mindfulness and like robbers steal away the merits that I have so carefully accumulated and I go to the bad migrations.

This gang of thieves and robbers, the afflictions, is seeking an opportunity and having found one will steal away my virtue and destroy lives in the happy migrations too.

Therefore I shall never let mindfulness depart from the door of mind. If it does go away, I shall remember the harms of the bad migrations then firmly place it there once more.

Due to keeping company with the guru, staying under the influence of the preceptor, and fearing being ashamed, the fortunate ones who show respect will easily have mindfulness arise.

Due to thinking, "The buddhas and bodhisatvas possessing unhindered sight of all, I am always in the sight of all of them", I come to have embarrassment, respect, and fear. And having done that, the recollection of buddha will also arise in me again and again.

When mindfulness has been stationed at the door of mind for the purpose of guarding it, then alertness will come about and the mindfulnesses that had gone away before will return again.

Having become aware in the first moment before acting that there is a faulty sort of mind, I will hold myself like a piece of wood, remaining capable of withstanding it.

I will never look around distractedly for no purpose, but with an ascertaining mind will always keep my eyes looking down. In order to rest up from looking that way I will sometimes look about.

If someone appears in my field of view, I will look at him then say, "Hello". In order to check for dangers on the path and so on, I will look again and again in the four directions.

On resting, I should look ahead then look behind. Having examined ahead and behind, I should proceed either to go forward or go back.

Having understood the need for that in all circumstances, that is how I will conduct myself.

Having prepared for an action with the knowledge, "My body will remain like this", I should periodically look to see, "How is it situated?"

I should make every effort to examine the drunken elephant of mind that now has been bound to the great pillar of minding the dharma to see how it is bound and to ensure that it has not wandered off elsewhere.

When striving by whichever means at concentration, in order not to wander off for even an instant I must individually examine my mind thinking, "Whereabouts is my mind focussed?

If someone is not able to practice this in the circumstances of being frightened by enemies, involved in festive activities, and so on, then he should do what is comfortable for him. It is like the Buddha's teaching that at the times of giving one could be indifferent to the disciplines.

I should undertake what I have thought of and not think of anything else. With mind focussed on that task, I should set about accomplishing it for the time being.

If that approach is taken, all will turn out well. If something else is also undertaken, then neither of the two will turn out well. If one acts in that way, the subsidiary afflictions that are not alertness will not grow.

I must abandon attachment to conversations filled with baseless stories and to being entertained by many kinds of wondrous spectacles.

If I do meaningless things like digging at the earth, picking at grass, drawing patterns on the ground, and so on, I should remember the trainings spoken by the Sugata then out of fear immediately stop.

When I want to move or want to speak, I should first examine my mind then should proceed with composure to do what is right.

When I see that my mind is attached or angry, I should not act nor speak, but should remain like a piece of wood.

When I am agitated and about to laugh derisively or if am puffed up with pride and about to reveal others' hidden faults, or am about to deceptively claim faults in others while making every effort to praise myself, or am about to revile and criticise then quarrel with others, then at such times I should remain like a piece of wood.

When I want gain, honour, and fame, or seek a circle of assistants, or have a mind wanting to be venerated, at that time I should remain like a piece of wood.

When a mind arises that wants to speak out about my wishes to forsake others' aims and look after my own aims, then I should remain like a piece of wood.

When minds of attachment to my side arise of impatience, laziness, cowardice, and likewise impudence and speaking without shame, then I should remain like a piece of wood.

Having examined his mind in that way for afflictions and meaningless undertakings, the hero should then hold his mind steady using the antidotes.

I should be extremely certain, utterly faithful, steadfast, respectful and deferential in body and speech, having a sense of shame and fear, and pacified.

I should strive to make others happy.

I should not be disheartened by the wishes of the childish when they are in disagreement and when afflictions have arisen for them; with love I will think, "These are produced by the mind".

And in doing the things that are not the despicable acts, I will always hold this mind to taking the standpoint of myself and sentient beings and acting like an apparition which is without a sense of "I".

Having contemplated again and again that I have gained supreme freedom after a long time, I should hold as unmoving as Mt. Meru that kind of mind.

If you, mind, will not be happy when the body is being torn apart and carried away by vultures greedy for flesh, then why do you counsel that it should be guarded now?

If you think, "It is due to grasping this body as mine", you must ask, "Why mind do you guard this body?" "If you and it are two separate things, then what use can it be to you?"

Why stupid mind, do you not grasp at a clean form made of wood? This machinery that is a mass of impurity is rotten, so what point is there in guarding it?

To begin with, mentally separate off the outer layer of skin. Then with the scalpel of prajñā separate the flesh from the skeleton of bones.

Separate the bones as well, then look into them down to the marrow, and examine yourself asking, "Does this have an essence?"

If you exert yourself at searching like that but do not see an essence in it, why are you still guarding this body out of attachment?

If your excrement is not fit to eat, your blood is not fit to drink, and your intestines not fit to be sucked, then what use is this body to you?

As a second-best proposition, could it be reasonable to guard it for the purpose of making food for the jackals and vultures? This human body of ours is something to be employed only for virtue; it is not right to consider it as something to be tossed away.

It is like this: you may have guarded it, but if the merciless Lord of Death steals it away and gives it to the birds and dogs, what will you be able to do?

If people are not given clothing and so on when they will not be able to serve with the other menials, why do you sustain this bag of meat broth when even though you hand-feed it, it will go elsewhere?

Having paid my body its wages, now let me put it to work for my sake! If it is of no benefit, I will not give it anything.

I will regard the body as a boat, simply a support for coming and going, or, in order to accomplish sentient beings' aims, I will transform it into a wish-fulfilling jewel of a body.

Having control of myself like that, I must always show a smiling face! I must completely give up frowning and scowling and be a friend and counsellor to migrators.

I will not be noisy whilst taking a seat on chairs and the like. I will not open doors with un-necessary force; I will always take joy in humility.

By moving stealthily without a sound, the stork, cat, and thief all accomplish what they desire to do, so the Capable Ones always conduct themselves in the same way.

When someone says something for my benefit that admonishes or advises me wisely and without confusion, I should accept those words with high respect; in general I should always be a student of all.

To all those who speak well I should say, "Well said!" If I see others creating merit, I should cheer them on by praising them.

If others have good qualities that are not apparent, I should express them, and if another's good qualities have been expressed by someone else, then I should follow along and express them too. If others express my own good qualities while I am present, then I should simply be aware of them.

All the undertakings of enlightenment mind are because of others' joy, a joy that would be rare even if it could be bought with money. Therefore, I should live in the happiness of finding joy in the good qualities made by others.

By doing so, in this life I will suffer no loss and by it in future ones too, there will be a greater degree of happiness. The fault of disliking their good qualities will cause me not to be joyful and to suffer in this life and to have a greater degree of suffering in future ones too.

When I speak, what I say should be pleasing to others because of inspiring trust and being clear in meaning; it should be free of the expressions of desire and anger; and it should be gentle and in moderate tones.

And when I am looking at sentient beings with my eyes, thinking, "I will become a buddha in dependence on these very beings", I should look at them with sincerity and loving kindness.

Because of always being motivated by great aspiration or by the antidotes, the virtues made in the field of good qualities, the field of beneficial providers and the field of suffering, and so on will be very strong.

I will always do the activities of the six paramitas having equipped myself with expertise and joy. All of those activities will be done without relying on anyone else.

The paramitas of generosity and the rest are carried out in an upward progression, with each one more distinguished than the last. One of greater meaning should not be put aside for the sake of one of lesser meaning. However, one should consider others' sakes as most important.

When that has been understood, I should remain diligently working for the sake of others. Those of compassionate activity having looked on from afar have prohibited some actions but allowed them for the bodhisatvas.

Having divided food received into four parts, a bodhisatva must share three parts among those who have fallen into the bad migrations, those who are without a guardian, and those who are staying in the yogic discipline of the pure conduct of brahmacharya. Then he should eat moderately.

All of my articles except for the three robes, can be given away. This body that is being used to carry out the holy dharma should not be harmed on account of something of little meaning. Taking that approach the intentions of all sentient beings are quickly fulfilled. When the mind of compassion is impure, this body should not be given away. By all means the body should in this and future lives be given over to becoming the cause of accomplishing a great purpose.

The dharma should not be explained to those who do not respect it, nor to those who, like a sick man, have wrapped a cloth around the head, nor to those carrying an umbrella, mendicant's staff, or weapon, nor to those wearing a covering on the head.

The profound and vast Great Vehicle should not be explained to followers of the Lesser Vehicle and not to a woman unaccompanied by a man. I should in every way respect the lesser and supreme dharmas as equal.

I should not connect those who are vessels for the very vast dharma with the lesser dharma. I should not completely cast aside the bodhisatva trainings. I should not seduce others by means of the sutras and tantras.

When I spit or discard a tooth-cleaning stick, I should cover it up. To urinate and so on in water or on land that is used by others is condemned.

When eating I should not stuff my mouth, eat noisily, nor eat with my mouth open. I should not sit with my legs outstretched nor should I rub my hands together.

I should not stay in vehicles, on beds, or in isolated places together with the women of others. Having observed and inquired as to everything that the world finds improper, I will abandon all such behaviour.

I should not give directions with one finger, but instead indicate the way respectfully with my right arm with all my fingers fully outstretched.

Nor should I wave my arms about, but should communicate with slight gestures and a little sound, such as with a snap of the fingers, and so on, otherwise I shall become unrestrained.

Like the Guardian lying down to pass into nirvana, I should lie in the desired direction and with alertness first of all make a firm decision to quickly arise.

The conducts of a bodhisatva are immeasurable, so I must carry out the conduct of cleansing the mind until it is certain that the stains of mind have been purified.

I will recite *The Sutra of the Three Heaps* three times during the day and three times at night, for by relying upon the conquerors and bodhisatvas my remaining downfalls will be alleviated.

Whatever I am doing in any situation, whether it is for myself or for others, I will exert myself and train in whatever training has been taught for that situation.

There is not anything that is not learned by the conquerors' sons for the purpose of all-knowing; for someone who is skilled at living like that there is no such thing as merits not arising.

I should not do anything, either directly or indirectly, other than for the sake of sentient beings and should dedicate all I do exclusively for the sake of sentient beings attaining enlightenment.

I will always attend a virtuous spiritual friend who is expert in the meaning of the Great Vehicle and possesses the supreme yogic conduct of the bodhisatva, and even at the cost of my life will not abandon him.

I will train in how to attend the guru according to *The Emancipation Story of Śhri Saṃbhava*.

I should know this and other instructions given by the Buddha through reading the sutras. The trainings appear extensively in the sutras, therefore I will read them. To begin with I should look at *The Sutra of Ākāśhagarbha*. Why? Because in it the conduct that is to be constantly carried out is very extensively shown.

Apart from that, I definitely should look again and again at *The Compendium of Trainings*. Alternatively, I should look at something more condensed, such as *The Compendium of Sutras*. I should also make an effort to look at the two works by noble Nāgārjuna.

I should carry out whatever conduct is not forbidden in those works. However, when I see a training that has to be done in order to guard worldly beings' minds, it will be all right to truly undertake it.

I shall examine again and again the situations of body and mind. When that is summarised, it has the characteristic of guarding alertness.

I shall use my body to put these conducts into practice, otherwise, what would be accomplished merely by talking about it? Will a sick man be benefited merely by reading medical texts?

That was the fifth chapter of *Entering the Conduct of a Bodhisatva*, called "Guarding Alertness".

CHAPTER SIX

Patience

One moment of anger destroys all the good conduct of generosity, offering to the sugatas, and so on that has been accumulated over the course of a thousand aeons.

There is no evil like anger. There is no fortitude like patience. Therefore, I should work assiduously at cultivating patience in various ways.

If I hold onto painful thoughts of anger, mind will not experience peace and, not finding joy and happiness, sleep will not come and I will be unsettled.

Even those who have come to depend on a person of high position because out of kindness he has provided them with funds and considerate treatment, will attack in order to kill him if he has become filled with anger.

By it, close ones and friends become disheartened and, although they are drawn in by my generosity, they will not trust me. In short, be it myself or others, no-one stays happily with someone who has hatred.

The enemy, hatred, will be the creator of sufferings such as those, whereas someone who persistently overcomes hatred will be happy in this life and others.

Having found its sustenance—a mind unhappy at having to do what I do not want to do and being prevented from doing what I do want to do—anger grows in size and then destroys me.

Therefore, I will completely destroy the sustenance that makes my enemy grow. This is how it is: this enemy has no function other than to do me harm.

Thus, whatever happens, I will not allow my happy state of mind to be disturbed. I could make myself unhappy over something, but then my wishes would not be accomplished and my virtues would deteriorate.

If something that happens can be remedied, what is there to be unhappy about? And if it cannot be remedied, what benefit will come from making myself unhappy over it?

I do not want any of the things called "suffering, contempt, harsh words, and unpleasant words" for myself or my friends, but for my enemies it is the opposite.

The causes of happiness only sometimes arise, but the causes for suffering are very many.

Without suffering there would be no renunciation. Therefore, you mind, should have a firm resolve.

If the ascetics who put faith in the turning back of Iśhvara and the people of Karṇāṭa who tolerate the pains of burning, cutting, and so on exercise patience for the sake of that sort of thing that has no meaning, then why do I not have the armour of courage for emancipation which is meaningful?

There is nothing anywhere that will not become easier through familiarization. Therefore, if I familiarize myself with small harms now, I will be able to exercise patience with great harms later on.

CHAPTER SIX

"Who has not seen a need to do this with the meaningless sufferings caused by snakes and flies, sensations of hunger and thirst, and so on and with rashes and the like?"

I should not lose patience easily with heat and cold, wind and rain, and so on, nor with sickness, bondage, and beatings, and so on because if I do, it will increase the harm caused.

Some become extra brave when they see their own blood. Some faint and fall unconscious when they see the blood of others. These reactions come from mind being either steadfast or timid respectively. Therefore, when something harmful occurs, I must dismiss it and remain un-affected by the suffering!

When those who are expert meet with suffering, even then they keep their minds lucid and un-defiled as they do battle with the afflictions, for during the battle much harm can be inflicted. It is those who have defeated the enemies of hatred and so on by dismissing all suffering that are the warriors who have been victorious over the enemy. The rest are slayers who kill corpses.

Furthermore, suffering has good qualities: being disheartened by it dispels haughtiness; it rouses compassion for those in samsaric existence; and it results in avoiding evil and taking joy in virtue.

I do not become angry at the greater sources of suffering, such as jaundice, and so on, so why should I be angry with those who have a mind when all of them are pressed on by conditions too?

For example, in the same way as this sickness will arise although unit is unwanted, likewise these afflictions will persistently arise although they are unwanted.

Beings do not deliberately think, "I will get angry", but just become angry. Likewise anger without deliberately thinking, "I will produce myself", is just produced.

All wrong behaviour as much as there is and all the various types of evil arise through the force of one's own conditions, so it is not that they exist independently.

These conditions that assemble together do not have a mind that is thinking "I will produce" and neither does what is produced by them have a mind thinking, "I will be generated".

That which is asserted as "the primal substance" and that which is designated as "the self" do not arise having deliberately thought, "I will arise".

If in not having been produced the self does not exist, any wish it might have to be produced also would be non-existent .

The self would be permanently involved with apprehending objects, hence would not cease doing so.

If that self were permanent, it would clearly be devoid of action, like space. Even if it met with other conditions, it being changeless what effect could be apparent?

If, even when there is a condition that has become present for it to do something, it remains as it was before, then what effect could its doing something have had on it?

How could saying, "This is its doer" make them related?

Thus all things are dependent on something else and due to that whatever arises from them arises without independence. If I have that sort of understanding, I will not become angry with any of these apparition-like things.

And then there is the question, "What turns away which anger?", to which one person says, "It would not be all right to turn away anger". However, there is nothing not all right with doing so because it is asserted that in dependence on doing so the sufferings will have their continuity cut.

If I see someone, whether enemy or friend, who because of that is doing something that is not all right, I must reflect that "this has happened due to some sort of condition" and take up a happy frame of mind!

If things came about by choice, then since no one wants to suffer, suffering would not arise for any of the bodied beings.

Being heedless some people harm themselves with thorns and other such things. Some become obsessed and stop eating, and so on because of trying to obtain a woman and other such things.

And there are some who harm themselves by hanging themselves, leaping from cliffs, eating poison or unhealthy foods, and doing other such merit-less deeds.

When they have fallen under control of the afflictions, people will see themselves as worthless and even kill themselves. At such time, how could they be expected not to harm the bodies of others?

If I cannot give rise to compassion for such people who have set out to kill me and the like because their afflictions have been aroused, the last thing I should do is become angry with them.

Just as the nature of fire is to burn but it is not right to be angry with it, so the nature of these childish ordinary beings might be to injure others, but it is still not right to be angry with them.

Well, if that fault was a temporary occurrence and if sentient beings' nature has been ascertained, it is not right to be angry, for that would be like begrudging space for allowing smoke to arise in it.

In the case of a stick or the like that is actually used to harm me, if I become angry with the wielder, since the wielder in turn was incited by anger, further examination will show that it would be correct to be angry at the hatred.

Before now I must have done this sort of injury to other sentient beings. Therefore it is right that this harm comes back to me, the one who has injured other sentient beings.

Both the weapon of that harmful one and my body are causes of my suffering. Since he came up with the weapon and I came up with the body, with whom should I be angry?

If, blinded by craving for this abscess of a human form that cannot bear to be touched and suffers I grasp at it, then with whom should I be angry in response to this body being hurt?

The childish beings do not want suffering yet are greatly attached to its causes, so it is their own fault that they are harmed. In that case why should I bear a grudge towards others?

For example, as with the guards of the hells and the forest of sword-like leaves this was created by my own karmic actions, so with whom should I be angry?

Brought on by my own karmic actions of the past these ones who harm me now arise and if their actions now send them on to becoming hell beings later on, I will be the one who has brought them such loss, will I not?

These ones have become a basis for cultivating patience through which many of my evils will be cleared away, but based on me, they will be sent on to the hells where they will suffer for a long time.

I am causing them harm and they are benefiting me. Why then unruly mind, do you become angry in such a mistaken manner?

If I have a good attitude, I will not go to hell. In that case I have protected myself, but how could the same happen for them?

However, if I were to harm them in return, it would not protect them and it would degrade my conduct, with the result that my capacity for withstanding difficulty would fail.

Mind does not have a physical body, so cannot be destroyed in any way by anyone. However, it does cling strongly to the physical body, so the body is harmed by sufferings.

If abusive speech, harsh speech, and unpleasant words will not result in harm to my body, why, mind, do you become so angry at them?

If those others not liking me will not devour me in this or another life, why do I not want it?

I may not want these because they will create an obstacle to material gains in this life. However, want them or not, I will have to leave material gains of this life behind, whereas my evils will remain firmly in place.

It would be better that I die today than live long with bad livelihood. Someone like me might stay long but the suffering of death cannot be avoided.

Suppose someone wakes up from a dream in which happiness was experienced for one hundred years and someone else wakes up from a dream in which happiness was experienced for a short while. For both of them, that happiness will never return. In both cases, whether the lives are long or short, at the time of death it will end up like that.

Although I might have had many material gains and lived happily for a long time, I will go on empty-handed, like having been robbed by bandits.

I may say, "If material gains enable me to live a long time, I will be able to end evil deeds and make merit". However, if I become angry on account of material gains, will not my merits be ended and evil deeds increase?

If the purpose of my life is undermined and only evil deeds are done, what meaning would such a life serve?

If I say, "I should be angry with those who say things unpleasant to hear that cause other sentient beings' liking for me to be undermined", then why is it, mind, that you are not also angry with those who express unpleasant things to others?"

If you can be patient with this loss of faith in someone else, why can't you be patient with someone who says unpleasant things about me because of afflictions that have been aroused in him?

Others might speak irreverently about or destroy statues, stupas, or the holy dharma, but even then it is not right to be angry about it because the buddhas, and so on cannot be harmed.

I will also turn back anger towards those who do harm to gurus, their relatives, and so on and to close ones, due to seeing in the manner shown before this that their actions have come about through conditions.

If bodied beings are injured both by beings with a mind and things without a mind, why single out beings with a mind and be hostile towards them? It follows that I must be patient with all harm!

If someone out of stupidity does wrong to another and the other stupidly becomes angry in return, which one would be without fault? Which one would be with fault?

Why did I previously do those karmic actions because of which others now do me harm? If everything in the end depends on my karmic actions, why should I have hostility towards these harmful beings?

Having seen that to be so, I see that a mind of mutual loving kindness is needed for everyone, so I will conscientiously make the merits for that to happen.

For example, if a fire burning in one house has spread to another house, flammable matter like straw should be removed from the other house. Similarly, when the fire of anger spreads to whatever my mind is attached to, I should immediately get rid of it out of concern that my merit will be burned.

What about it is not fortunate if a man condemned to death is released after having his hand cut off? What about it is not fortunate if my human suffering will be enough to free me from hell?

If I am unable to be patient with this relatively minor suffering of the present, then why do I not turn away from anger, the cause of the suffering of the hells?

For the sake of my desires I have experienced being burned, and so on thousands of times in hell, but have accomplished nothing of my own or others' sakes.

Only gladness for this suffering is appropriate here, for this suffering does not involve even a fraction of that much harm, but very meaningful things will be accomplished through it that will dispel the harms of migrators.

If a person who praises another with good qualities gains the happiness of a joyful mind, why, mind, do you not praise him and make yourself joyful too?

This joyful happiness of yours would be a source of happiness and would result in an absence of wrongdoings. Permitted by those having good qualities, such commendation of another is also a supreme means for gathering disciples.

It is said that others will be made happy like that. However, if you do not want them to be happy, you could do things such as stop paying their wages, though if you do that, there will be results both seen and unseen that will cause you to degenerate.

When people speak of my own good qualities, I want others to be happy too, but when they express the good qualities of others, I do not want happiness even for myself. There is that and there is wanting all sentient beings to be happy due to which the mind for enlightenment has been aroused. Having aroused that mind, why am I angered by sentient beings finding happiness for themselves?

If I want sentient beings to become buddhas who are worshipped by the three worlds, why are you tormented on seeing them receive the most basic service and respect?

If a relative who you support and provide for has been able to find his own livelihood, wouldn't you take joy in this, rather than becoming angry?

If I do not wish for migrators to have even that, what meaning is there in my wishing that they become enlightened? How could there be enlightenment mind in someone who becomes angry when others receive something?

Whether a donor gives a recipient something or it remains in the donor's house, because you will never have ownership of it, it makes no difference whether it is given to the recipient or not. What use is the envy involved?

Why do I throw away my merits, the faith of others, and my good qualities? By throwing them away I am not keeping what turns into material gains, so tell me, why am I not angry with myself?

Not only do you not despair over the evils that you have done, but you want to compete with others who have done meritorious deeds?

If an enemy becomes unhappy, what cause is there for you, mind, to be glad about it? Your simply wishing for that will not cause your enemy to be harmed.

And even if he suffers as you had wished, what cause is there for you to be glad about it? If you say, "I will be satisfied by it", what will come of that is ruin for you and what else?

The fishing line cast by the fisherman of the afflictions has an unbearably sharp hook; having been caught on it it is certain that I will be cooked by the guards of hell together with other sentient beings in the cauldrons of hell.

The honours of praise and fame will not turn into merit nor a longer life. They will not give me strength, will not bring absence of illness, and will not provide physical well-being.

If I knew what would be meaningful for me, what value would I find in these things? If all I want is mental happiness, I must apply myself to its causes—gambling, and so on and liquor, too.

If for the sake of becoming renowned I lose my wealth to others or get myself killed, what use would those words be then? Once I have died, who will they make happy?

When their sandcastles collapse, children cry in despair. Likewise when my praise and fame decline, my mind becomes like that of a child.

Short-lived sounds have no mind therefore they cannot possibly have a mind that thinks to praise me. However, the audible sound "He is liked by others" is counted as a cause of joy, so it makes the person doing the praising happy and makes me happy too.

What benefit does the other's joy bring me? That happiness of joy belongs to him so I will not get even a part of it.

If his happiness makes me happy, then I need to have that approach with everyone else as well and if that is so, how could I be unhappy when others are made happy by what brings them joy?

In the same way my own joy produced from thinking, "I am being praised", also is not acceptable and ends up being nothing else than the behaviour of a child.

Praise and so on distract me. They destroy my disenchantment with samsara. They make me envious of others who have good qualities. They destroy a perfection of virtue.

Therefore, "Those who are closely involved with tearing down my praise and the like are also here in order to guard me from falling into the bad destinies, are they not?"

For I who seek liberation, being bound by material gains and honour is unnecessary. How then could I be angry with those who have liberated me from being bound by them?

And how could I be angry with those who want me to suffer when, like buddhas giving a blessing, they close the door that leads to suffering?

I might recognize someone as an "obstructor of merit", but it still would not be right to be angry with such a person. If there is no fortitude that withstands such difficulties as patience, I should dwell in it, should I not?

If due to my own faults I am not patient with this person, it will end up that I have made this cause of merit who is present right in front of me into an obstructor of merit.

If there is none at all of what is called "a cause", a result will not arise and if there is, it will. If one thing is the cause of another, how could I say that it is "obstructive"?

At the time of giving, a beggar is not considered to be an obstructor of generosity and it does not work to call those who participate in an ordination "obstructors of ordination".

There are indeed beggars in this world, but those who would harm me are scarce, for if I have not harmed others, none will harm me.

Therefore, I should be glad to have an enemy for, like a treasure that has come forth in my house without need of tiring effort, he assists me in my enlightenment conduct.

I accomplish patience in concert with this enemy, therefore he is worthy of being given the fruits of the patience first. It is so because he has become the cause of my patience.

"If this enemy does not have the thought that I must accomplish patience, he is not to be worshipped", you say. Then why would I worship the holy dharma given that it too is fit to be a cause for accomplishment?

"If this enemy has the thought that I should be harmed, he is not to be worshipped", you say. Then how would my patience be accomplished if others, like physicians, always strove to do me good?

Therefore, since patience is produced in dependence on another who has a very aggressive mind, that person having become a cause of patience is, like the holy dharma, worthy of worship.

Because of that the Capable One spoke of "the field of sentient beings and the field of conquerors". By seeing that these sentient beings are to be pleased, many have gone to the other shore of gaining the perfection of their own and others' sakes.

The buddha qualities are accomplished through sentient beings and the conquerors and since it is that way, how is it that do I not respect sentient beings in the same way that I respect the conquerors?

This is not about the good qualities of their intentions being equivalent, but about their results being equivalent. Because of that equivalence, sentient beings have good qualities, too.

The merit that comes from worshipping someone having the enlightenment mind is due to the greatness of sentient beings, and similarly the merit that comes from having faith in the Buddha is due to the greatness of a buddha.

They each have a share in accomplishing the buddha qualities, therefore they are asserted to be equal. However, none are equal to the buddhas who are limitless oceans of good qualities.

Their collection of supreme good qualities is that of the buddhas alone. And for those few in whom a mere portion of their good qualities appears, if for the sake of worshipping them the three realms were offered, it would be insufficient for the task.

Sentient beings have a share in giving birth to the supreme buddha qualities, therefore, in conformance with just that much of a share, it is correct to worship sentient beings.

Furthermore, what else except for pleasing sentient beings will repay the kindness of those who befriend us without deceit and provide us with unfathomable assistance?

Benefiting them will repay the kindness of those buddhas, the ones who have given their bodies and even entered the hell of Unremitting Torment for the sake of sentient beings. Hence I will behave impeccably in everything that I do, even if these sentient beings do me great harm because of it.

When those who have now become my lords have no regard even for their own bodies, how is it that I, so stupid, act towards them with pride and not act as a chattel, their servant?

The capable ones are gladdened by sentient beings' happiness and made unhappy by their being harmed. Thus, by making sentient beings glad I make all of the capable ones glad and by harming them I harm all the capable ones.

If my body were totally ablaze with fire, my mind would not be happy even if all desirable sense-objects were piled up before it. Likewise if sentient beings are harmed, there is no way that the greatly compassionate ones could be glad.

Therefore, since I have done harm to migrators, today I individually lay aside whatever evils I have done that have not gladdened the compassionate ones. Please forgive me for the unhappiness I have caused you.

In order to gladden the tathāgatas, from today onward I shall definitely tame myself and be a servant of the world. Though many migrators stamp upon my head or even try to kill me, I will not retaliate. Thereby may I gladden the guardians of the world!

There is no doubt that the buddhas, whose nature is compassion, regard all of these migrators as themselves. And they see sentient beings' entity, which is the hidden-from-view guardian that is none other than the buddha's enlightened mind. Why then would I not respect the functioning of their buddha nature?

This pleasing of sentient beings is what pleases the tathāgatas. Just this is also what truly accomplishes my own aims. Just this is also what dispels the suffering of the world. This being so, I should always do just that.

For example, if some of the king's men were to harm many people, farsighted men would not return the harm even if they could do so, for they would see that the men were not acting alone but were a force representing the entire might of the king. Similarly, I should not underestimate a few weak beings who do me harm, for they are a force representing the guards of the hells and the compassionate ones. Proceeding like the subjects of that fierce king, I shall please all sentient beings.

If someone such as a king were to become angry, could he make me experience the harms of hell that will be experienced because of not pleasing sentient beings?

And if someone such as a king were to be pleased, he could not possibly grant me the buddhahood that will be obtained by pleasing sentient beings.

Why do I not see that, putting aside the fact that the future attainment of buddhahood comes from pleasing sentient beings, in this very life great glory and fame and happiness all come from the same?

The benefits of patience are that while circling in cyclic existence, it brings a beautiful body and so on, absence of sickness, renown, an extremely long life, and the vast happiness of a wheel-turning emperor.

That was the sixth chapter of *Entering the Conduct of a Bodhisatva*, called "Patience".

CHAPTER SEVEN

Perseverance

Having become patient like that, perseverance must be undertaken given that enlightenment is present in those who have perseverance. Just as there is no movement without wind, merit does not arise without perseverance.

What is perseverance? It is delighting in virtue. Its non-conducive side is explained to be laziness, which comes from clinging to what is bad, procrastination, and low self-esteem.

Because of experiencing the pleasurable taste of idleness and because of craving for sleep, there is no disenchantment with the suffering of samsara and laziness grows strong.

Having been caught in the trap of the afflictions, I have entered the trap of birth and gone into the mouth of the lord of death. How is it that I am still not aware of that?

The lord of death is systematically slaughtering our species, but you do not see it! Nevertheless, those who prefer to sleep are like buffaloes facing a butcher.

Having blocked off every path of escape the lord of death is looking to kill, so how can you enjoy eating and how can you enjoy sleep?

Death will be here quickly, but for as long as it is not, I will gather the accumulations.

I might attempt to abandon laziness when death arrives, but it is not the time for it, so what will be the use?

When something has not been undertaken, or has been started, or is only half finished, the lord of death will suddenly come. I will think, "Oh no, I have failed!"

Those close to me, their eyes red and swollen in sorrow and tears running down their faces, knowing that there is nothing that could help finally lose hope and I see the faces of the messengers of Yama. Tormented by the memory of my evils and hearing the sounds of hell, I will be so afraid that I will clothe my body in excrement and then what could I do in such a crazed state?

If in this life I become filled with fear like that of a live fish being rolled in hot sand, what need is there to mention the sufferings in the unbearable hells that will be made by the evils I have done?

If those of youthful flesh come into contact with boiling water, they will not be able to bear the pain. Why then do I remain at ease like this when I have done karmic actions that will result in the Extreme Heating Hell?

Much harm befalls those who want results without being diligent and those of little tolerance who in the clutches of death will, like the gods cry out, "Oh no, I am overcome with sufferings!"

Rely on this boat of a human body to liberate yourself from the great river of suffering! In the future it will be difficult to obtain this sort of boat, so "You stupid fool!", this is not the time to fall asleep!"

Why do you abandon the supreme joy of the holy dharma that has limitless causes for joy then become distracted by causes for suffering and find joy in things that make your mind agitated, and so on?

I must do the following: be without procrastination, have the supporting forces assembled; be industrious; be in control of myself; see myself and others as equal; and practise exchanging self for other!

I should never indulge in procrastination by entertaining thoughts such as, "How could I possibly gain enlightenment?" This is how to judge that. The tathāgata, one who speaks the truth, has told this truth: "If they develop the strength of their diligence, even those who are flies, meat flies, insects in general, and likewise worms will gain this difficult to gain, unsurpassed enlightenment."

For someone like myself who has been born in the race of humans and can recognize what is beneficial and what is harmful, as long as I do not let go of the conduct of enlightenment, what could stop me from obtaining enlightenment?"

"Well yes, in the long run I will obtain it, but it frightens me to think that I will have to give away my arms, legs, and so on". Being stupid in regard to what is heavy and light, I have ended up being afraid of the light one.

During countless tens of millions of aeons I have been cut, stabbed, burned, and split apart many times, but it has not resulted in my gaining enlightenment.

Yet this suffering that comes with my accomplishing enlightenment has a measure of being light. It is like the suffering of having an incision made on the body in order to remove the greater pain of something such as an arrow lodged inside and damaging it.

All doctors use somewhat unpleasant medical procedures to remove major illnesses and in the same way I should tolerate smaller discomforts in order to overcome manifold sufferings.

The supreme physician does not employ common medical procedures such as these, but treats fathomless great illnesses with extremely gentle techniques.

The Guide taught giving cooked food and the like as a beginning preparation. Later, having become familiar with that, one could gradually reach the point at which one could even give away one's own flesh.

When a mind has been produced that regards one's own body like cooked food, and so on, what difficulty would there be in giving one's own flesh, and so on?

Such things are done in order to abandon evil, so there will be no suffering involved and they are done in order to develop expertise, so there will be no unhappiness involved. This is how it is: we have been producing wrong concepts and doing evil actions that have harmed body and mind, whereas if we had been making merit, we would have been making the body happy and if we had been developing expertise, we would have been making the mind happy. Thus, the Compassionate Ones may have to stay in samsara for a long time for the sake of others, but how could they ever become disheartened by it?

This one, using the strength of his enlightenment mind exhausts his previously-done evil deeds and collects an ocean of merit, therefore he is said to be supreme when compared to the śhrāvakas.

Having mounted the horse of enlightenment mind which dispels all despondency and physical weariness, he goes from happiness to happiness, so who on knowing of this mind would procrastinate?

CHAPTER SEVEN

The forces to be developed in order to accomplish sentient beings' aims are intention, steadfastness, joy, and rejection. Intention and the others are developed through being afraid of suffering and through considering their benefits and abandoning what is not conducive to them.

Industriously working at intention, pride, joy, and rejection will develop the strength of my control over myself and because that can increase perseverance I must exert myself at them.

The wrongs of myself and others are fathomless, but I must eradicate them. It will take an ocean of aeons to eradicate each one of those wrongs, but if I do not see in myself even a fraction of the diligence needed to exhaust all of those wrongs, why doesn't my heart burst on seeing this place of fathomless suffering?

The good qualities needed for myself and others will be many, so I will have to work at familiarization for an ocean of aeons in order to accomplish every one of them.

However, I have never gained familiarization with even a fraction of those good qualities, so what have I gained? I am amazed at how meaningless I have made this birth!

I have not worshipped the Bhagavat with offerings and not found happiness in the celebrations honouring him; I have not done the activities required by the teaching; I have not fulfilled the wishes of the poor; I have not provided those who have fear with no fear; and I have not given comfort to those who are downtrodden. I have ended up doing nothing more than making pains in my mother's womb, and following that, creating only suffering for her.

In past lives and the present one too, I have kept away from the intention to follow dharma because of which this sort of paucity has arisen. Who would ever relinquish the intention to follow the dharma?

The Capable One said that intention is the root of everything virtuous. And its root in turn is constant meditation on full-ripening results.

Suffering, mental unhappiness, the various fears, and separation from what is desired come from doing evil.

By doing virtue with a beneficial intention, I will go here to the higher levels or there to emancipation but here or there wherever it is, the merit involved will offer up manifest good results.

The evil done might come from wanting happiness, but wherever I go that evil will cause the weapons of suffering to overwhelm me completely in that place.

By doing virtue, I will dwell in the spacious, fragrant, and cooling heart of a lotus, my radiance developed by the food of the Conqueror's sweet speech, my supreme body arising from a lotus opened by the Capable One's light, and will stay before the conquerors as a son of the sugatas.

Because of doing many non-virtues in the past, my whole skin will be peeled off by the henchmen of Yama and in that extremely feeble state, molten copper melted by an extremely hot fire will be poured into my body. Stabbed by flaming swords and daggers, my flesh will be cut apart into hundreds of pieces and I will collapse onto the fiercely blazing iron ground.

That is how it is, so I should have the intention to accomplish virtue and cultivate it with respect.

Having undertaken the accomplishment of what is meaningful using the rite in *The Vajra Victory Banner*, I should then cultivate pride.

First of all I should examine a task to find out whether I should undertake it or not. Not to start might be best, for once it has been started, there is no turning back.

If I try to accomplish what I am not capable of, in future births I will have a habit of that and evil and suffering will increase and also in other births at the time of the result there will be a low-grade result and as well as that, the task undertaken will not be accomplished.

Pride should be applied to the three of action, affliction, and capability. Saying, "I alone will do it" is pride applied to action.

Made powerless by the afflictions, the migrators of this world are incapable of accomplishing their own aims. They are not capable in the way that I am, therefore I will do it for them.

Others may be working at lesser tasks, but how could I just stand by? If I do nothing because of pride, it would be best for me to have no pride.

When a crow encounters a dead snake, it behaves as though it were a king of birds and if I have a weak personality like that, even small adversities will trouble me.

Could someone who has shrunk from this task and given up trying have emancipation through such poverty mentality? Someone who is using pride to develop exertion will be very difficult to overcome, even by great adversities.

Therefore with steadfast mind I shall overcome all adversities, for if I am defeated by an adversity, my desire to conquer the three realms will be worthy of ridicule.

Therefore, I will conquer everything and no-one will conquer me! I, a son of the lion-like conquerors, will dwell in this sort of pride.

The migrator who is overpowered by pride which is an affliction is not the person with pride being shown here. The person with pride shown here does not fall under the enemy's control, whereas the other does fall under the control of the enemy, pride.

The one who is puffed up with the pride of the afflictions will be led to the bad migrations and will have the festival of being human destroyed, be turned into a servant dependent on another's food, and be stupid, ugly, weak, and despised everywhere. If that sort of person also were included among the ones with pride, tell me, what could be more demeaning than that?

Someone who carries pride in order to conquer the enemy pride is the one with pride and also a totally victorious one and a hero. Someone in whom the enemy pride has taken hold but who then defeats it completes the fruition of becoming a conqueror, fulfilling what is wanted for migrators.

If I find myself amidst a crowd of afflictions, I will withstand them in a thousand ways; like a lion not being bothered by jackals and the like, I will not be bothered by the afflictions.

Just as people will guard their eyes to prevent them from being hit in the midst of a terrible beating, likewise in the midst of terrible upheavals, I will prevent myself from falling under the control of the afflictions.

It would be better for me to be burned to death or have my head cut off, than to bow down to the enemy, the ever-present afflictions.

Similarly, in all circumstances I will not conduct myself in any way other than what is correct. Like those who want the enjoyment that comes from a game, this sort of person is attracted to whatever tasks are to be done and he never has enough of such tasks, which only bring him joy.

People work for the sake of happiness, but with no certainty of whether there will be a happy outcome or not. On the other hand, this work of mine will have a happy outcome, but if I do not do the work, how could it have a happy outcome?

If there is no satisfaction in desirable objects that are like honey on a razor's edge, why would there be satisfaction with the merit for the peace of enlightenment whose full-ripening is happiness?

In view of that, in order to finish an activity I shall enter it again and again like an elephant who, tormented by the heat of the midday sun, on finding a lake plunges into it.

When my strength declines, I should put aside whatever I have been doing for a while so that I will be able to pick it up and continue with it later.

When it has been done well, it can be abandoned while wishing to accomplish what comes next.

Like old warriors who are expert at dodging an enemy's weapons meeting the enemy on the battlefront, I will dodge the weapon-like afflictions and skilfully deal with the enemies that are the afflictions.

If someone drops his sword during a battle, he quickly picks it up out of fear and likewise, if I lose the weapon of mindfulness, remembering the fears of hell I will quickly retrieve it.

Just as poison spreads throughout the body due to the circulation of blood, likewise if the afflictions find an opportunity, wrongs will spread throughout the mind.

Those who practise the yogic disciplines should be as attentive as a frightened man carrying a vessel full of mustard oil who is being followed by someone holding a sword and threatening to kill him if he spills it.

Just as I would swiftly stand if a snake came into my lap, should sleep or idleness come, I will quickly repel them.

Each time something wrong occurs, I should berate myself then contemplate for a long time that, "In future, I will do whatever it takes so that this does not happen to me again".

"How in these circumstances will I develop familiarization with mindfulness?" Because of such a thought I will want to meet with spiritual friends or obtain appropriate tasks from them.

Before having such a task, one needs to be prepared in all ways and for that I should recall what was talked about in the chapter on heedfulness. Then I should rise to any task with a lightheart.

Just as the wind blowing back and forth governs the movement to and fro of cotton wool, so shall I be governed by delight.

That was the seventh chapter of *Entering the Conduct of a Bodhisatva*, called "Perseverance".

CHAPTER EIGHT

Meditative Concentration

Having developed perseverance in that way, I should set my mind in the equipoise of samadhi. The person whose mind is distracted dwells between the fangs of the afflictions.

Through solitude of body and mind distraction does not arise. Therefore I will abandon the world and entirely discard conceptual thinking.

The world is not abandoned because of past attachments or by craving for material gain and the like, therefore I should entirely abandon these things, given that those who are expert see it this way.

Having understood that the afflictions are destroyed by superior seeing fully equipped with calm abiding, to begin with I will seek out calm abiding which will be accomplished through the strong joy of being unattached to worldly life.

The true attachment that impermanent beings have for other impermanent beings means that they will not see their beloved ones again for thousands of lives.

Not seeing them makes me unhappy. My mind will not settle into equipoise and, even if I do see them, I am not satisfied, so like before am tormented by craving.

When I become attached to sentient beings it totally obscures the authentic, destroys my disenchantment, and in the end tortures me with anguish.

By thinking only of them this life will pass without meaning. These impermanent relatives and friends will even destroy the thoroughly good, everlasting dharma.

If I live at the same level as the childish, it is certain that I will go to the bad migrations. If by not living at that level I lead myself upwards, what would be gained from entrusting myself to the childish?

They will become close friends in an instant and turn into enemies a short time later. Even joyful situations make them angry. It is difficult to please the ordinary beings.

If something is said for their benefit, they get angry and attempt to turn me away from what is beneficial. If I do not listen to what they say, they become angry and because of that will go to the bad migrations.

They are envious of superiors, competitive with equals, proud towards inferiors, haughty when praised, and if something unpleasant is said, they become angry; nothing of benefit can be gained from the childish.

If I associate with the childish, some kind of non-virtue will definitely arise, such as praising myself and reviling others and discussing the joys of samsara.

The mutual support and association of myself and others will end up in nothing but ruin. They do nothing for my sake and I do not work for theirs, so I should go far away from these childish people.

When I do meet them, I should please them by making them happy, but without becoming too familiar with them should behave well out of simple courtesy.

In the same way as a bee takes honey from a flower, I should take but remain unfamiliar with all of them, as though not having seen them before.

"I have many material gains and am more honoured, so many people like me". If I maintain that kind of self-importance, I will become afraid at the time of death.

Thus, out of total stupidity I become attached to this and that, adding to them one after another, with the result that suffering a thousandfold will ensue.

That being so, the learned do not make attachments because fear is born from the attachment. With an unflinching mind fully understand that by nature these things will be discarded!

I might have many material gains and be famous, and be well spoken of, but the gain and fame I have amassed will have no power to accompany me to my destination.

If there are others who deprecate me, what joy would there be in being praised by some? And if there are others who praise me, what sorrow would there be in being deprecated by some?

If even the Conqueror could not please sentient beings of varying inclinations, what need to mention a bad person such as I? Therefore I should give up all ideas of being in accord with the world.

Sentient beings deprecate others who have no material gain and express unpleasant things about others who do. They are by nature hard to be with, so how could any of them be a source of joy?

The tathāgatas have said, "Do not befriend the childish at all, because they are not happy unless their own purposes are being fulfilled.

In forests, the gentle creatures, birds, and trees do not express unpleasant sounds, so being with them is a happy event, and one day I shall stay together with them.

May I while dwelling in a cave, empty shrine room, or at the foot of a tree not look back one day, but be without attachment.

May I dwell in places that, not being held to as "mine" by anyone, are naturally spacious for the mind, where I can behave as I wish and without attachment.

One day I will dwell there with just a begging bowl and a few other articles and with the robes that no-one wants for their use, not having to hide myself, yet not at all afraid.

Having gone to the charnel ground, one day I shall understand that the skeletons of others and my body are the same in having the feature of being subject to decay.

This body of mine will smell so bad that even the foxes will not come close to it; such is what will become of it.

Although this body first arose as one whole thing, it and the flesh and bones with which it was created will break down and separate into pieces. If so, what will I say about the others whom I hold dear?

At birth I was born alone and at death I shall die alone. If others cannot take on a share of this suffering, what use are close ones who create obstructions?

Like travellers of the roads find a place and stay in it, travellers of the paths of rebirth find a place to be born and stay in it.

I shall retire to the forest until, supported by four pall-bearers and with the world standing there with tears on their faces and stricken with grief, I have to go on.

Befriending no one and begrudging no one, this body will dwell alone in solitude. Having already been counted as a dead man, there will be no mourners when I die.

There will be no one around to trouble me with their mourning, so there will be no one to distract me from my recollections of the Buddha and the others.

That being so, I shall dwell by myself alone in the forest of exceptional beauty and joy where having only minor difficulties leaves me at ease and with all distractions quelled.

Having completely let go of all other ideas and with single-minded purpose, I shall persevere in order to set the mind in equipoise and tame it.

In this world and the next one too, desires bring down ruin; in this one they produce being killed, bound, and flayed and in the next, they produce the hells, and so on.

For the sake of a woman many requests are first made through messengers for her and evils and notoriety are not avoided for her sake; I engage in fearsome deeds and even exhaust my wealth for her. However, the woman who is the source of supreme joy at the time of total sexual embrace, is a skeleton obscured by the machinery of skin and flesh, and nothing else. Then instead of utterly wanting and thoroughly clinging to this thing which is not autonomous and not mine, why do I not go to nirvana?

The first time, I made an effort to lift her veil and, when it had been raised, she bashfully looked down. Previously, whether anyone could see her or not, her face was covered with a cloth.

Now afflicted one, with its skin torn off by the vultures' beaks you see her face clearly as it actually is, as though you were seeing it directly. Now that you see it for what it is, why do you run away?

Although other men fixed their eyes upon it, I thoroughly guarded it, so why jealous one, do you not guard it while it is being eaten by vultures?

If vultures and others—jackals, and so on—having seen this flesh are eating it, there is no offering of flower garlands and sandalwood ointments to be made now that it has become the food of others.

And, having seen her bleached skeleton, if I am frightened by it even though it does not move, why am I not frightened by zombie corpses which are propelled by a few impulses?

Although I was attached to it when it was covered, why do I not desire it when it is not covered? If I have no need for that, why do I embrace it when it is covered?

At the time of sexual activity, I will swallow the woman's saliva. If excrement from below and saliva from above come solely from food, why do you not like excrement yet like saliva?

A pillow, whose cotton is soft to the touch, does not give me sexual enjoyment, whereas I believe that the pores of a woman's body do not emit a bad odour. Thus you, desirous one, are deluded as to what is unclean!

Some stupid fools saying that they cannot sleep on cotton although it is soft to the touch, become angry towards it.

If you think, "I am not attached to what is unclean", why do you copulate with a cage of bones linked together with muscle and plastered over with the mud of flesh?

Yours too has many unclean parts that you have to live with, yet your obsession with what is unclean makes you want another bag of uncleanliness.

"I enjoy the flesh", so I want to touch it and gaze upon it. But you do not want the flesh that by nature is without mind!

The mind of a woman desired cannot be touched or viewed and anything that could be touched would not be a consciousness. Thus, sexual embrace is meaningless, so what use is it?

It is not so strange not to realize that the bodies of others are unclean in nature, but it is very strange not to realize that one's own body is unclean!

Having abandoned a fresh lotus flower opened by rays of the sun in a cloudless sky, how is it that, with a mind that has clung to this uncleanliness, I am finding joy in a cage of the unclean?

If you do not want to touch places such as the ground that are smeared with excrement, how is it that you want to touch the body from which it came?

If you have no desire for the excrement, why do you embrace another's genitals? You do not want an unclean little maggot that came to life in a pile of unclean excrement and whose seed was nourished by the excrement, but you want to touch a big worm that was born from impurity.

Not only do you not condemn your own uncleanliness, but your obsession with what is unclean makes you want another bag of uncleanliness as well!

Attractive things such as camphor, and so on, and savoury foods or cooked rice having been put into the mouth then spat out make the ground unclean. Although such uncleanliness is obvious to the senses, if I still have doubts, I should go to charnel grounds and look at the bodies and other uncleanliness thrown away there!

Knowing that if the skin is opened up it will give rise to great fear, how will that body give rise to joy again?

The scents rubbed on a woman's body are sandalwood and the like, not the scents of that woman's body, why then do I become attached to others' bodies because of scents that are other than their own?

If I am not attached to this body because of its naturally bad odour, that is good is it not? How is it that those who crave the meaningless things of the world apply pleasant scents to the unclean body?

Well, if it is the pleasant scent sandalwood, how could it come from this body? Why then do I become attached to others' bodies because of scents that are other than theirs?

The long hair and nails, yellowish teeth, smell, and taint of dirt of that woman's body shown naked in its natural state is frightening. Why do I make such an effort to pretty it when that is like sharpening a weapon that will cause me harm? The efforts of my stupidity are the bases for the world's being totally disturbed by a crazed mind.

When, having seen some skeletons, renunciation is produced in the charnel ground, will there be any joy in charnel grounds of cities that are filled with moving skeletons?

Women, who are in that way unclean, are not obtained without paying a price. I exhaust myself gathering wealth for that purpose and will be harmed in the hells, and so on.

As a child I am not able to increase my wealth. As a young man how could that be an easy situation? At the end of a life of amassing wealth when I have become aged, what use will sex be then?

One type of bad, desirous person wears himself out by working all day and then after arriving home in the evening, leaves his exhausted body lying there like a corpse.

One type has the suffering of becoming afflicted by having to travel and go far away from home. That person longs for his spouse, but does not see her for years at a time.

Some who want to benefit themselves through stupidity sell themselves for their own purposes, but not getting what they want are aimlessly driven by the winds of others' actions.

Some sell their bodies and powerless are employed by others. And if their wives give birth, the children end up at the foot of a tree in an isolated place.

Some fools who are deceived by desire, thinking, "I want sustenance to stay alive", go to war all the while apprehensive that they might lose their lives. Some go into the service of others for the sake of a small recompense.

Some desire-filled people have their bodies cut up on account of women or wealth. Some because of being sentenced to it by the law, get impaled on the impaling stick. Some others are stabbed with a dagger. Others still are burned. Such things as these are readily seen.

Due to the pains involved in amassing, guarding, and losing it, I should realise that wealth is the root of infinite problems. Those who become distracted by their attachment to wealth have no opportunity to be liberated from the suffering of rebirths in becoming.

There are many disadvantages to having desire, such as the ones listed above, and little profit. People like that are like the livestock used to draw carriages who get to eat just a few mouthfuls of grass.

For the sake of a little recompense—which is not so rare given that even animals manage to get some—this perfect leisure and endowment so difficult to find is destroyed by the deep suffering created by previous actions.

The things of desire will certainly perish and cause me to fall into the hells, and so on. Because this is not very meaningful, it comes with the constant difficulty of total weariness, whereas the attainment of buddhahood comes with difficulty that is a ten-millionth fraction of that. Thus, compared to those following the conduct of enlightenment, those having desire experience greater suffering yet have no enlightenment.

If I have contemplated the sufferings of the hells, and so on, I will understand that the ruin brought on by weapons, poison, precipices, fire, and enemies cannot compare with the harm caused by desire, and in that way having become disenchanted with desire, I shall arouse joy for isolated places.

Inside forests that are peaceful without disputes and without the sights and sounds of others, fortunate ones, mindful of their purpose to benefit others, tread in pleasing places of excellent houses of broad flat stones that are cooled by the sandal-scented moonlight, in the forest peaceful without enemies, a place fanned by gentle breezes.

They dwell for as long as they wish in empty houses, at the foot of trees and in caves, having abandoned the suffering of guarding and caring about possessions.

Not relying on anyone, they live carefree, independent and detached, having no ties to anyone. Even the leader of the gods has difficulty finding a life that is as contented and happy as this.

Having in those ways and others contemplated the good qualities of isolation, I should take joy in that.

There, I will completely pacify discursive thought and meditate on enlightenment mind. First I will make an effort to meditate on self and other being equal.

All sentient beings, myself and others, are equal in wanting happiness and not wanting suffering. Like me, all of them equally guard against suffering.

My body has many parts such as the hands, but as a body to be guarded all of them are one. Likewise, migrators in their particular happinesses and sufferings might not be the same, but myself and all of them are one in being something that guards against suffering and produces happiness.

Although my suffering does not harm another's body, that suffering of mine is, because of clinging to a self, unbearable. Similarly, when I am cherishing another with compassion, although the other's sufferings do not come down on me, I suffer because I am clinging to a self in the other's person whereby the other's suffering becomes something difficult to bear.

Hence I should dispel the suffering of others because it is suffering, like my own suffering, and I should benefit others because they are other sentient beings just like me.

When both myself and others are matched in wanting to be happy, what is so special about me? Why do I work for my happiness alone?

When both myself and others are matched in not wanting to suffer, what is so special about me? Why do I guard myself alone?

"Because their suffering does not harm me, I am not guarding them against it", then also for future sufferings, why guard against them if they are not harming me now?

If I think, "I will experience the suffering of my next life", that is a wrong-minded concept, given that it is one person who dies in a past life and another who is born in a later one.

"When another has some sort of suffering, that other person will have to guard himself against it." The suffering of the foot is not also that of the hand, why then does the hand guard against the suffering of the foot?

If I say, "It might not be correct, but because of this world's style of grasping a self there is the idea of foot and hand being mutually one", then grasping at dual self and other also is not right and whatever is not right should be thoroughly rejected.

What are referred to as "a continuum" and "a collection" are false in the same way as a rosary, an army, and so on. There is no sufferer who has the suffering, in which case who governs it?

There being no owner who has the suffering, there is no special case among us. It is suffering, therefore it must be removed. Then why am I so sure about dispelling my suffering and not that of others?

"Why should everyone's suffering be turned away?" There is no argument over this. If it is to be turned away, then all of it should be turned away. If not, then I too am to suffer just like other sentient beings.

You might ask, "Compassion brings much suffering, so why should I persistently develop it?" When the suffering of migrators is considered, the person with compassion suffers much more.

However, if a compassionate person by the single suffering that would come from giving away the body for the sake of others was to eliminate many sufferings of himself and others, out of love he would accept that one suffering for himself and others.

The bodhisatva Supuṣhpachandra, although aware that a vicious king would harm him, did not try to prevent his suffering in order to prevent the suffering of many.

When the bodhisatva's mindstream has become familiarized like that, he takes joy in pacifying the suffering of others, so will, like a swan entering a lake of lotuses, enter even the hell of Unremitting Torment.

Will the ocean of joy gained when sentient beings have been liberated not be most excellent? What does wanting emancipation achieve?

Although the bodhisatva works for others' sakes like that, he has no conceit and does not consider himself to be wonderful. Due to having joy only in working only for others' sake, he has no hope for a full-ripening result.

Proceeding like that, just as I guard myself against unpleasant words however small, so I should cultivate a mind to guard others and I should cultivate a mind of compassion.

Familiarization has led me to regard the drops of semen and blood of others as "me" even though they are not things of mine. In the same way, why do I not also apprehend the bodies of others as "me"?

It is not difficult following on from that to see my body as also that of others.

Moreover, having made myself aware of the faults in cherishing myself and the ocean of good in cherishing others, I will completely reject all cherishing of myself and will take up cherishing others. That is to be cultivated in meditation.

In the same way as the hands and so forth are maintained to be limbs of the body, why are bodied beings not claimed to be limbs of migrators?

In the same way as familiarization with this body that does not have a self gives rise to a mind thinking, "It is myself", why would familiarization with other sentient beings not give rise to a mind that thinks, "They are myself?"

When doing that sort of familiarization, even though I am working for the sake of others, I should not be thinking that I am wonderful nor having conceit arise. It is similar to feeding myself then not having hope for something in return.

Therefore, just as I guard myself from unpleasant words however small, so I will familiarize myself with a mind that guards migrators and a mind that has compassion for them.

Therefore, guardian Avalokiteshvara, lord of great compassion, has even blessed his name in order to dispel fears of being amongst migrators.

I should not turn away from it because it is difficult. This is so given that, because of the power of familiarity, I could become unhappy later upon hearing that someone whose name was previously frightening to hear was not around.

Therefore, someone who wants quickly to protect himself and others should carry out this holy secret, the exchange of self and other.

Because of attachment to my body there is fear of smaller things, so who would not be hostile towards this body that gives rise to great fear?

Wanting a means to cure the body's distress of hunger and thirst, and so on, I might kill birds, fish, and gentle creatures, and lie in wait at the sides of roads.

If for the sake of profit and respect I were to kill even my father and mother or steal the property of the Three Jewels, I would burn in the hell of Unremitting Torment. In that case, what wise person would worship this body by desiring and guarding it? Who would not regard it as an enemy?

"If I give it away, what will be left for my use?" A mind that thinks of my own sake like that is going the way of the malicious spirits. "If I use it, what will be left for me to give?" A mind that thinks of the other's sake is taking the approach of the gods.

If I harm others for myself, I will end up suffering in the hells, and so on, but if I harm myself for others, I shall gain everything.

Wanting for the higher levels will end me up in the bad migrations, ugly and deeply stupid. If I shift that attitude to others, I shall obtain an honoured place in the happy migrations.

If I use others for my own purposes, I will experience being a servant to them, and so on. If I use myself for others' purposes, I will experience being a lord over others.

However much happiness there is in the world all of it comes from wanting others to be happy and however much suffering there is in the world all of it comes from wanting myself to be happy.

What need is there to explain it further? The childish act for their own sake and the capable ones work exclusively for others' sakes. Look at the difference between the two!

If I do not genuinely exchange, like trading one for the other, my happiness for others' suffering, I will not accomplish buddhahood and even in samsara will have no happiness.

Put aside the next world—between my servants not working and my masters not paying me a wage the aims of this life will not be accomplished in this life either.

Confused beings completely cast aside the happy situations they could have gained as the result of having made a perfect set of causes for the production of happiness seen and not seen, and, through the cause of having made suffering for others, take on unending suffering.

If all of however much injury, and fear and suffering exists in the worlds arises from grasping a self, then what use is that great malicious spirit to me?

If I do not completely let go of my own such self, I will not be able to abandon suffering, in the same way as I will not be able to avoid being burnt if I do not let go of a fire that I am holding.

Having seen that, then in order to alleviate my own harms and pacify the sufferings of others, I shall give myself over to others and hold them as I do my self.

I must be certain of the mind that thinks, "I am governed by others"! Now, except for the sake of all sentient beings, you mind must not think of anything else.

And, it is not correct to do anything for my own sake using these eyes, and so on that are now governed by the other. Hence, it is not correct to do anything with these eyes, and so on that would be contrary to their sakes.

Thus, sentient beings should be my principal concern. Anything I see on my body that would be useful I will take then use for the benefit of others!

Setting those lesser than myself and the others as myself and myself as the other, and using a mind without conceptual thought of a self, I should cultivate envy, competitiveness, and pride.

This one is honoured but I am not. I have not acquired material things like this one has and this one is praised by everyone, whereas I am deprecated. This one is happy, whereas I suffer.

I do all the work while this one sits about at ease. This one is renowned as greater in the world, whereas I am reputed to be inferior, with no good qualities at all.

What is gained from this talk of no good qualities? We all possess good qualities! Compared to some this one is inferior, that is how it is, and compared to some I am superior, that also is how it is.

The degeneration of my discipline, views, and so on happens because of the force of the afflictions, it is not something I have control over, so you must cure me to the best of your abilities and if it causes harm, I must be willing to accept that as well.

However, if I cannot be cured by him, "Why does he berate me?" What use then are his good qualities to me?

This one has the good quality that I have yet has no compassion for migrators who are caught in the cruel mouth of the bad migrations. This one who outwardly displays conceit over his good qualities wants to join ranks with the experts.

In order to make myself better than this one who is regarded as equal with me, I certainly will amass material gains and honour for myself, even if it means taking them by verbal dispute.

I shall by all means make my good qualities evident to the whole world and furthermore shall not let anyone hear of this one's good qualities, whatever they are.

And for my faults too, I will hide them and be worshipped but this one will not. In the coming days I will abundantly obtain material gains and will be honoured, but this one will not.

I shall make this one appear horrid then watch for a long time with pleasure as he is made into a laughing stock of all migrators, someone whom they revile back and forth.

It is well known that, "This afflicted one is attempting to compete with me", but how could this one be equal to me in hearing and prajñā or in bodily appearance, family line, or wealth?

Upon hearing of my good qualities that have become in that way well-known to all, I shall be thrilled with joy, my body hairs standing on end.

Even if this one has some possessions, if he is working for me, I shall give him just enough to live on and take any extra by force.

I will spoil his happiness and perpetually bring him harm, for in samsara for all of hundreds of lives he has harmed me.

You mind, while wanting to act for your own sake have seen countless aeons pass by, but the great weariness involved has meant that you have accomplished nothing but suffering.

Thus, I certainly shall fully engage in working for the sake of others! The command of the Capable One is not deceptive, so I shall see its good qualities in the future.

If in the past you had done this sort of act, then this situation of not having gained the perfect happiness of a buddha could not possibly have come about.

Therefore, just as you have come to grasp an "I" in these drops of semen and blood of others, likewise you shall also familiarize yourself with others!

Having made a grand concept about others, I will steal away any good quality that appears on my body and then you must live benefiting others!

"I am happy, others are sad. I am high, others are low. I benefit myself, not others", why am I not envious of myself?

I will separate myself from my own happiness and connect myself with the sufferings of others. Asking, "At this point now, what exactly am I doing?", I must examine myself for faults.

Although others do wrong, I will transform the wrongs into faults of my own! Although I do even a small wrong, before many people I will totally lay it aside!

By describing another's renown in the best of terms I will make it outshine my own renown! Like the lowest of servants, I will employ myself for the sake of all!

I should not praise this naturally fault-ridden self for some little transient good quality it may have. No matter which good qualities this self has, not letting even a few people know, I shall hide them!

In short, may the harm that I have done to others for my own sake from now on descend upon me!

I should not become aggressive and overbearing but should have the manners of a new bride—bashful and timid, and restrained.

You mind are to remain in that sort of conduct and not behave as you did before. If you stay within that mode of conduct, you will be governed by the antidotes, but if you go outside it, that will be your destruction.

However, even though you mind have been advised like that, if you do not act in that way, since all wrongs will depend on you, they will end up in your destruction in particular.

Mind, that previous time when you could ruin me is another time; now that I see you and where you go I shall completely destroy your haughtiness.

I reject you, mind that thinks, "Still, I have my own sake to take care of"! I have traded you to others so do not be downhearted but offer them all your strength.

If having lost heedfulness I do not give you over to sentient beings, it is certain that you will give me over to the guards of the hells.

Up till now you have given me over like that many times and I have suffered long. Now, recalling all my grudges I will defeat you, the mind that thinks of its own sake.

If you want joy for me, it will not happen by making me joyful in relation to my own sake. If I want to be guarded, it will happen through constantly guarding others.

The more I take enormous care of this body, the more I fall into a state of extreme fragility, unable to tolerate anything.

For falls like that, if nothing on earth can satisfy the desires, who could fulfil them?

Those desires give rise to afflictions and also to a dissatisfied mind. However, by not being attached to any desired thing I end up not depending on anything at all and because of that will never know the exhaustion of an excellent accumulation of desired things.

Therefore, I shall never allow an opportunity for the desires of the body to increase and not grasping at attractive things will be the finest of all things. In the end, my body will turn to dust and, unable to move itself, will be moved by others with a mind. This unclean form of thirty-six constituents is unbearable. Why do I grasp a self in it?

Whether it lives or whether it dies, what use is this machine to me? What difference is there between this body and clods of earth, stones, and so on? Oh my! Why do I not dispel the pride that comes with thinking, "There is an I in this!"

Concerns for the body have led me to an accumulation of meaningless suffering, then produced attachment and anger towards it, but what use is this thing that is equivalent to a lump of wood?

Whether I am taking care of my body as I am now or whether it is being eaten by vultures, and so on, it has no attachment and no hatred. Why then do I become attached to it?

When someone belittles it there could be anger, when someone praises it there could be pleasure, but if they are not recognized by the body, all that I do for it does nothing but wear me out.

You say, "I want this body to be happy for it and I are friends", but, since all beings want their own body to be happy, why do I not find joy in theirs?

Therefore, I shall without attachment give up this body in order to benefit migrators. In that case, though it may have many wrongs connected with it, I will look after it while experiencing the results of my previous actions.

The childish behaviour that has gone before has been enough! Now I shall follow along after the experts and having recalled the talk about heedfulness, shall turn back sleep and mental dullness.

Like the compassionate Sons of the Conquerors, I shall bear what is right to do, for if I do not exert myself single-mindedly day and night, when will my suffering come to an end?

Therefore, in order to dispel the obscurations I shall withdraw my mind from mistaken ways and constantly place it in equipoise upon the perfect object.

That was the eighth chapter of *Entering the Conduct of a Bodhisatva*, called "Meditative Concentration".

CHAPTER NINE

Prajna

Because all of those branches were taught by the Capable One for the sake of prajñā those wanting to quell the sufferings will develop prajñā.

Truth is twofold—Fiction and Superior Fact. It is said that Superior Fact is not the domain of rational mind and rational mind is the Fictional.

Regarding that, the world is seen to consist of two types: the yogins and the commoners.

The world of commoners is harmed by the yogins' world and amongst the yogins also, those of less refined view are harmed by those who are successively higher with their more refined rational minds.

When both worldly ones and yogins are using the examples that go with their assertion in common but are not analysing for the purpose of the fruition, the worldly ones are seeing substantial things and moreover conceiving of them as real. Because of that the worldly ones are not seeing them in the way that the yogins do, as illusion-like. Thus the worldly ones and yogins have a dispute over this.

They say that visual forms and so on are established by direct perception. We reply, "Yes, but that is establishment through renown not through valid cognition. It is false the same as what is actually unclean, and so on is renowned in the world as being clean, and so on."

For the sake of bringing worldly ones in the Guardian taught substantial things which in suchness are not momentary. If they say, "For the fictional too, it would be contradictory", we reply that the yogins have no fault in regard to the fictional for, in contrast to the world, they see the fictional in actuality. Otherwise their perception that women are unclean would be harmed by the world.

Merit from an illusory sort of conqueror is gained in the same way as with a truly existent one.

If they say, "If sentient beings are an illusory sort of thing, how could they, after having died be reborn?", we say, "For as long as the conditions for it are assembled, illusion will arise." We say, "How could sentient beings exist in truth merely because of having a longer duration?"

We say, "There is no mind involved in the killing, and so on of a being of illusion, hence there is no evil." We say, "For someone possessing an illusion-like mind merit and evil will occur."

We say, "Minds of illusion never happen because the mantras, and so on do not have the ability to create mind. The illusions that arise from a variety of conditions arise in a whole variety of ways that additionally have mind. There is no single condition existing anywhere that has the ability to produce all such effects."

They object, "If this is how it is—that in superior fact all sentient beings are the nature of nirvana and that in cyclic existence they occur in the fictional—then the buddhas also would be in cyclic existence, so what use would enlightenment conduct be?" We reply, "When the continuity of the conditions for the illusion of cyclic existence has not been cut, the illusion will not have been brought to an end, whereas when the continuity of the conditions has been cut, birth in the fictional will not occur again."

The Chittamatrin says, "For you, when the confused consciousnesses do not exist, what will reference the illusions?" The Madhyamika says, "When for you Chittamatrins illusions do not exist, what can be referenced at that time?" The Chittamatrin states, "If in suchness they exist as other, the aspect is mind itself." The Madhyamika replies, "When it is illusion manifested by mind itself, then at that time what will be seen by what? The Guardian of the World himself said that 'mind does not see mind'. Hence, just as a sword's blade does not cut itself, so it is for the mind."

The Chittamatrin states, "It is like the way that an oil lamp truly illuminates itself." The Madhyamika says that the oil lamp will not illuminate itself by itself for the reason that it was not obscured by darkness.

In regard to that the Chittamatrin states, "There is the blue colour like that of a crystal and the blueness which does not exist in relation to something else, likewise some things are illuminated in reliance upon something else and some other things are seen even without reliance on something else." The Madhyamika replies, "If it is not a blueness, then it has not made itself blue by itself."

Saying that "the lamp is illuminating" is about your idea of consciousness being known by consciousness. If we talk about that, it is saying that "rational mind is what illuminates itself by itself", but this begs the question "known by what knower?"

If mind is never seen by anyone, any description of it as self-illuminating or not would, like a description of the beauty of a barren woman's daughter, be meaningless.

The Chittamatrin says, "If self-knowing does not exist, how will a consciousness be recalled?"

When something other is experienced in consciousness, there is a connection due to which it will be remembered, as with a rat's poison.

If you, the Chittamatrin, say, "Because a mind possessing other conditions sees another's mind, one's own mind is self-illuminating", we say that due to the application of a consecrated eye-lotion a vase can be seen, but the eye-lotion itself will not be seen.

Here, it is not how the objects of the consciousnesses are known—the eyes seeing visual forms, the ears hearing sounds, and so on—that is being negated. Here, it is the cause of all suffering, conceiving substantial things as true, that is to be repelled.

You Chittamatrins say, "The illusion-like phenomena are neither thought of as other than nor not other than mind." We reply, "If they are substantial things how could they not be other than the mind? And if you say, "They are not other than it", then they do not exist as substantial things.

The Madhyamika says, "We accept that, like an illusion is not true but can be viewed, so it is for the viewer, the mind." The Chittamatrin says, "Samsara has a basis in substantial things, otherwise, it would become the same as space."

The Madhyamika replies, "How could those non-existent things of samsara because of being dependent on a substantial thing come to have the ability to perform the functions of samsara?"

And, for you, mind is an unaccompanied singularity. When mind has been freed from grasping, at that time all sentient beings would have effortlessly become tathāgatas. Even if so, what good will come from considering everything to be false aspect mind only?

Chittamatrin: Even if all phenomena are understood to be illusion-like", how will afflictions be repelled? The illusionist who has manifested a beautiful woman could have desire for her arise.

Madhyamika: The illusion can make him desirous because he has not eliminated the latencies for becoming afflicted towards knowables. Therefore, when he sees her, his latencies of emptiness meditation are weak.

By starting to familiarize himself with the latencies of emptiness, his latencies of substantial things will start to be eliminated and by familiarization with their being "nothing whatsoever" that also will later be eliminated. Then, when "there is nothing existing", the substantial things to be examined are not being referenced. At that time how could non-existent things free of basis be present before rational mind?

When things and non-existent things are not present before a stain-free rational mind, at that point there is no superfice, so there is the utter peace of being without references.

Question: "If buddhahood is like that, then nothing else but that would appear to a buddha, because of which a buddha would not enact other's sakes, would he? If he did, it would be necessary to appear to others, which contradicts what was explained before."

Answer: Like wish-fulfilling gems and wish-fulfilling trees completely fulfil others' wishes, bodhisatvas' prayers of aspiration for those to be tamed causes a conqueror's form to appear to those to be tamed.

For example, a person once made a Garuḍa-bird pillar for worship then passed away and, even for a long time after he had passed away, it could alleviate poisons, and so on. Similarly, in accord with a bodhisatva's enlightenment conduct done in the past a conqueror's pillar for worship is accomplished in the present and even though the bodhisatva who created it has passed into nirvana, he is still enacting the sakes of all sentient beings.

Lesser Vehicle follower: "But how would worshipping buddha who has no samsaric mind bring about a result of the worship?"

Madhyamika: Because it has been explained that the merits derived from worshipping a buddha both while he is present and from worshipping his relics after he has passed into nirvana are the same.

Madhyamika: It is established through scripture that there is equally a result of offering to a buddha whether in fiction or suchness. For example, as with how a result accompanies a truly-existing buddha as asserted by you.

Vaibhāṣhika: Seeing the four truths will liberate us. What use then is there in seeing emptiness?

Madhyamika: Because a scripture says, "Without this path of realizing emptiness there can be no enlightenment."

Vaibhāṣhika: "The Great Vehicle is not established." The Madhyamika replies: "How can it be that your Shrāvaka scriptures are established?" The Vaibhāṣhika responds, "Because they are established as the buddha-word for both of us."

The Madhyamika says, "It is the case, is it not, that they were not established for you at first but, later on, due to certain circumstances, you developed trust in them? It is the same for the Great Vehicle as well."

If something is true simply because two parties other than ourselves assert it, there would be the consequence that the Vedas, and so on, also would be true.

CHAPTER NINE

If he says: "Our scriptures are not disputed at all, but those of the Great Vehicle are disputed by one party, therefore the Great Vehicle is to be rejected", we reply, "Because your scriptures are disputed by the Tīrthikas and because some scriptures of the eighteen Buddhist sects are disputed by you and others, your scriptures should be rejected also."

If the root of the teaching is the full monks, the full monks are in a difficult position. And, their minds will have referencing, so nirvana also will be a difficult position for them.

If he says, "Liberation happens when the afflictions have been abandoned", then we say that as a consequence, immediately an arhat has abandoned the afflictions he must be liberated from suffering.

If he says, "That is what we assert", we say the arhats have no afflictions, but they have been seen to have the suffering of the potentials of karmic actions done previously."

He responds, "It is ascertained that in a subsequent birth, craving, the cause of appropriation, 'does not exist'."

The Madhyamika replies: "Why could they not have craving that is not an afflicted type of craving, but a total stupidity type of craving?"

The condition of feeling brings about craving and they do have feeling. The mind having referencing will dwell on some objects.

In a mind that is separated from the realization of emptiness, causes of movement can stop functioning for a while and then start up again, as happens with the meditative equilibrium "non-perception". Therefore, one should cultivate emptiness.

In general, the task of staying in samsara for the sake of all those sentient beings who are suffering as a result of their stupidity of believing in a self, is accomplished by becoming liberated from the extremes of remaining in attachment and fear. This is a result of emptiness.

Therefore it is not acceptable to reject such emptiness and hence, without doubting emptiness, one must meditate on it.

Emptiness also is the antidote to the darkness of the obscurations of the afflictions and of the knowable, so, wanting to have all-knowing quickly, how could one not meditate on it?

The advice is given: "Grasping substantial things brings suffering, so why, given that emptiness is what quells suffering, would one be afraid of it?"

If there were a self somewhere, then one could become afraid due to anything at all, but there is not a self anywhere, so who is there to be afraid?

Teeth, hair, and nails are not the self. The self is not bones and not blood. It is not nasal mucous nor phlegm, nor is it lymph or pus. The self is not fat nor sweat and the lungs and liver are not the self. The other internal organs are not the self nor is the self excrement or urine. Flesh and skin are not the self nor are warmth and the energy-winds the self. The orifices are not the self. Never are the six types of consciousness the self.

The Madhyamika refutes the Sāṃkhya's self: Regarding the self, if the consciousness that grasps sound was permanent, there would be the consequence of the apprehension of sound at all times. If you say, "We assert that", then when there is no sound knowable, what sound would be known? What would result in its being called "consciousness"?

If you say, "Although there is no object consciousness there can be consciousness of an object", then we say that there would be the consequence that wood also could be conscious of an object. Thus it is certain that, "There will not be a consciousness unless its knowable object is within range."

If you say, "That sound consciousness later becomes conscious of visual form", then we ask, "At that time why is sound not also heard?" You say, "Because there is no sound within range." We say, "Therefore, the consciousness of it also would not exist, so sound is proved to be impermanent."

Madhyamika: How could that whose nature is to apprehend sound apprehend visual form? We say, "One person being father and son is a conceptual designation, not the actual situation. This is how it is: the individual qualities of rajas, tamas, and sattva are not son and not father either.

Moreover, if you say, "That apprehender of visual form is not seen to have the nature of possessing an apprehender of sounds, but like an actor, the apprehender of sounds assumes another guise and sees", then as a consequence, that apprehender of visual form is not permanent given that it is produced in another guise and ceases from it. That oneness is an unprecedented oneness!

If you say, "If another guise is not the true one", well then, tell us the actual nature of that conscious knowing self! If you say, "It is consciousness that operates at all times continuously", then we say, "In that case, there is the consequence that all beings would become identical."

And, not only that, that which has a functioning mind and that without mind also would become of one nature because of being the same in being existent. If that is asserted, when all the specifics are up-ended in that way, what basis would there be for positing similarity?

The Madhyamika refutes the Naiyāya's self: That without mind is moreover not a self because of its quality of being without mind, as with a piece of cloth, and so on. The Naiyāya follower says, "Yes, but due to including the rational mind of mind it does possess mind and because of that it is conscious meaning that it does function as an object consciousness." The Madhyamika says, "If so, there is the consequence that when it—the self—due to possessing the mind of rational mind becomes somewhat unconscious in the circumstances of being intoxicated, in a faint, and so on, it could perish in the circumstances when the rational mind is included.

If you say, "If the self is not subject to change at either of the two times, what effect would the mind that includes the rational mind have on that self?", we say that it would have none because the self is changeless. In accord with that assertion of a self which has a consciousness like that which has not the slightest effect on it and which is free of activities because of its permanence, space also could be made out as a self.

Rishi Kapila and others like him say, "If the self that having made karmas in this world goes on to the next world does not exist, a relationship between karmas done and their results would be not be tenable; if having done a karma the doer were to perish, then whose karma would it be?

We reply that we both concur that the bases of an action and its result are different in this and a future life respectively and that the self has no bearing on this matter, hence it is meaningless to argue about this, is it not?

"The one possessing the cause is the one who has the result" is something that could not possibly be seen.

Nevertheless, in dependence on the world's clinging to the belief that it is one continuum of mind that is involved with the things of both cause and effect, the Buddha taught that "the doer is the experiencer of the result" out of consideration for those to be tamed.

If you think, "Mind is the self", past mind and future mind are not the self because having ceased and not been produced respectively, they are not existent. You say, "Yes, but the mind produced now in the present is the self." We say, "If so, given that it perishes in the second moment, there is no permanent self."

For example, if the trunk of a Plantain tree is pulled apart, nothing will be found. Similarly, if you search using attribute analysis, a truly-established self also will not be found.

You say, "If sentient beings do not exist, for whom will compassion be produced?" We say that it is for whoever has been imagined in the fictional by the stupid ones who have promised to work for the sake of their gaining the result, buddhahood.

You say, "If in superior fact there are no sentient beings, then who gets the result of the compassion, given that there would be not be anyone having a fruition?" That is true. Nevertheless, there are the needs of the world of those stupid ones. The stupid ones who see a need for the beings of the world to achieve the fruition for the sake of thoroughly pacifying their sufferings are not rejected.

The pride of grasping an I that is the cause of samsaric suffering is to be rejected because it will increase the stupidity of a self. If you say, "There is no method for getting rid of it", we say that there is a method; meditation on the non-existence of self is the supreme one.

If attribute analysed, the body is not the legs above the ankle bones and not the shanks. The thighs and waist also are not the body, nor are the abdomen or back the body. The chest and the shoulders also are not the body. The body is not the ribs, and so on nor the arms. The armpits and shoulders also are not the body. The inner organs also are not it. The head and the throat also are not the body. If not, what here in these individual parts is the body?

The Sāṃkhyas and others say, "The individual parts are not the body, rather, there exists something having parts that pervades all the parts, a singular thing that enters all the parts." We say, "If you assert that this body becomes resident in all parts in a partial way, if you were to examine to find in which particular place it is resident, you would find that it does not reside anywhere. You might think, "The pieces of the body do indeed become resident in a piece at one time", but even then, where would that body asserted to be a singular body itself be residing?

If that body having parts was in its entirety and not just partially resident in the hands and other parts, then there would have to be as many bodies as those hands, and so on.

If there is no body outside or inside, how could the hands, and so on have a body? If the body does not exist somewhere other than the hands, and so on, how could it exist?

Therefore the body does not exist. However, stupidity in regard to the hands, and so on results in the impression of a body conceived of in the rational mind. It is like the shape of a cairn of stones results in a rational mind apprehending the cairn as a human.

For as long as the conditions for it are assembled, the body appears as a person. Similarly, for as long it exists in the hands, and so on, a body continues to appear in them.

In the same way, because the hand is a collection of fingers assembled together, what will be the hand? It is the same for the fingers because each one being a collection of segments will not be found, and the segments too having been separated into their own pieces will not found, and the pieces too having been separated into their own atoms are broken down, and the atoms too by separation into their directional parts of east, and so on, are not established as singular. Because the separated directions also are free of pieces, they are like space, with nothing about them established at all, so even atoms do not exist.

Therefore, who of analytical mind would become attached to this dream-like form of ours that appears to confusion? When in that way there is no body, what man attached to a woman is there and what woman attached to a man is there?

If suffering feeling actually existed, why wouldn't it obstruct great enjoyment? If happy feeling actually existed, why would tasty foods, and so on not bring pleasure to someone afflicted with grief, and so on?

You say, "They do exist in actuality, but are not experienced because of being overridden by something which is stronger". If so, when there is a feeling that does not have the property of experiencing, how could it be feeling?

You say, "At the time of a happy feeling, suffering feeling exists in a subtle form even though its gross form has been removed by the happy one, isn't that so? It is a mere feeling of enjoyment other than that gross happy one."

We say that that subtle one moreover does not depart from its own class. Thus, if a condition that opposes suffering arises and therefore suffering does not arise, it is established, isn't it, that feeling conceived of as true is what is called "manifest clinging"?

On account of that manifest clinging that has come from conceiving of feeling, there is its antidote, the cultivation of this attribute analysis which is the thorough placement of mindfulness of feeling. The meditative concentration that comes from that field of thorough examination is the food of yogins.

If sense faculty and object have an interval between them, where would they meet? And if you say that there is no interval between them, they would be oneness. In that case, what sense faculty would meet with what object?

There is no entering of one atom into another atom because atoms do not have space that would provide the opportunity and are equal in size. When there is no entry, there is no merging, and if there is no merging, there is no meeting of the two.

For the partless case moreover, how could what is called "meeting" be acceptable when there are no parts? For meeting, one part is necessary. If you have seen a mutual meeting and one which is partless yet without contradiction, then show it to us!

It is not possible for consciousness, which is without body, to have a meeting and as a consequence it also is not possible for an assembly of sense faculty, object, and consciousness. This is similar to the way that attribute analyses were done earlier.

If in that way contact does not exist, from what would feeling arise? If it does not arise, what meaning is there to this tiring effort?

What feeling of duḥkha would harm who—what feeler of it—given that feeler and feeling are without nature?

Because of that, when there is no feeler at all and the feeling also does not exist, then, having seen this situation of all phenomena being primally pacified, why craving are you not expelled?

If you say, "For Rishi Kapila, the substances of clay pots and so on exist as visible and touchable", then we say that something can be seen by the eye faculty or touched by the body faculty, but mind with its dream-like and illusion-like personality is produced simultaneously with feeling, because of which it does not see the feeling.

Feeling produced earlier is remembered by mind produced later, but when they are produced simultaneously, mind does not experience the feeling. Mind does not itself experience its own personality, feeling, nor is it experienced by something else.

There is no existence of a feeler at all, hence feeling is not real, not established in actuality. How could this assembly which like that has no self be harmed by this feeling?

Mental mind does not reside in the sense faculties. It is not in the objects—visual form, and so on. It is not somewhere in between, either. Mind is not inside nor outside the body and even if searched for is not found anywhere else either.

And, the mind is not the body nor something other than the body. It is not mingled with body and its flesh; nor is it somewhere apart from the body. The mind is not established in the slightest because of which sentient beings are primally nirvana by nature.

If the sense consciousnesses exist prior to their knowables—the objects of visual form, and so on, how could a consciousness be produced after having referenced its object? If consciousness and knowable arise simultaneously, how could the consciousness be produced after having referenced something?

Moreover, if the consciousnesses exist after the knowable, at that point from what object would the consciousness be produced? In that way, production for any phenomenon is not something that could be known.

Objection: "If it is like that, there would be no fictional truths that are produced and perish in which case how would there be two truths? Moreover, if fictional truths existed due to others, how could sentient beings pass into nirvana?

Reply: This talk of "passed into nirvana" is about the conceptualizing of another's mind, it is not about one's own fictional posited by one's own rational mind. Later, if that exists as an ascertained phenomenon, then at that point that fictional exists; if it does not exist, it is a nonexistent fictional.

That being so, both the conceptualizer and the object conceptualized by it are mutually dependent just as all of these attribute analyses which are expressed in dependence on what is well-known.

Objection: When an analysis is done using attribute analysis on an attribute analysis already done, at that point the second attribute analysis also will have to be analysed by a third attribute analysis because of which there would be no end to it.

Reply: When that thing to be analysed has been attribute analysed and determined, no basis for the attribute analysis will exist and because there now is no basis for it, it will no longer be produced. That non-production moreover will be described as "having gone to nirvana".

According to the advocates of substantial things being true, the two of knowable and knower are true, but that position is extremely difficult to maintain. If they say, "An object to be evaluated is established through the power or force of a consciousness which is a valid cognizer", then we ask what basis or proof is there for positing the existence of consciousness which is a valid cognizer?

If they say, "Yes, but consciousness is established as true through the knowable being established as true", we ask what basis and proof for the knowable existing is there? If they say, "Both consciousness and knowable exist by way of being mutually dependent", then we say that both would become non-existent.

Objection: For example, if without a son there is no father because the convention of father would not apply, then from where would a son come? Just as in the absence of a son a father does not exist, likewise consciousness and knowable being mutually dependent, both of them are non-existent.

They say, "Just as a sprout is produced from a seed and what the seed is is understood through that sprout, similarly, why for a consciousness—a result—that has been produced from a knowable—a cause—would the knowable not be understood as existing through the consciousness?" We say that if a consciousness which is other than the sprout were to understand through the sign of the sprout that "this seed exists" through what would the consciousness that understands that that knowable exists be understood to be existent?

The Charvakas state, "All substantial things are produced without a cause." The Madhyamikas refute it: "Everyone in the world directly sees all causes. The variations in the stalks of lotus flowers, and so on, are created by variations in their causes."

If you the Charvakas ask, "What makes the variations of cause?", we say that it is the variations in earlier causes. You ask, "Why do causes have the ability to create a result?" We say that it is due to the power of earlier causes.

The Naiyāyikas and Vaiśheṣhikas state that Īśhvara is the cause of all migrators. We say, "If so, then tell us what is this Īśhvara?!" If you say, "He is the elements", then we say that that is indeed true, but why tire both of us out arguing over a mere name? Nevertheless, earth and the other elements are manifold and impermanent, are without movement, are not divine and are trodden upon and are unclean, thus they cannot be Īśhvara himself.

Īśhvara is not space because it is without movement. He is not the self because that called the "self" has previously been refuted. If you are thinking, "Īśhvara is the Inconceivable One", then we say that the Inconceivable One whose function as creator of migrators also is something that cannot be conceived of, so what use is there in describing him as the creator?

Moreover, we question, "What result does he desire to create?" If you say, "a self", then we say that the three things of that self, the four elements of earth and the others, and the entity of Īshvara are permanent, aren't they?

If you say, "Īshvara's result is consciousness and with that is happiness and suffering", we say that consciousness is produced from knowables and the happiness and suffering experienced without beginning is from karmas. Tell us then, what has he created?! If the cause, Īshvara, does not have a beginning, how could the result produced by him, the formation of the world, have a beginning?

Moreover, why wouldn't he, a permanent cause, not be perpetually making the result? You say, "He, Īshvara the cause, is not reliant on anything else." We say that if there is nothing else—no other assembly of causes—not made by him, on what would this assembly made by him rely?

If he is reliant, because the cause would be an assemblage of conditions, Īshvara would not be the cause. If all the causes for the creation of a result have assembled, he will be powerless to prevent a result being produced and in the absence of such an assembly will be powerless to produce.

If Īshvara himself makes a result while not desiring to do so due to the power of causes and conditions having assembled, as a consequence the result would be under the control of other because Īshvara would have no control over it. And if you say that he desired to create a result, even then he would be dependent on newly-created desires. However, if he acts that way, given that such desire is something other than Īshvara, where is the activity of Īshvara?

Those who advocate permanent atoms had their assertions refuted earlier.

The Sāṃkhya assert "the primal substance", which is permanent and is the cause of migrators, meaning the cause of the animate and inanimate worlds. When the qualities called "sattva, rajas, and tamas" are equally present, they refer to it as "the primal substance" and when not equally present, they refer to it as "migrators."

For the refutation of that, there are six positions to be rejected. For the first of the six, it would not be all right for one thing, the primal substance they assert, to have a personality of three natures of sattva, rajas, and tamas. Thus there is no primal substance, so it and everything that results from it does not exist. Likewise the qualities do not exist and, moreover, because each one of the three qualities would have three aspects the qualities do not exist in which case the existence of sounds, and so on—the twenty-three transformations produced from them—is very far-fetched.

The refutation of happiness, and so on being material. If you say, "Migrators are the personage of the three qualities, so clothing, and so on are of the nature of happiness", then we say that clothes, and so on being matter without mind could not possibly have happiness, and so on—meaning happiness, suffering, and neutral states.

If you say, "Substantial things of clothes, and so on have the nature of being happiness, and so on's cause", then we say that we have already done the attribute analysis of substantial things, haven't we?"

Furthermore, if everything illuminated is the nature of happiness, and so on, it follows that clothing, and so on are not your cause, happiness and so on, because the clothing, and so on are evident. If we make that assertion, then saying, "Moreover, from your cause which is happiness, and so on there is no arising of cloth, and so on and from the cloth, and so on there is the production of happiness, and so on" shows that the result comes after the cause. And if those things—the cloth, and so on—are absent, there will be no happiness, and so on.

The refutation of the assertion that the happiness, and so on are permanent follows. If you say, "That happiness, and so on being the personage of the three qualities are permanent, so clothing, and so on are not produced", then we say that the happiness, and so on are never observed as permanent because the qualities, and so on do not exist. The pervasion: If the illuminations of happiness, and so on perpetually exist, why are they not apprehended as the experience of happiness?

If you say, "If that happiness, and so on which is a co-present illumination that later on not being referenced has become subtle, like stars in the daytime sky", then how can it be coarse and subtle?

If you say, "It is not that there is the sudden existence as two, coarse and subtle, rather, having left its coarse state, it has become the subtle state", then we say in which case the coarse and subtle states would be impermanent. Coarse and subtle being impermanent like that, why do you likewise not assert all of the twenty-five substantial things to be impermanent?

If the coarse state is not other than happiness, the coarse state which is happiness will be illuminated and thereby will be impermanent.

Refutation of the assertion that cause and effect are of the same substance contains two refutations: firstly of the non-existent not being produced and secondly of being existent but not seen. Here, three arguments made by opponents are dealt with and removed in connection with the consequence of the two being equivalent.

For the first of the three, if you assert that "something not existent is not produced at all because of being non-existent", then you will not assert production later of an illumination when the illumination that happens in the circumstance of not illuminating is not existent, but not doing so you are caught at being an advocate of existence.

If the entity of the result is present in the cause, then someone eating food would be an eater of excrement. If you want to wear cotton clothing, you should use the money for the cotton clothing to purchase seeds of cotton then wear them.

Refuting the assertion of existing but not being seen is as follows. If you argue that in superior fact the result exists in the cause, but the stupid people of the world do not see it, then we say that is the case even for others who know about suchness.

That knowledge of the result existing in the cause exists even for the world, so tell us why is it not seen by the world! If you argue, "It is because worldly people do not have valid cognition", then we say that they see the illuminations—sounds, and so on—but that is not true.

The argument of the consequence of matching it to itself is as follows: If a conventional type of valid cognizer is not a valid cognizer, would not an evaluation done by it and even if it were an overall analysis become false?

Madhyamika: You assert that then say, "Meditation can be done in suchness on emptiness, but because of that situation in which everything will be evaluated as false there will be the consequence of it not being accepted." We then say that, not having detected the substantial thing under investigation, its non-existence will not be apprehended. Therefore, for any substantial thing that is false that is to be refuted, its non-existent thing is clearly false is what is asserted. That false thing to be refuted is therefore a preventative false valid cognizer; on the death of a dream child, the conceptualizing thought that thinks, "That child does not exist" functions to prevent the previous conceptualizing thought, "That child exists". It too is false.

Performing attribute analysis as just explained reveals that there is no production at all of a result without a cause, nor is there such a result present in either its individual or combined conditions that produce the result.

It has not come from somewhere else, does not dwell, and does not go off to another place. What difference is there between this that stupid fools make out to be true and the illusions of an illusionist?

Examine where the illusions manifested by illusionists and the things manifested by causes come from and also to where they go.

Any given thing will be seen due to the causes and conditions for it being nearby. If they are not there, it will not. It is a contrivance analogous to a reflected image, so how could there be any truth to it?

If at the time of the cause, the result is already existing as a substantial thing, what need would there be for a cause? Nevertheless, if you think, "Although that result does not exist now at the time of the cause, later it will become a result that is a substantial thing", then what need would there be for a cause?" This is so because even with a thousand million causes there is no turning a non-existent thing into a substantial thing.

In that situation, how would that result be a thing or not? What else could change later into a thing?

If at the time of being non-existent, the result could not possibly exist as a substantial thing, when would it become an existent substantial thing? A thing for as long as it has not been produced is a non-existent thing and will not be separated from being so.

If not separated from being a non-existent thing, the time of being an existent thing is not possible. A thing also does not change to being a non-existent thing because if it did there would be the consequence of it having two natures.

When analysed in that way there is no cessation and there is no thing that has been produced because of which all of these knowables in the migrations have not been produced and do not cease in a permanent way.

If you say, "Well yes, but what would it be like, this appearance of production and cessation?", we say that the migrations are like a dream; when attribute analysed, they are similar to the Plantain tree with its layers of covering.

If attribute analysed, there is no difference between those who have and have not passed into nirvana.

What is there to gain and what is there to lose in regard to things which are empty like that? What is there in being honoured or totally abused by someone?

Where do happiness and suffering of body and mind come from? What is there to be liked and what is there to be disliked? When I look into the nature of it, who is craving and what is craved?

If analysed, who in this world of the living dies? Who will come into life and who has come into it? And who are relatives and who are friends?

You must thoroughly grasp as I Śhāntideva have done, that everything is like space.

Those wanting happiness here in this life who rely on the causes of fighting and delighting create utter conflict and overwhelming joy.

Their desires failing, they are miserable and strive to accomplish them; they argue, beat and stab one another, and intimidate each other all of which causes them to live very difficult lives.

They come again and again into happy migrations where many types of happiness are available for their use, but then they die and fall into the long and unbearable sufferings of the bad destinies.

They wander in becoming, a place of many pitfalls where there is no mention, no understanding, of suchness. And there, these two sides of samsara and emptiness meditation are mutually incompatible, therefore in becoming there is no mention, no understanding, of this sort of suchness.

And there in that becoming too, because it is a limitless ocean of suffering whose difficulty to bear is beyond analogy, there is little strength for that sort of thing—abandoning suffering and accomplishing virtue—and life is very short as well.

And there too, they work at meaningless activities for the purpose of living long and without illness, attending to hunger and weariness, sleeping, being injured, keeping company with childish associates, and so on. In that way their lives pass quickly without meaning and as a result, it is extremely difficult for them to find the prajñā that does this sort of attribute analysis.

And there too, how could there be the samadhi that is the method for turning away from familiarization with complete distraction?

And there too, the maras are striving to ensure that they fall into the great bad destinies, the hells.

There are many wrong paths in there and it is difficult to get past doubt; it will be difficult to gain leisure again and extremely difficult to have the occurrence of a buddha because the river of afflictions is difficult to stop. E MA Compassion! Suffering arises in a non-stop succession.

For those in samsara like that there is extreme suffering, but not seeing their own suffering they stay in the river of suffering. For them, whose sufferings are unbearable, it is right that I should be pained and exclaim "Oh my!" because I cannot bear their suffering.

For example, there are some ascetics who pour water over themselves again and again then enter fire again and again. They stay like that, suffering in the extreme but priding themselves on being happy.

Like them, there are others who carelessly continue to perform such activities, going ahead as though there were no aging and no oncoming death. First they will be killed by the lord of death, then they will fall into the three bad destinies where they will have unbearable suffering.

For those who like that are pained by the fires of their sufferings I will one day become a rain of all that is needed for sentient beings' happiness, a rain that falls nicely from the clouds of my merit accumulation and quells their sufferings.

I will one day, in the mode of not referencing, out of respect have gathered the accumulation of merit within an illusion-like state and will teach emptiness to those ruined by referencing.

That was the ninth chapter of *Entering the Conduct of a Bodhisatva*, called "Prajñāparamita".

CHAPTER TEN

Dedication

By the virtue I have obtained through composing *Entering the Conduct of a Bodhisatva* may all migrators enter the bodhisatva's conduct.

May all beings everywhere as many as there are who are sick with the sufferings of body and mind obtain an ocean of happiness and joy by my merits.

While they are arousing the enlightenment mind in order to gain the happiness of buddhahood, may their happiness never decline and moving along may they obtain an uninterrupted flow of the unsurpassed happiness.

May the bodied beings in all of the hells as many as there are in the world realms enjoy happiness of the sort enjoyed by the sentient beings in Sukhāvati.

May those feeble with cold find warmth. May those feeble with heat be cooled by limitless rivers of water pouring down from the great clouds of the bodhisatva's miracles.

May the forest of trees with sword-like leaves become a beautiful pleasure grove. May the forest of Śhalmari tree trunks turn into wish-fulfilling trees.

May the regions of hell become places of joy beautified by exquisite calls of wild ducks, geese, and swans and have lakes with fragrant lotuses.

May the heaps of burning coals turn into heaps of jewels and the burning ground become a polished crystal floor. May the iron mountains of Crushing Hell turn into celestial palaces of worship then be filled with sugatas.

May the rains of lava, blazing stones, and weapons from now on become a rain of flowers. May all the exchanges of the blows of weapons from now on be a playful exchange of flowers.

May those sinking into fiery pits at the Fordless River, their flesh falling away and their lily-white bones revealed, by the force of my virtues obtain the body of a god and stay together with goddesses in gently flowing rivers.

"Why are these unbearable henchmen of Yama, the crows, and the vultures afraid? Through whose excellent strength is darkness everywhere dispelled and joy brought upon us?" On thinking that, they look up and see, in the centre of the firmament above, the blazing form of Vajrapani! May they, by the force of the utter joy born within them be free from evil then go together with him to "Adakavatī".

When they see hell's heaps of fire extinguished by a rain of falling flowers mixed with incense-scented water, immediately satisfied they wonder whose work this was and in this way may these beings in the hells see Padmapani.

"Friends, come here, come here quickly! Do not be afraid! The fearless youthful one with long tresses has arrived, the one whose power removes all of our suffering and relieves us with the force of joy, the one who has produced for us the enlightenment mind that protects all migrators and love."

Upon seeing Mañjughoṣha may the beings in hell cry out, "Friends! See him in a delightful palace resounding with praises and songs sung by a thousand goddesses, with the tiaras of a hundred gods being offered to his lotus feet, with eyes moist with compassion and a rain of many flowers falling upon his crown."

Like that, having seen by my roots of virtue a pleasant fall of cooling, sweet-smelling rain coming from clouds created by the bodhisatvas Samantabhadra and the others, bodhisatvas with no obscurations, may all beings in hell be truly happy.

May all animals be free from the fear of being eaten by one another. May the hungry ghosts be happy like the men of Unpleasant to Hear.

May they be satisfied by a stream of milk pouring from the hand of the noble Lord Avalokiteshvara and by bathing in it may they always be cool.

May the blind see with their eyes, may the deaf always hear the sounds of dharma, and just as it was for Mayadevi, may pregnant women give birth without harm.

May the naked find clothing, the hungry find food; may the thirsty find water and delicious drinks.

May the poor find wealth. May those weak with sorrow find joy. May the forlorn find a cheerful mind. May they find steadiness of mind and an excellent situation.

May those who are sick with any of the types of disease there are quickly be freed from their sickness. Henceforth may every one of the sicknesses of migrators permanently not happen.

May the frightened cease to be afraid. May the imprisoned be freed. May the powerless have power, and may people have a mind that is flexible.

May all travellers find happiness and no fear everywhere they go. May they accomplish their purpose in going without need of effort.

May those who sail in boats and ships accomplish their wishes and having safely returned to the shore may they joyfully reunite with their relatives.

May wanderers who have lost their way in dangerous places meet with other travellers, and without fears of thieves, tigers, and so on, may their going be easy and without fatigue.

May those who find themselves in isolated and other such places, intimidating places without a path—the children and the aged without a protector, those stupefied and the insane—be guarded by divinities.

May beings be free from all states of no leisure and have faith, prajñā, and love and with excellent food and excellent conduct, may they be always be mindful throughout their lives.

May all sentient beings have unending resources like those in the storehouse of space. May those resources being free of dispute and injury be theirs to use as they please.

May those who have little splendour come to great splendour. May those whose form has become degraded through facing difficulties come to have a most excellent form.

May the females however many there are in the world come to be males. May the bad types gain a higher position in a future life and the proud ones also be overcome.

By the merits I have accumulated, may all beings, none left out, abandon all forms of evil and perpetually engage in virtue.

May those who are arousing the mind for enlightenment not be parted from the enlightenment mind and diligently perform the conducts of a bodhisatva and may they be cared for by the buddhas and abandon the works of the maras.

May all of those sentient beings who are arousing the enlightenment mind have lives that are unfathomably long. May they always live happily and not even hear the word "death".

May all directions be filled with gardens covered in wish-fulfilling trees, gardens in which the sweet sounds of dharma are being proclaimed by the buddhas and the buddha sons.

May the lands everywhere be places devoid of stones and the like and level like the palm of the hand, of the nature of lapis lazuli and smooth.

There are several circles of disciples, but may the majority, the bodhisatvas, be present in every land adorning them with their excellences.

May bodied beings uninterruptedly hear in all their places the sounds of dharma issuing from birds and trees, rays of light and even space itself.

May they always meet with buddhas and buddha sons. May those gurus to migrators be worshipped with infinite clouds of offerings.

May celestials bring timely rains so that harvests are bountiful. May kings act in accordance with dharma. May the people of the world be happy.

May all medicines be effective and those who recite mantras be successful. May dakinis, rakshasas, yakshas, and so on be endowed with compassionate minds.

May no living creature ever be sad, commit evil, or ever fall ill. May none ever be afraid or berated, or develop an unhappy frame of mind.

May reading and recitation flourish and stay nicely present in all viharas. May the sangha always be in harmony and the sangha's aims be fulfilled.

May members of the sangha who want to do the trainings find isolated places. May they, in having abandoned all distraction cultivate the mind so that it becomes workable.

May the fully-ordained nuns be materially sufficient and abandon quarrelling with and harming each other. Similarly may all ordained ones never let their discipline become corrupt.

May I, on seeing that my discipline has become lax, give rise to renunciation then always put an end to evil acts. May I moreover obtain a happy migration then in that place guard my yogic conduct so that it does not become corrupted.

May the experts be honoured and receive alms. May their minds be completely pure and may they be renowned in all directions.

May beings not experience the suffering of the bad destinies and without hardship obtain a body better than that of the gods, and thereby quickly accomplish buddhahood.

May sentient beings make offerings many times to all the buddhas and as a result always have the happiness of the inconceivable happiness of the buddhas.

May the bodhisatvas accomplish the welfare of migrators just as they have intended. May sentient beings receive the happiness that the guardians intended for them.

Similarly may the pratyeka buddhas and the śhrāvakas also find happiness.

Until by the kindness of Mañjughoṣha I have gained the first level Utter Joy, may I always remember my lives and immediately upon birth obtain ordination.

May I be sustained by basic foods that will nourish me. May I in all my lives have a place with all of the qualities needed for staying in isolation.

May I, whenever I want to see guardian Mañjughoṣha or want to ask him a small question, see him without hindrance.

May I, in order to accomplish the sakes of all the sentient beings who reach as far as the ends of space in the ten directions, have a conduct like the conduct done by Mañjughoṣha.

For as long as space remains and for as long as migrators remain, for that long may I too remain in order to dispel the suffering of migrators.

May all the sufferings of migrators big or small whatever they might be ripen on myself. May the sangha of bodhisatvas set all migrators in happiness.

The sole medicine for dispelling the suffering of migrators, the source of every happiness is the Buddha's teaching; may it together with material support and honour remain for a long time.

I prostrate to Mañjughoṣha through whose kindness virtuous minds arise. "I prostrate to my virtuous spiritual friends through whose kindness I have developed my body of analytical thinking through hearing, contemplating, and meditating."

That was the tenth chapter of *Entering the Conduct of a Bodhisatva*, called "Dedication". *Entering the Conduct of a Bodhisatva*, by Śhāntideva is complete.

PART TWO

Entering the Bodhisatva's Conduct
with the Interspersed Commentary
by Drukchen Padma Karpo called
"A Lamp for the Path of
the Middle Way"

PREFACE

There have been three major translations into Tibetan of *Entering the Conduct of a Bodhisatva*. The earliest was made by Kawa Paltseg; the next was made by the great translator Rinchen Zangpo; and a more recent one was made by the great translator from Ngog. An edition was made from those translations at this time and used for this commentary by Tsang Nagpa who compared them to find places of agreement. In regard to those three earlier translations, Buton has said, "Ngog's translation is not good."

There are four Indian commentaries preserved in the Tibetan *Tangyur* or *Translated Treatises* that cover all of Śhāntideva's text. They were composed by Kalyāṇadeva, Prajnākaramati gatekeeper of the western gate of Vikramaśhila, Vairochanarakṣhita, and Vibhūtichandra. There is also a small tika commentary by Dānaśhrī that covers only the prajñā chapter. On the Tibetan side, Buton made a lengthy commentary and the translator Ngog made a commentary based on the foremost instructions of the Kadampa tradition that he followed that were based on the Kadampa geshe 'tsho sna pa chen po's annotated edition. My investigations led me to believe that it would be good to make a fresh commentary and the result is the commentary here which is an interspersed style of commentary called "Lamp for the Path of the Middle Way".

The commentary came about in this way. Tenzin Norbu, a chief who protects the vast southern kingdom, and the lake-born vajra's relative who came with nuggets of gold, urged me to do it saying that it must be composed. I accepted the task but did nothing about it for a long time. Later, wanting to study *Entering the Conduct of a Bodhisatva* well and knowing that I had to go to see the great master again, I, the paṇḍita from East Kongpo, Padma Karpo, set myself in an isolated monastery in the area of Chim named Or Shod Thil. It took one month to do the work.

I prostrate to the precious All-knowing Drukpa, Ngawang Chokyi Gyalpo[8].

The virtue of offering even a hair from the body is enough
To please all the buddhas whose forms without exception are clearly
    visible on it.
To that indisputable wonder, at the feet of the all-knowing Drukpa,
I respectfully prostrate.

Having completed every part of actual bowing, there is the teacher, a
    tree able to grant every wish,
From whom the whole nectar of peace descends as the excellent
    speech, a moon water crystal itself,
Producing a most excellent harvest of merit here, the holy field of the
    good qualities of the saṅgha;
In this glorious system of that King of the Śhākyas, worthy of having
    praise heaped on it,

There is the might of the experts who are victorious over the enemy
    of not knowing
Without need of entering the battle-field of a long training
Who have entered the lofty position of softened glory[9];
I bow to their great force descended from the heavens.

---

[8] This is Padma Karpo's guru.

[9] Skt. Mañjushrī, Tib. 'jam pa'i dpal. "Softened glory" is a play on words against the name of Mañjushrī. Mañjushrī means "he who, having totally softened his mind, is glorious".

Śhāntideva, the god who dwells in the gem of peace,[10]
Made his entrance into the ocean of
The bodhisatva's conduct and thereby
Eliminated the lower level of the rivers and valleys of this world[11].

The lotus of the commentary within it smiles
To reveal its anthers, the power of analysis contained within,
And like Sarasvati coaxing her vīṇā,
The pure white swan atop the drum of my throat[12],

gives the explanation of this holy dharma that is to be given here, whose name is, in Indian Sanskrit language, "bodhisatvacharyāvatāra", in Tibetan language, "byang chub sems dpa'i spyod pa la 'jug pa", and in English language, *Entering the Conduct of a Bodhisatva*. The author is the great being Śhāntideva. The size of the text is one thou-

---

[10] Śhānti is "peace" and deva is "god".

[11] He showed a higher dharma, one that belongs to the heavenly realms, as just described, which equates with Buddha Śhākyamuni and his system of teacher, dharma, and saṅgha, which is a heavenly kind of dharma compared to the ordinary levels of this world.

[12] It is worthy of note that the section of poetry just completed has been done in the style that shows the greatest level of mastery of composition. That style is one in which the metre is changed as the verses are written. The first verse is done in eleven units to the line, the next in fifteen units to the line, the next in nine units to the line, the next in seven, and the last in nine. These are the main metres of Tibetan verse and he shifts through all of them, something which is very difficult to do. Moreover, it is usual in Tibetan composition to end the verse section and then explicitly start the prose section. However, Padma Karpo just shifts directly from verse into prose. Again, this is a sign of someone who has not only totally mastered composition but who is willing to use that mastery to make a high level of eloquence.

sand śhlokas divided into ten chapters[13]. The text belongs to the sūtra piṭaka of the three piṭakas, therefore the translator's homage is worded "Prostration to all of the buddhas and bodhisatvas."

---

[13] A śhloka is a four-lined verse of Sanskrit poetry. It tends to read more like English prose than English poetry. Because of that similarity, the text contained in the verses is usually best read as prose.

CHAPTER ONE

The Benefits of Enlightenment Mind

This is the first bundle[14].

The purpose for writing the text can be known through the explanations contained in it, so how are the explanations are arranged? They are arranged in three parts: the goodness of the beginning, the prefatory matter; the goodness of the middle, the main matter; and the goodness of the end, the concluding matter.

1 The Goodness of the Beginning, the Prefatory Matter

The prefatory matter comes in two parts: the expression of worship and the declaration of composition.

1.1 The expression of worship

The expression of worship begins "**I respectfully prostrate to the ones gone to bliss**" where "ones gone to bliss" translates the Sanskrit term "sugata". Sugata is used here because it shows what buddhas are in

---

[14] Tib. bam po. Texts in India were written on palm leaves which were then held together by a thread that was passed through a stack of leaves on either side with a needle, resulting in a bundle of leaves. Long texts might be spread across several bundles. For example, the Sanskrit edition of this text was spread across two bundles, with the second bundle beginning in the sixth chapter.

essence: they are those who have gone to bliss because of having abandonment with three specific features and realization with three specific features; as Dharmakīrti said,[15]

> The ones gone to bliss—those who have abandoned the causes of samsara and gained three qualities of realization ...

"Sugata" is a term of the Sanskrit language of India. It is comprised of the upasargaḥ "su" and the main term "gata". "Su" has many usages, but is understood here to have the three meanings of "beautiful", "non-regression", and "every one without exception". The term "gata" means "gone" as in "gone across samsara to the other side". By combining su and gata, we get "gone to the beautiful", "gone to non-regression", and "gone from every karmic trace", which are three specific features of a buddha's abandonment of samsara. Or, by taking "gata" to mean "realized" and making the combinations as before, we get "realization of the beautiful", "non-regressing realization", and "realization that has left all karmic traces behind", which are three specific features of a buddha's realization of enlightenment.[16]

---

[15] Buddhas are most generally defined as "those who have abandonment and attainment", meaning that they have abandoned samsara and its causes and have attained a realization that has infinite good features. The term sugata was used by Śhāntideva because it embodies that meaning.

[16] According to the *Pañjikā* great commentary, "su" in relation to sugata has four meanings. Padma Karpo follows Dharmakirti's explanation which gives it as having three meanings. There is no contradiction here because the three meanings of Dharmakirti are simply three of the four meanings presented in the *Pañjikā* commentary. Of the three meanings, "the beautiful" means that the sugatas gone to or realized the beautiful state of having abandoned all of the delusions of samsara, including grasping a self; "non-regression" means that they have gone to or realized a level from which they never fall back; and "every one without exception" means that they have gone to or realized a level in which they have eliminated every one of their karmic imprints.

The ones gone to bliss are those **who have the dharmakāya**, where "dharma" refers to both "realization of the dharma" and "the dharma teaching" and where "kāya" means a "body" or an "assemblage". Because they have such a body, they show the function of a buddha, turning the wheel of dharma. As it says in *The Two Truths*,

> In the commentary when it says, "because it is a body of all dharmas ...", it means that being a body of all dharmas it is the dharmakāya, because of which migrators as a whole never depart from being the entity of the tathāgata. The meaning of body is "an assemblage", so dharmakāya refers to an assemblage of dharmas.

Then, in **together with their sons**, "sons" translates the Sanskrit "suta" which, ascertained through the Sanskrit grammatical procedure called "erasure and addition", has the meanings "born into the family", "upholder of the family line"[17], and "doing the activities". These three mean "son" in general. In this particular case it means "son of the tathāgata", that is, a member of the group who is training in enlightenment mind. Someone who is "doing the activities" of this group is referred to as "someone who has properly entered the activities of the Great Vehicle saṅgha".

Within Jowo Atisha's classifications of the places of refuge, the sugatas together with their sons mentioned here have the characteristics of the suchness Three Jewels explained in the Maitreya's text *The Highest Continuum*. Thus, to them **and then to all the other worthy ones as well**—where "all worthy ones as well" means all of the other Three Jewels, which consists of the ones who have manifested realization and the ones who are the cause of manifesting it.

1.2 The declaration of composition

---

[17] "Upholder of the family line" has the sense in English of "a pillar who supports and maintains the family line".

Now, having paid homage like that, what is to be expressed in this text? Śhāntideva says **I will present the topic of engaging in the vows of the sugatas' sons**[18] because what bodhisatvas take up as their practice is contained within those vows or because the conduct of bodhisatvas is just exactly the keeping of those vows. How will it be expressed? It will be expressed **in accordance with scripture and in summary form.**

What is the purpose of writing it? From the perspective of the meaning he says, "**nothing will be expressed here which has not already been said before**" and from the perspective of the words he says, "**and I have no skill in the art of composition, therefore**" given both of those, "**without thought of benefit for others, I compose it in order to cultivate my own mind.**" If you wonder, "What does cultivating one's own mind involve?", the Buddha said,

> It is the process of considering something again and again,
> Evaluating it and cultivating a correct concept of it.

Thus it involves considering something again due to a need for easily grasping its meaning.

Because it is a cultivation of virtue, doing it will increase the force of my faith for a while and similarly, if others whose circumstances[19] **are similar to mine see it, it will be meaningful for them, too.**

---

[18] Skt. saṃvara, Tib. sdom pa. What is usually translated as vow actually means a restraint or binding. Therefore, the phrase here is the "vows of a bodhisatva" with the specific sense of the conduct to which a bodhisatva binds himself.

[19] "Similar circumstances" translates a Sanskrit term that literally reads "equal fortune", but which in this context means that if there is someone else whose circumstances of life are similar enough to those of Śhāntideva—shared interests, shared language of the text, shared outer circumstances such as being a Buddhist monk, and so on, then that sort of person could benefit from his work too.

That ends the declaration of composition. Next comes the validation of the treatise.

The conduct of a bodhisatva is what is to be expressed. By setting out the words in a way that is easy to grasp, the need, which is easy familiarization with it for oneself and others, is present. From that, the core need, which is gaining unsurpassed enlightenment, is present. Without the earlier of those two the later one would not arise whereby a connection between them is shown. The above is set out so that those who understand it will be able to engage in the treatise with respect for it.[20]

---

[20] In the Indian Buddhist system of composing a treatise, it was necessary for the composed treatise to pass a test in order to be accepted as valid. The treatise had to have all of what are called, "the four things of a treatise". The *Illuminator Tibetan-English Dictionary* gives the following.

> They are: 1) that which is to be expressed, that is, the specific meaning to be transmitted by the written expressions in the treatise; 2) the need, that is, what purpose is being addressed by the expressions of the treatise; 3) the core need or the real, inner purpose being addressed by the expressions of the treatise and which is an extension of the need; and 4) the connection, which is that the previous three must connect together or the treatise will not fulfil its function. In other words, that system required that a treatise fulfilled a purpose and a core purpose, and that the former and latter were properly connected, the first leading to the second.

A commentator on a Buddhist treatise usually does a validation after the declaration of composition and prior to the actual body of the text. It is done at that point because the validation cannot be done until the declaration of composition has been made and because if the test fails, the treatise will be invalidated and there would be no point to continuing the commentary.

In this declaration of composition, Padma Karpo has stated that the "vows of a bodhisatva" are "what is to be expressed" in this treatise. Then, after the declaration of composition, he has shown the remaining three items of
(continued ...)

2 The Goodness of the Middle, the Main Matter

This has three parts: the conduct of entry, arousing the mind for enlightenment; performing the conduct that goes with accomplishing enlightenment mind, training in the paramitas; and the conduct that goes with accomplishing buddhahood.

2.1 The conduct of entry, arousing the mind for enlightenment

This has three parts: a basis that is fortunate, a support that has the family line; the basis for joining with the conduct, arousing the enlightenment mind; the basis for accomplishing great enlightenment, practising by following the trainings.

2.1.1 A basis that is fortunate, a support that has the family line

Of the two types of family line, the one that resides in the dharmatā is the one spoken of in "every sentient being has the buddha essence". Because of it, in the end all sentient beings will become buddha. That buddhas arise earlier and later is due to the size larger and smaller of accumulated roots of virtue which in turn are the conditions that make for awaking being closer or more distant. Closer conditions have been defined as having a perfect body support and an excellent mind support.

2.1.1.1 Perfect body support

Leisure and endowment are a set of eighteen good qualities that someone with a human body can possess. Leisure, defined in terms of the adverse side, is to be free of eight unfree states. Endowment, defined in terms of the conducive side, is to be in receipt of a complete set of ten circumstances. **This human body possessing the eighteen good qualities of leisure and endowment is extremely difficult to gain and with it what is meaningful for mankind—buddhahood—can be obtained, so if the benefit it offers is not accomplished, is not used to arouse enlightenment mind, when in the future could such a support be**

---

[20] (... continued)
the validation of a treatise. Thus he has just validated this treatise.

truly received again considering that we have been wandering in samsara from time without beginning until now?

As for the unfree states, a set of eight unfree states is defined as a state of non-freedom, but there is scripture that elaborates, showing non-freedom as more than one item:[21]

> Monks, these eight states of non-freedom are not times when a person could dwell in brahmācharya.[22]

And it goes on to say,

> This support alone is defined as "leisure", but it is just one of the times when a person has the leisure to dwell in brahmācharya. The tathāgata having appeared in this world, he also teaches the dharma ...

Of the eight items constituting non-freedom, the long-life-god category is usually asserted to be birth in the non-perception of the Greater Result abode of the four meditative absorptions[23] and birth as an ordinary being in the formless realms[24]. However, Vīra[25] defines it as

---

[21] He is saying that when the leisure of leisure and endowment is defined, it is defined as the opposite of the one thing, "non-freedom", which is a set of eight circumstances. There is scripture that expands on that one thing and here it is ...

[22] Brahmācharya, literally meaning "pure conduct", refers here to being a monk, someone whose life is dedicated to spiritual practice.

[23] Greater Result is the highest of the three ordinary abodes of the fourth meditative absorption of the form realm. The gods there have the *greatest* attainment or *result* of all of the three levels comprising the fourth meditative absorption. They have the highest attainment in the form realm possible in samsara.

[24] For ordinary being, see the glossary.

[25] Vīra was a very learned Indian man also known as Aśhvagoṣha, well-
(continued ...)

birth in the Heaven of the Thirty-Three and others like it[26] from the standpoint that birth in them does not have the possibility of entering homelessness[27] and that a body not having non-freedom was referred to by the Buddha as "a body more special than that of the gods". I consider the latter of the two understandings to be the acceptable one[28].

As for endowment, *The Buddha Essence*, which explains endowment extensively, says,

---

[25] (... continued)
known in Tibet for writings such as *The Fifty Verses of Guru devotion*.

[26] "Others like it" are the other god abodes at the top of the desire realm, such as Tuṣhitā heaven.

[27] Sanskrit pravrajita, Tib. rab byung. This means that one leaves worldly household life and goes forth into a spiritual life. In Buddhist literature, it then comes to mean taking ordination as a monk or nun which in turn means entering the pure conduct of brahmācharya .

Having ordination is seen as one of the requirements for being able to make the cause of another excellent support, that is, a precious human birth in the future. Padma Karpo does not draw this point out explicitly, but it is yet another thread of meaning contained in his commentary.

[28] "Long-life god" is a general term for the higher births in samsara, from the gods of the desire realm and up. In the eight states of non-freedom, the category "long-life god" is usually defined as birth in the "non-perception" just mentioned or as birth in any of the four levels of the formless realm because birth in those places is not only very long in length but has a loss of perception associated with it such that it is not possible to recognize that one is in cyclic existence and must get out. However, the Indian master Vīra, based on the Buddha's statement that the precious human body can take on brahmācharya whereas the gods of the Heavens of the Thirty Three and above cannot, and based on Buddha's calling that human body "a body more special than that of the gods", defined long-life god here as birth in any of the god realms in samsara above the Heavens of the Thirty Three.

Monks! Endowment is tenfold: five external endowments
and five personal endowments ...

The ten, being conducive conditions, are defined as "endowments", like the resources that rich people have for their use. It is difficult to find a person who has gained this type of support for it requires the appearance of a buddha in this world, a circumstance which is rare. As *The White Lotus of the Holy Dharma* sutra says,

Monks! It is difficult to meet with the appearance of the tathāgata, arhat, true complete buddhas. In many hundreds of thousands of tens of millions of hundreds of thousands of millions of aeons a tathāgata might be seen but also might not be seen in the world. A buddha's appearance is like the Uḍumbara flower.[29]

The cause of a support with the eighteen qualities of leisure and endowment is perfect discipline[30] because it makes for meeting with the appearance of a buddha in the world. As *The Sutra of Authentic Discipline* says,

A person possessing discipline meets with the appearance of a buddha.

2.1.1.2 Mind support

The author advises,"Just as in the gloom of a dark night, a flash of lightning inside rain clouds instantly illuminates all around, similarly in the worlds by the power of the buddhas or the presence of their teaching, for a minute fraction of the time intelligent minds

---

[29] This is a flower that only flowers once in an extraordinarily long time.

[30] Tib. tshul khrims phun sum tshogs pa. The Buddha stated that the cause of having a support of leisure and endowment is the vowed disciplines given to his disciples. Moreover, he said that the vowed disciplines of a fully-ordained person are best for creating the cause and that it is not merely a matter of having the vows but also of keeping them purely. Thus "perfect" here means both a full set of vows and keeping them purely.

seeking what is meritorius—enlightenment—sometimes arise." And when they do arise, enlightenment mind should be aroused.[31]

When that sort of thing happens, it brings about a connection to faith that is present as one of the good mental qualities possessed by the excellent mind support. *The Sutra of the Ten Dharmas* says,

> For men without faith
> The white dharmas do not arise.
> For seeds singed by fire
> How can there be green shoots?

and *The Precious Garland* says,

> Because they have faith
> They rely on the dharma.

Faith is of three kinds. The first kind is admiring faith so-called because, through knowing the good qualities of the Three Jewels, the mind admires them. Coming after that, there are both trusting and longing faiths; *The Sutra of the Lamp of the Jewels* says,

---

[31] This verse does not mean that a bolt of lightning appears in the sky on a dark night; the Sanskrit and Tibetan both say "within the depths of clouds". The verse refers to lightning flashing *inside* rain clouds on a dark night because of which there is a sudden brightness illuminating everything around, a metaphor for the buddha mind existing deep within a person's thick clouds of ignorance appearing and its all-knowing quality illuminating everything for just a moment. The imagery of lightning that is powerful and has the ability to illuminate these dark depths is joined to the idea of the power of buddha mind and its ability to manifest as a moment of illumination in the ignorant minds of beings. Also, Śāntideva is not saying that a meritorious samsaric mind appears but that the meritorious enlightenment mind appears once in a while. What causes it to appear is the buddha-mind's inherent drive to return from the darkness of ignorance to the state of enlightenment. When it happens, it should be a condition for going further by arousing enlightenment mind then training it, which is what the rest of the text is about.

Having developed faith in the conquerors and their dharma
And then working at faith in the conduct of the conquerors' sons
The development of faith in unsurpassed enlightenment comes about.
That is called "the birth of the mind of the great beings".

Faith leads to being oriented towards what one has faith in. Due to having that orientation and actively seeking what is meaningful, a condition for waking up the family line is obtained[32]. In regard to that condition, Ngog Lotsāwa gives a nice explanation[33]; he says that this condition is simply having taken refuge with the nature of that refuge simply being a wish to attain enlightenment. Thereby, the first factor conducive to enlightenment has been obtained. For just that much, the arousing of enlightenment mind does not have to be done beforehand; *The Ornament of The Sutra Section* says,

Family line, interest in dharma, and
Likewise arousal of enlightenment mind, and ...

---

[32] "Family line" refers the enlightened family line to which all beings belong because of having the buddha nature. "Waking it up" refers to bringing it into manifestation.

[33] Atisha was an Indian master who went to Tibet where he taught extensively on refuge. Ngog Lotsāwa, a disciple of his, was a leading early Tibetan translator. In a formalized style of presentation, the waking up of enlightenment mind does not happen until enlightenment mind has been formally adopted. In a more organic approach, a flash of the enlightenment mind which is always present in all beings illuminates the good qualities of the Three Jewels, which in turn leads to faith and then to taking refuge in them. In that way, taking refuge in the Three Jewels is already a manifestation of pursuing enlightenment mind even if it has not yet been formally aroused. Here, Śhāntideva is beginning his text with the very organic process by which the family line of enlightenment awakens. He then presents the formal waking of the family line in a later chapter.

which is to say that having an interest in the Great Vehicle dharma is included in the causes of arousing enlightenment mind.

Moreover, in regard to the topic of the support, scripture explains that for a beginner and also for someone who is ordained, they may have a support that is destined for bad migrations, but there can be the arousal of enlightenment mind for the first time, so their falling into the bad migrations is not fixed.

2.1.2 The basis for joining with the conduct, arousing the enlightenment mind

There are three chapters connected with this: this chapter which teaches the benefits of enlightenment mind in order to rouse enthusiasm for it; the chapter following that on laying aside, one of the most important preparations for it; and the chapter following that on fully adopting it, one of the most important topics of the main part.

2.1.2.1 The chapter which teaches the benefits of enlightenment mind in order to rouse enthusiasm for it

This chapter has three parts: the common benefits of enlightenment mind; the divisions of enlightenment mind; and the individual benefits of the two types of enlightenment mind.

2.1.2.1.1 The common benefits of enlightenment mind

Thus, the intelligence that pursues **virtue** does not happen easily and even when it does happen is short in duration, so is perpetually feeble and evil is overwhelmingly strong, so what root of virtue other than the mind of complete enlightenment could overpower it? Nothing else could.

It is not just about the removal of what is to be abandoned, evil deeds, expressed in the previous paragraph. The leaders among Capable

Ones[34], who have given the matter their utmost consideration for many aeons, have seen exactly this to be beneficial; by it, the immeasurable mass of beings easily attain what is to be accomplished, the supreme bliss of buddhahood.

That being so, one who wants to defeat his own abundant sufferings of becoming and wants to dispel the unhappiness of all the other sentient beings and who wishes that all—both himself and others—will live in abundant happiness will never let go of the enlightenment mind.

Furthermore, when the enlightenment mind has been produced, instantly those who previously had been wretches—wretched ordinary beings—bound in the prison of samsara will be described as "sons of the sugatas" and will become objects of prostration in the worlds of gods and men like a person who, on being let out of prison, is immediately appointed to the position of king's regent. *The Āgama of Shāridvipa* says,

> Shāri's son said, "Bhagavat, I prostrate also to the bodhisatva who for the first time has aroused enlightenment mind".

If it says that, then is there any need to consider others?

And it does not end there, for like the alchemist's liquid that transforms iron into the supreme form of gold, it transforms this impure body that has been taken up into the priceless jewel of a conqueror's body, therefore it is right that this particular alchemical extractor of the essence called "enlightenment mind" should be most firmly adopted. As *The Gaṇḍavyūha Sūtra* says,

---

[34] Capable ones, a term used by Buddhists and non-Buddhists alike which has mostly been mistakenly translated into English as "sages", refers to those who, having been capable of withstanding whatever hardships and difficulties arise on the spiritual path, have reached or are reaching their goal. Here it refers to the buddhas.

> Son of the family, it is like this. For example, there is what is called "the mercuric substance that makes things have the appearance of gold". Just one ounce of it will transform one thousand ounces of iron into gold. That single ounce of mercuric substance will be exhausted by the one thousand ounces of iron but will not be transformed into iron in the process. Similarly, the all-knowing ones' full adoption of enlightenment mind[35] also is an extractor of the essence, one that functions to draw out wisdom; through it, the roots of merit are wholly dedicated, the iron-like obscurations of karma and affliction are entirely exhausted, and all dharmas are made into the golden colour of an all-knowing one. However, the iron of karma and the afflictions cannot ever cause that extractor of the essence which is the arousing of enlightenment mind to turn into affliction for the all-knowing ones.

Furthermore, if the sole captains of migrators, the buddhas, have thoroughly examined it with their measureless and immeasurable intellects and seen it to be a thing of great value, then because of that those wanting to be free of birth in the five abodes of migrators should properly and firmly adopt the precious enlightenment mind, the precious jewel that provides all wants and wishes both short and long term. In regard to this *The Gaṇḍavyūha Sūtra* says:

> Son of the family, it is like this. For as long as the sun and moon's disks carry on illuminating with light, for that long, all of the gems, grains, Saley[36] gold, silver, flowers, incense, garlands, lotions, clothes, and property, as much as there are, will never be able to match the value of the foremost gem of the conquerors. Similarly, throughout the three times for as long as the wisdom of the conquerors carries out the illumi-

---

[35] "Full adoption" means fully taking up the enlightenment mind, which usually done through a ritual of proclaiming that one is doing so. When that is done, the bodhisatva vows are also adopted up at the same time.

[36] "Saley" was the name of the finest gold in Ancient India.

nation of the dharmadhātu realm, then for that long all the roots of virtue with outflow and without outflow as many as there are of gods, men, all sentient beings, śhrāvakas, and pratyekabuddhas will never be equal in value to the arousing of enlightenment mind that is the foremost great precious gem of the conquerors.

The enlightenment mind is more efficient at increasing what is to be accomplished, virtue, and is more effective at destroying what is to be abandoned, evil, and moreover, in addition to those two features, **all other virtues are like the Plantain tree in that, having produced their fruit once, they are exhausted, but the living tree of the enlightenment mind perpetually bears good fruit without being exhausted by doing so and steadily grows ever larger.** Following on from that, *The Gaṇḍavyūha Sūtra* also says:

> For roots of virtue also, when gripped by the enlightenment mind and dedicated to the state of all-knowing, they only ever increase.

Like someone who has done unbearable evil but relies on a strong man for an escort will be freed from very great fears, a person who relies on the enlightenment mind will for a little while be freed, so why do small-minded people not rely on it? *The Gaṇḍavyūha Sūtra* says:

> Someone who truly relies on an heroic type of being will not be frightened by any enemy. Similarly, the bodhisatva who truly relies on the heroic type of being who has aroused the enlightenment mind will not be frightened by any of the enemies, bad conducts.

Furthermore, **like the fire of the end of time** that incinerates a world system[37], it definitely incinerates great evils in an instant. It does that

---

[37] An example of this is that our solar system is forecast to run out of
(continued ...)

by generating the path of seeing which absorbs evils in the first moment of acceptance[38]. The overcoming of fears happens because of the arousing of the fictional enlightenment mind and the incineration of great evils happens as one of the benefits of the arousing of the superior fact enlightenment mind. In the last two examples, a distinction is made between other force and then own force[39].

And those various benefits are not all. **Its fathomless benefits were explained by the very intelligent Guardian[40] Maitreya to Good Wealth.** The abbreviated story of Good Wealth is as follows. Youthful Good Wealth, son of the trader Stable Wealth, aroused enlightenment mind in the presence of Mañjuśhrī, fully adopting it in the city Source of Glory. Starting out from there, he travelled all roads to the south, where he took teachings in general from one hundred and ten spiritual friends. Śhāntipa was the eleventh of them and Good Wealth posed one thousand and one hundred questions to him. Finally, Good Wealth went to a place on the shores of a lake where there was a house whose walls were decorated with images of Vairochana. He went inside with

---

[37] (... continued)
nuclear fuel, grow to an enormous size because of it, and incinerate the entire solar system in the process.

[38] This is the one of the sixteen moments passed through from the beginning to the end of the path of seeing.

[39] The fictional arousing of enlightenment mind, which is concerned with love and compassion for others, can temporarily overcome fears that would be caused by others. The superior factual arousing of enlightenment mind, which is concerned with insight into emptiness, has the ability to destroy, for good, the negativities of one's own mindstream, bringing with it the realization of the path of seeing and putting an end to one's own samsara in the process.

[40] For guardian, see the glossary.

the special thought free of all birth[41] and met Guardian Maitreya who asked whether his journey had gone well. Good Wealth replied then asked him, "Noble One, if I were to enter unsurpassed, true complete enlightenment, I would no longer have to seek the bodhisatva's conduct. Would you, noble one who has the great qualities that come with being separated from enlightenment by one life only, please advise me on how to do the trainings?" Guardian Maitreya praised him, saying, "You have aroused the enlightenment mind. It is good, it is good!" Then he explained to Good Wealth at length, "Why is that? Son of the family, the enlightenment mind is like the seed for all of the buddha qualities. It is like a field because it totally increases the white dharmas of all migrators. It is like the ground because it shows the whole world. And it is like a synopsis because it incorporates every conduct and prayer of the bodhisatva. It is like a stupa in the worlds of gods, men, and asuras. Son of the family, enlightenment mind has in that way those good qualities and also has measureless other specific qualities".

2.1.2.1.2 The divisions of enlightenment mind

That enlightenment mind when summarized is understood to be of two types: a mind that aspires to enlightenment and one that engages in enlightenment.

Like the way that wanting to go somewhere and actually going there are understood, intelligent people will understand that there is a sequence to these two.

The basis upon which the divisions are made is exactly that entity that possesses the previously discussed benefits of arousing the fictional enlightenment mind. That mind which is a mental consciousness

---

[41] "Free of all birth" means that it was not produced in a dualistic mind, in other words, it was the superior factual enlightenment mind. "Special" refers to the final level of the various levels of development of bodhichitta on the fictional side. Altogether, he had a very high level of development of enlightenment mind.

referencing the enlightenment mind—emptiness having an core of compassion—is something that has the ability to lead one to inexhaustible virtuous good qualities. When it is sub-divided in a more detailed way, it is sub-divided on the basis of the levels[42], and so on, into twenty-two sub-divisions, and when it is sub-divided in a medium way, it is divided on the basis of the intentional[43], and so on, into four sub-divisions. Those twenty-two and four sub-divisions as they are generally discussed are arousings of the fictional enlightenment mind, but each of them does also have an arousing of superior factual mind goes with it.

The two of wanting to go and going, which are exclusively fictional enlightenment mind, have the following difference. As with wanting to go somewhere, first there is the aspiration, "For the sake of sentient beings, I will become a buddha." It is not a mind that has set off on the journey, but one which just aspires to it. As with going somewhere, second there is having set off on the journey to enlightenment that was aspired to.

Having set off on the journey to enlightenment, the aspiration is included within the engagement, for example walking where the walking has been motivated by the aspiration to walk. Yet the mere starting out on engagement is the work only of aspiration for, as *The Avataṃsaka* says,

> Son of the family, it is like this. Even when broken, a precious vajra still outshines every fine gold ornament and on top of that the name "precious vajra" will not be rejected—all

---

[42] "Levels" here means all levels of the path to enlightenment, those on the samsaric paths of accumulation and connection and on the non-samsaric paths of seeing, meditation, and no more training.

[43] "Intentional" refers to the levels of the path within samsara. The other three are the impure bodhisatva levels, the pure bodhisatva levels, and the level of a buddha. Each of these circumstances is said to have a particular type of enlightenment mind.

impoverished people will completely turn towards it. Son of the family, similarly, the precious vajra which is arousing the mind for all-knowing does, without any effort, outshine all the ornaments of the śhrāvakas and pratyekabuddhas' good qualities and on top of that, the name "bodhisatva" will not be rejected—all impoverished people of samsara will completely turn towards that being.

You might think, "If we assert that the refuge of the Great Vehicle includes the intent to attain buddhahood for the sake of others, then there would be no difference between that and the aspiring to go", but it is not so. The first is asserted to be a mental event. The second is, because of the sake of others, an orientation and drive that wants true complete enlightenment and that being a consciousness that produces the two minds is very different from the first[44]. The first is the simple thought, "I will obtain it", whereas the second is total dedication to it through the thought, "I will attain it, may it be so!" whereby it has turned into something that is not operating at the level of a mental event.

2.1.2.1.3 The individual benefits of the two types of enlightenment mind

The mind that aspires to enlightenment and that is all **gives rise to** many **greater** types of **results**—such as birth as a chakravartin emperor—**while** cycling about **in samsara, but unlike arousing the mind of engagement does not give rise to a continuous stream of merit.** That is so because the former being merely a commitment is without any attempt to accomplish it.

---

[44] This is a technical way of talking based on an Abhidharma understanding of the differences between main minds (Skt. citta, Tib. sems) and mental events (Skt. caitta, Tib. sems byung). The first thing is merely a mental event; the second is a mental event but causes a consciousness or main mind. In particular, it produces the consciousness that is the two types of enlightenment mind.

From the time that the mind of engagement has with an irreversible attitude genuinely been adopted by taking the vows of enlightenment mind, from that time on, even if asleep or not paying attention, there will be a force of merit that does not start and stop but is continuous in terms of time and equal to space in terms of vastness.

This explanation given in the preceding paragraph can be accepted on trust because of what the Tathāgata himself said in *The Sutra Petitioned by Subāhu* for the sake of sentient beings who are inclined towards the lesser vehicles, as follows,

> If someone who, because of having the aims of a sentient being intent on the lesser way, is wanting the stated[45] good qualities of a pratyekabuddha or good qualities of a śhrāvaka, also, moment of mind by moment of mind, develops infinite and infinite again roots of merit and has the expansion of infinite and infinite again roots of merit, then what need to mention a son of the family or daughter of the family who wishes for and is intent on and aspires to the buddha qualities with infinite good qualities and limitless good qualities, limitless, infinite strengths, and limitless strengths, to the realization of them in their entirety, and to their total completion when the four causes, four conditions, and four references of those[46] who even have fallen into not paying attention or being asleep result in four infinite and limitless heaps of roots of virtue that lead to four infinite and limitless heaps of enlightenment accumulation that, moment of mind by moment of mind, will develop and expand.

---

[45] "Stated" means stated by the Buddha to be the case.

[46] ... sons and daughters of the family who are not merely wanting, intent on, and aspiring to these qualities of complete buddhahood but who are engaging in the conduct that leads to the qualities of complete buddhahood ...

If someone in thinking, "I will remove just the headaches of sentient beings", is having a beneficial thought that will result in gaining an unfathomable amount of merit—like the offspring of a dear friend—what need is there to mention the result of wishing to dispel all the sufferings of samsara, the unfathomable unsatisfactoriness of each sentient being and of wishing to produce in each one of them buddhahood with its unfathomable good qualities? The previous sutra continues,

> Subāhu, furthermore, a bodhisatva trains authentically like this, thinking, "If someone wanting to dispel for just one moment of mind of the moments of mind the connection to suffering of the infinite and infinite again mass of sentient beings, also, moment of mind by moment of mind develops infinite and infinite again roots of merit and has the expansion of infinite and infinite again roots of merit, then what need is there to mention someone who, for future, not yet come infinite, unfathomable aeons has the wish to dispel the suffering of birth up through the suffering of becoming of the infinite and infinite again mass of sentient beings?"

Who of the ones close to you, your father or mother, either one, has this kind of beneficial mind? Do those who the world takes as a refuge, gods and ṛishis either one or Brahmā even, have this sort of beneficial mind or not?

Those sentient beings in cherishing only themselves up till now have not even dreamt of this kind of mind for their own sake, so how could they have given birth to it for others' sakes?

This special, precious mind that in thinking of sentient beings' sakes thinks of others without thoughts of one's own sake arising, a wonder that has not previously existed in this world, has now been born!

How could the merit of the precious mind that is the cause of gladness in all migrators, that is salve for dispelling the suffering of sentient beings, be measured? It says in *The Sutra Petitioned by Shrī Dāna*,

> Enlightenment mind's merit,
> If it developed form,
> Would fill the whole of space;
> Therefore it is special.

If even just the aspiration that is a thought to be of benefit is more special than offering to the buddhas ... The immediately preceding sutra says,

> Compared to a buddha field filled not
> With the amount of the sands of the Ganges
> But with the seven precious things
> And offered to the guardians of the world,
>
> The offering made by anyone who
> Puts his hands in añjali and
> Arouses the enlightenment mind
> Has no limit to it, so is superior.

... then what need is there to mention the mind of engagement that is striving for the sake of the happiness of every one of the sentient beings without exception?

You might think, "Sentient beings are expert at removing their own suffering themselves and making their own happiness themselves, so there is no point to the enlightenment mind striving for their sakes", but it is not so. They—the sentient beings—have a mind that wants to get rid of their own suffering themselves, but in their attempts to do so they rush to manifest suffering as though doubting that they already have it. They want happiness, but their delusion of the four perversions[47] defeats all possibility of their own happiness as though it were an enemy. That is why it is correct for the enlightenment mind to strive for their welfare.

This is someone who will satisfy with every happiness those having little happiness and will eliminate all of the sufferings of those having many sufferings, and who will even dispel their delusion. Where is there virtue equal to this? Where is there a spiritual friend like this? Where is there something as meritorious as this?

Because of that, if any beneficial response is deemed worthy of a little commendation by the world which says of the doer, "He is a good person", what need is there to mention the praiseworthiness of the bodhisatva who unconditionally does only good for others?

Furthermore, if someone provides a few migrators with food on a regular basis or gives just food for the moment—just food and only enough for one meal—or gives in an abusive way enough to last for half a day, even then beings will honour it, saying, "This is virtuous activity".[48] What need then to mention someone who perpetually gives to sentient beings beyond count for a long time—for as long as

---

[47] The four perversions are four wrong ways of looking at one's world which serve to bind one into samsara: seeing the impure as pure, seeing the impermanent as permanent, seeing the unsatisfactory as satisfactory, and seeing the compounded as uncompounded.

[48] There are four different ways of giving here that are mentioned in the sutras as being inferior in one way or another. Giving to a few beings on a regular basis is a case where the object of the practice of giving is limited; giving only food is a case where the substance is limited—after all one could give more than just food; giving just once is a case where the duration is limited; and giving in abusive manner, which was a fact of gifts of food to beggars in Asia where they might have been beaten as well as offered food, is a case of limited quality of treatment. A bodhisatva's giving exceeds all of these as is pointed out in the rest of the verse.

space remains—the unsurpassed bliss of the sugatas and the fulfilment of all yearnings, none left out? It says in *The Sutra Petitioned by Nārāyaṇa*:

> If I am willing to give and give totally even this body of mine to sentient beings, then what need to mention external things? Whatever it is, this and that, that this and that sentient being might need, I will give it, this and that, to this and that one.

The Capable One said in *The Sutra Showing Complete Ascertainment of Illusion* that someone who gives rise to a negative mind towards a son of the conquerors who acts as a donor like that to all sentient beings, will dwell in hell for as many aeons as moments the negative mind was produced. He said,

> A bodhisatva who rouses a mind of anger and rouses a mind of condescension towards a bodhisatva will for as long as it lasts himself reside in hell for aeons.

Furthermore, he said in *The Sutra On Creating Strength of Faith*,

> Son of the family or daughter of the family, if someone were to destroy or burn stupas numbering the sands of the Ganges and, son of the family or daughter of the family, someone were to rouse a harmful mind or much negativity or anger towards a bodhisatva mahāsattva intent on the Great Vehicle, and to try to bring him down with bad talk because of it, this in comparison would produce a level of evil action that was incalculably greater than the first. Why is that so? From bodhisatvas bhagavat buddhas are born, and from buddhas arise stupas, every item of happiness, and every one of the gods' levels.

You might ask, "That being the result that comes from harming a bodhisatva, what sort of result comes from being respectful of him?" However, anyone who develops great admiration for him will have a result that will be even greater than that previously mentioned evil produced by that negativity. *The Sutra on Certain and Not Certain* says,

> Mañjushrī, what if there is someone whose full adoption after thorough examination results in his becoming an eye of all sentient beings of the realms of the worlds of the ten directions and also if there is full adoption after thorough examination, if some sons of the family or daughters of the family abiding in the mind of loving kindness are the ones who are creating the eye of all of them[49]? Mañjushrī, another son of the family or daughter of the family who looks on a bodhisatva intent on the Great Vehicle with a mind of admiration would produce merit especially greater than that.

Even when someone creates a major problem for the conquerors' sons, even to the point of losing their lives over it, the enlightenment mind itself has no thoughts of anger, and so on, in it, so evil does not arise and, on their side, there is patience and a special kind of compassion with force like that of a king's loving kindness produced by the circumstance for whatever is causing the harm, so **their virtue naturally increases.**

Therefore, in order to show that, "The bodhisatva is worthy of veneration", Śhāntideva says, "**I prostrate to the bodies of those in whom the precious jewel of that holy mind has been produced in the mindstream and I take refuge in those who are sources of happiness because of joining those who have assisted them and even those who have harmed them with happiness.**" The bodhisatva is a source of happiness for he not only connects a person who has helped him with happiness, but also connects a person who has harmed him with happiness, which he does because of totally accepting everyone for the person for the long term.

---

[49] An "eye of the world" is a person who has developed compassion for the beings of world and looks on them with that compassion. From this, we can know that admiration for a bodhisatva is very meritorious, which is the point being made.

You might ask, "Does this not contradict the earlier statement about doing harm to those who are creating great evil?" No it does not; if there is no repair of the evil created, the full-ripening follows immediately from it. All of that kind of harm and so on turns into the cause of happiness for the long term; for others samsara is endless, but please look at the bodhisatva with faith! Someone might have harmed him, but because of that person and the surrounding circumstances, he then totally ripens all of the sentient beings, none of whom he rejects; that person causes him to keep his mind on changing their situation so that there will be an end to samsara for them!

That was the first chapter of *Entering the Conduct of a Bodhisatva*, called "Explaining the Benefits of Enlightenment Mind".

CHAPTER TWO

Laying Aside Evil Deeds

2.1.2.2 The chapter on one of the most important preparations for arousing enlightenment mind, laying aside evil deeds

This chapter has three parts: making offerings, the basis for accumulating merit; going for refuge, the basis for awakening the family; and laying aside, the basis for purifying evil deeds.

2.1.2.2.1 Making offerings, the basis for accumulating merit

The explanation of the ritual which is to be done in order to adopt the precious mind has three parts—preparation, main part, and conclusion—of which this topic is the preparation.

2.1.2.2.1.1 The object to whom the offerings are made

I nicely make offerings to the tathāgatas, to the stainless Jewel the holy dharma, and to those oceans of good qualities, the buddha sons. In regard to this, *The Compendium of Trainings* says,

> They begin with receiving all relevant scripture and adopting the vows and then conscientiously working to familiarize themselves with the topics of the bodhisatva trainings, all of which is done through someone having the vows. Once they have done that, transgressions of the trainings might cause them to have great shame and become scared that the guru will doubt their sincerity, however, putting aside a need to obsess over transgressions, they should practise the trainings

with joy and respect. Then the bodhisatvas, in full view of the buddhas, genuinely adopt whichever of the bodhisatva trainings that they wish to accomplish.

In relation to that, the conquerors having the supreme of all good qualities[50] have said this, "Vows are the dharma in general" and in *The Condensed* the Buddha said, "One attends a person who has the buddha dharmas, a spiritual friend."

If a person suitable as a guru[51] cannot be found, *The Compendium of Trainings* says,

Alternatively, if there is no spiritual friend of that sort, meditate on the buddhas of the ten directions and the bodhisatvas being actually present, then adopt the vows by connecting with them through your own force. If it is not so, then all the buddhas and bodhisatvas and the worlds having gods would become deceptive.[52]

Therefore, the vows are taken in front of a spiritual friend who is actually present or is seen with the mind.

2.1.2.2.1.2 The substances used for the offerings

There are five unsurpassed offerings: offering of unowned things; offering of the body; mentally manifested ones; pleasant-to-hear melodious praises; and practice.

2.1.2.2.1.2.1 Offering of unowned things

---

[50] Non-buddhists in the Buddha's time also claimed that their gods were conquerors. Thus, for Buddhists, the leaders among all conquerors are the buddhas.

[51] Guru here means a teacher who can show you the way to mastery of any given training. Here it means a spiritual friend.

[52] ... because they have explained that this is the way to do it.

In this human world: As many flowers and fruits as there are; whatever types of medicines made from roots, leaves, and trunks there are; as many precious things of the world as there are; whichever delightful pure waters there are; precious mountains and likewise precious forests and furthermore other solitary and pleasing places; trees decorated with ornaments of flowers and the like, trees whose branches are bowed with excellent fruits that are edible,

And as well as that, in all the realms of the worlds of the gods and others like them, fragrances, incense, wish-fulfilling trees, jewel trees, crops that grow without cultivation—unploughed and unplanted.

And furthermore, ornaments that are suitable to be offered that were not made through effort[53], such as lakes and ponds ornamented with lotuses and dotted with wild geese of extremely sweet cry and delightful plumage—

If I mentally imagine all of those un-owned things existing through to the limit of all-encompassing space then nicely offer them to all the Capable Ones supreme among beings together with their sons, then you superior places of offering, you of great compassionate activity, considering me with love accept those things I have offered!

Having no merit I am destitute and have nothing of value to offer at all. Therefore you guardians who are concerned with others' sakes, accept this through the force of doing it for my sake! This verse comes from the perspective of an ordained person, someone who keeps no valuables. For that sort of person, the mentally-made offerings

---

[53] This and the next are connected. He is offering ornamentation, both of the sort requiring some type of effort to accomplish the ornamentation and of the sort which naturally occurs, such as wild geese with their beautiful cry and beautiful plumage dotting lakes.

detailed in the verses prior to this one alone will be offered and nothing special apart from that. The great Śharawa said many times, "If you do have something to offer but repeat this last verse without offering it, you become a liar". If you do have something to offer, offer it then mentally imagine the remaining things. Then, when you say the verse, because you have nothing else of value to offer apart from what you have set out, there will be no contradiction.

2.1.2.2.1.2.2 Offering of the body

I forever offer not a part but all of my body to the conquerors and their sons. You supreme heroes accept me completely! I will respectfully be your servant who carries out whatever you command.

Now that I have been taken into your care, I am not afraid to be in becoming, and because of that I will benefit sentient beings; I will truly go beyond the karmas accumulated from my earlier evil deeds by laying them aside and henceforth shall do no more.

2.1.2.2.1.2.3 Mentally manifested offering

In very sweetly-scented bathing chambers which moreover are with brilliant crystal floors, with delightful four pillars ablaze with jewels, with pearl latticework hangings glowing with light, and fine silk canopies overhead, I bathe the bodies of the invited tathāgatas and their sons using many jewelled vases filled with delightful waters made pure with aromatics[54] to the accompaniment of much song and music in the style of bathing of a chakravartin emperor.

Then I dry their bodies with incomparable cloth such as fine Kaśhika cotton cloth[55] clean and well-moistened with fine scent. Then, having

---

[54] In ancient India, the aromatic substances used to make incense, for example sandalwood, were also put into water to freshen and improve it.

[55] In ancient India, Kaśhika was the finest of cotton muslin cloths available
(continued ...)

rubbed them down like that, I offer them nicely dyed—using the dyes allowed for the buddha and his shrāvakas[56]—garments that have been made fragrant with the finest scents.

I will adorn as I would adorn the leader of the gods[57], the great heroic beings[58], noble ones Samantabhadra, Mañjughosha, Lokeshvara, and the others with various raiments excellent, fine, and smooth—brilliant like Sa Og brocade having a thousand designs[59]—and with jewellery possessing hundreds of supreme qualities.

I anoint the bodies of the leaders among Capable Ones[60], bodies that blaze with a lustre like that of polished refined gold, with supreme perfumes whose fragrances waft throughout all of the third-order world.

---

[55] (... continued)
in the city Kashi (modern-day Varanasi) which was and still is famous for its fine textiles.

[56] These are the dyes that the Buddha sanctioned for use by his monks. The details are given in the Vinaya texts.

[57] The god Indra.

[58] Skt. mahāsattva. This term meaning "great being" is used in these teachings to refer to a bodhisatva. In some cases, such as the case here, it additionally refers to the very advanced bodhisatvas dwelling on the pure bodhisatva levels, the eighth level and up.

[59] Sa Og brocade, whose name is thought to be a corruption of the country name Sahor in which the cloth originated, is especially fine brocade with threads of precious metals woven into it in a few designs. Here, a level of quality with a thousand designs is mentioned.

[60] There are many levels of capable ones—both Buddhist and non-Buddhist—meaning strong practitioners capable of undergoing hardships for the sake of their spiritual journey; the leaders among all of them are the buddhas.

And to those leaders among Capable Ones, a supreme place for making offerings, I offer all the sweet-smelling flowers—the delightful Mandāravā, Lotus, Utpala, and others—and delightful well-designed garlands made of flowers and jewels, and all-pervading cloudbanks—pervading space—of the fragrant smoke of the best incense whose scent steals away the mind.

I also offer them foods of the gods that include a variety of foods and drinks. I also offer them rows of jewelled lamps mounted in lotuses of gold[61]. On the surrounding land over which incense water has been spread, I scatter the petals of delightful flowers.

I offer to those who have a nature of compassionate activity immeasurable palaces filled with praises expressed in delightful melodies, ablaze with the beauty of hangings made of pearls and precious ornaments that are swaying to and fro, and which, because these palaces are bigger than can be comprehended it is as though they fill space with beauty, so they have become ornaments of unfathomable space.

And I perpetually offer to the Capable Ones beautiful umbrellas made of precious substances—gold and so on—which are delightful in appearance with their golden handles and ornamentation around the rim and whose nice shape when held erect is lovely to behold.

2.1.2.2.1.2.4 Offering of pleasant-to-hear melodious praises

As well as that, may a mass of offerings resounding with delightful music and pleasing melodies, like thunder-bearing rain clouds that relieve the sufferings of sentient beings, be present.

2.1.2.2.1.2.5 Offering of Practice

---

[61] A lamp in ancient India was an oil-containing vessel with wick. These vessels are made from gold and designed as large lotus buds.

Making the offerings inexhaustible by thorough dedication: May a continuous rain of precious substances, flowers, and so on descend upon all the volumes of the holy dharma Jewel and upon the stupas and statues.

Just as Mañjughoṣha and the others—Samantabhadra and so on—made vast and unsurpassed offerings to the conquerors, so I too will make offerings to the guardian tathāgatas together with their sons.

And I will praise those oceans of good qualities with oceans of types of melodious praise that express their oceans of good qualities. May those clouds that broadcast sweet and pleasant-to-hear melodious praises certainly always arise for them in the oceans of their oceans of field realms.

Doing this with ordinary beings' purity of the three spheres absent and with thorough dedication makes the offering into paramita because of which it becomes an unsurpassed offering.

2.1.2.2.2 Going for refuge, the basis for awakening the family

This has three parts: the preliminary, prostrations; the causal refuge, proclaiming as one's support the Three Jewels which have already been accomplished in another's mindstream; and the fruition refuge, proclaiming as the fruition the Three Jewels which will arise in one's own mindstream.

2.1.2.2.2.1 The preliminary, prostrations

I prostrate where the prostrations are done with the five extremities touching the ground with imagined or mentally-manifested bodies as numerous as all the atoms within the oceans of fields—the field realms of the buddhas and each body having a hundred thousand tongues—bodies owed down to all the buddhas gone in the three times—past, present, and future—to the dharma Jewel, and to the supreme assembly.

I prostrate also to the bases of enlightenment mind—the supports for it of statues and volumes of texts—and the stupas. I prostrate to the preceptors, likewise to the masters, and to those of supreme yogic activity, that is, to the ones who have restrained themselves with the vows of a bodhisatva.

Prostrating like that results in births as a chakravartin emperor one thousand times the count of sand grains in the area covered by the five extremities when prostrating. As it says in a main text of The School of Those Advocating Everything Exists[62],

> Monks! As many sand grains as are covered beneath this monk … this monk will live one thousand times in the sovereignty of a chakravartin.

2.1.2.2.2.2 The causal refuge, proclaiming as a support the Three Jewels which have been accomplished in another's mindstream

What is the length of time for which one takes refuge? In the case of a śrāvaka it is for the length of one's life and in this case it is from the current time **until the heart of enlightenment has been reached.** "Heart of enlightenment" refers both to the place that is the heart of enlightenment and to the realization that is the heart of enlightenment. The former refers to the sambhogakāya's Akaniṣhṭha and to the nirmāṇakāya's Vajra Seat, the places created by the Vajra-Like Samādhi. Not the place but the realization is the one intended here, so one is taking refuge until arriving at the realization which is the heart of enlightenment meaning unsurpassed enlightenment.

What is the place in which one takes refuge? **I take refuge in the buddhas** who are defined as the suchness and so on refuges. **I likewise also take refuge in the dharma and in the bodhisatva assembly.**

---

[62] This is one of the eighteen branches of the śrāvaka school that arose after the Buddha's passing. They proclaim that all phenomena are existent.

What is the cause for taking refuge? In this case it is the compassion that wants to liberate sentient beings from unsatisfactoriness. The essence of that refuge is being having an aim in which one does not hold to the approach of the śhrāvaka trainings but wants to obtain buddhahood in order to finalize one's own and others' sakes.

Why does one go for refuge? One goes because of the faith that knows that the Great Vehicle Three Jewels have the ability to liberate from the failings of becoming and peace.

What is the mode of going for refuge? For the sake of those wanting to obtain buddhahood the path of fearlessness was taught and because of it, they accept the buddha as the teacher and understand him as the one who will provide them with support and assistance—if they did not see him that way, they would not have faith in his commands. They accept the holy dharma as what is to be directly known for the purpose of truly pacifying all unsatisfactoriness because if they did not see it that way, they would not engage in practising according to it. They accept the saṅgha as what is to be relied on, the ones who lead to the place of fearlessness, because if they did not see it that way, they would not train by following them.

Etymologically speaking, the Three Jewels are referred to as a *refuge* because they provide protection from fear and unsatisfactoriness. We speak of *taking refuge in* or *going for refuge to* them because, having adopted them as the providers of support and assistance, we want to be guarded in accordance with their command. It is similar to the situation in the world where someone taking refuge in another person does not transgress that other person's command.

The trainings to be done by those who have gone for refuge are stated in *The Sutra of the Great Nirvana*,

> Someone who has gone to the Buddha for refuge
> Is one who has become a true upāsaka;

He never goes for refuge
To other divinities.

If he has gone to the holy dharma for refuge,
He has divorced himself from the minds of violence and killing.
And having gone to the saṅgha for refuge,
He will not pay homage to those of Tīrthika ways.

That is saying that ordinary beings should: apprentice themselves to the holy ones; listen to the holy dharma; keep their minds properly directed; practise dharma according to dharma and keep the sense doors restrained; have heartfelt love for sentient beings; be diligent at offering to the Jewels; and take vows to the extent that they can.

Taking refuge accomplishes good qualities that bring benefit and ease to sentient beings, prevents one from becoming disheartened by while doing austerities, the good qualities it has are the cause of all vows, it protects from all fears, it enters people into holiness, and so on—in short, it is the basis for all the good qualities that come from following the three vehicles.

2.1.2.2.2.3 The fruition refuge, proclaiming as the fruition the Three Jewels which will arise in one's own mindstream

This is taught in accordance with what has been said. It says in *The Sutra of the Householder Uncouth*,

> Householder, what is it like for a bodhisatva householder to have gone for refuge to the buddha? Householder, for this, a bodhisatva householder actually forms the mind that thinks, "I will entirely accomplish a buddha's body nicely adorned with the thirty-two marks of a great being" ... When it is like that, householder, a bodhisatva has gone for refuge to the buddha.
>
> Householder, what is it like for a bodhisatva householder to have gone for refuge to the dharma? ... He achieves the reflection, "Because of possessing dharma in this way, I will achieve

unsurpassed true complete enlightenment, becoming a manifest complete buddha, then through dharma will share dharma with the world with gods, men, and asuras". Householder, when it is like that, a bodhisatva householder has gone for refuge to the dharma.

Householder, what is it like for a bodhisatva householder to have gone for refuge to the saṅgha? Householder, for this, a bodhisatva householder who has gone for refuge to the saṅgha fully achieves the reflection ... "I will attain unsurpassed tru complete enlightenment, becoming a manifest buddha, and then will teach the dharma in order that the good qualities of the saṅgha will be accomplished". Householder, when it is like that, a bodhisatva householder has gone for refuge to the saṅgha.[63]

2.1.2.2.3 Laying aside, the basis for purifying evil deeds

This has three parts: who the laying aside is done before; who undertakes the laying aside; and how the laying aside is done.

2.1.2.2.3.1 Who the laying aside is done before

I mentally invite before me the complete buddhas and the bodhisatvas seated in all ten directions, the ones who have great compassionate activity that works only for others' sakes.

2.1.2.2.3.2 Who undertakes the laying aside

Having prostrated to them, I drape my outer robe over my right shoulder and place my right knee on the ground **then supplicate them with palms joined** as explained in *The Sutra of Golden Light*.

---

[63] Padma Karpo has left out significant portions of what is actually said in the sutra and has also modified the words of the section on the saṅgha so that it refers to the good qualities of the bodhisatvas instead of the good qualities of the śhrāvakas. See PKTC's publication "The Sutra of the Householder Uncouth", by Tony Duff, ISBN 978-9937-572-56-9.

2.1.2.2.3.3 How the laying aside is done

This has three parts: the synopsis; the first three forces extensively explained; and the last force just briefly explained.

2.1.2.2.3.3.1 The synopsis

How the supplication is done is as follows. This is the laying aside for what has been done in the past and in the present: "In samsara having no beginning, in this lifetime and in others, I, due to not knowing the results of it, have done evil deeds myself and have ordered them done by others and I, taken over by the confusion of delusion, have rejoiced in what was done. Having seen those mistakes as mistakes, from my heart—that is, with great regret—I admit and lay them aside before the guardians. I am not concealing anything. I am not hiding anything. In future I will again keep the vows." There is no laying aside to be done for the future, because one has already turned away from bad behaviour. From *The Sutra Petitioned by Maitreya*[64],

> If a bodhisatva mahāsattva has four dharmas, he will overcome evil deeds done and accumulated. What are the four? They are the forces of complete rejection, thorough application of the antidote, turning away from bad behaviour, and the reliance.

---

[64] What follows is mis-quoted, though the explanation of the four dharmas needed for purification of evil deeds by laying them aside presented here is correct in itself. The sutra actually says: "Maitreya, furthermore, if a bodhisatva has four dharmas, he will abandon all bad migrations and not fall into the hands of degrading companions, and will quickly achieve an unsurpassed, true complete enlightenment, manifest complete buddhahood. 'What are the four?' They are: abiding within discipline, not being sceptical about all the dharmas, taking true delight in solitude, and to have entered the authentic and not be wavering from being in the authentic. Maitreya, if a bodhisatva has those four dharmas, he will abandon all bad migrations and not fall into the hands of degrading companions, and will quickly achieve an unsurpassed, true complete enlightenment, manifest complete buddhahood".

2.1.2.2.3.3.2 The first three forces extensively explained

This has three parts: the force of complete rejection[65], the force of reliance, the force of thorough application of the antidote, and the force of turning away from bad behaviour.

2.1.2.2.3.3.2.1 The force of complete rejection

Having aroused intense regret for evils done previously, the method is to do the laying aside with that intense regret. *The Condensed*[66] says:

> It is not done through the action of severing karmas of downfall that have arisen by the process of mind.

What the regret is for? It is for this. **Before this I have done wrongs in relation to the Three Jewels and parents, gurus, and others**—other sentient beings—**through the afflictions by way of body, speech, and mind and I, a person whose many wrongdoings have produced faults in me that have not pleased the buddhas who have arisen, a person of evil deeds, have done evil deeds that are utterly intolerable**—not fitting. **In the presence of the guides I lay all of it aside.**

If I wonder, "Is it all right to lay aside those evil deeds slowly?", the answer is no. I may well perish before the evil deeds have been cleaned away, so the way to do it as above is to please protect me in a way that will swiftly and certainly free me from them.

If I wonder, "What is the reason for this concern that I will perish before that has been done?", the answer is that **the untrustworthy lord of death does not wait for this and that to be done or not done; in every case whether I am sick** with a chronic disease that has brought me to the time of death **or healthy** yet death suddenly strikes, I should know that **this fleeting life cannot be relied on.**

---

[65] This is also known as the force of regret.

[66] This is a Prajñāparamita sutra that condenses the large Prajñāparamita sutra into approximately sixty four-line stanzas.

At the time of death leaving everyone behind I must depart alone, but not having understood that, I have done various kinds of evil deeds for the sake of my friends and foes.

When examined like that, the nature of the situation is that my foes will become nothing, my friends too will become nothing, I will become nothing and likewise all will become nothing.

That being the case, like experiencing a dream, the things I have had for my use will pass and so become memories and, having passed, all of it that I did see will not be an object of being seen again. The many friends and foes of this brief life of mine will have passed, but if I think, "It is not necessary to regret the individual evil deeds done on account of them because they are in that way no longer seen", then it is not so; the unbearable evil which I did without meaning for their sakes remains ahead of me and because of that is to be feared.

Not having realised in that way that "I am but a fleeting event", motivated by delusion, desire, and anger I have done many types of evil deeds. Day and night by turns, this life which cannot stay is always slipping away and if it cannot be extended, why would death not come to one like me? It is like a body of water whose source of water has been shut off cannot increase but can only decrease.

While lying in bed I may be surrounded by my friends and relatives, but the feelings of this life ending cannot be shared so will be experienced by me alone. That being so, when seized by the messengers of death what help will relatives be, what help will friends provide? I ask, "Is there nothing that would be of help?" At that time merit alone would protect me, but then I never did attend to that!

O guardians! Rejecting you who are what can be relied on, careless me who goes unaware of a fear like this has gone about producing many evil deeds for the sake of this transient life. Petrified at being about to lose his life is the person who having been subject to the law has been taken by an executioner and is today being led to the place of execution. If with dry mouth, bloodshot eyes, and so on his appearance has changed from how it was before, what need to mention someone being clasped by the frightening-to-see physical forms of the extremely frightful ones, the messengers of death, and having the total weakness that comes with being stricken with the disease of great fear?

At that time, I will say, "Who will give me good protection from these very great fears?" With terrified, wide-open, and bulging eyes I search the four directions for a refuge, but, similar to searching through the other passengers whose lot is the same as my own on a frightful sea journey, seeing no refuge in the four directions I will become enveloped in gloom. If because of that there is no protection there, then at that point what should I do?

2.1.2.2.3.3.2.2 The force of reliance

This has two aspects: the object relied upon and the thought relied upon.

Due to that being the case, from today I go for refuge to the conquerors, the guardians of migrators, the ones who strive to provide a refuge for migrators, the ones of great strength who have the capacity to dispel all strong fears.

Likewise I truly go for refuge to the dharma they have mastered that dispels all the fears of samsara and also to the assembly of bodhisatvas who are a field of great good qualities.

The former going for refuge is definitely needed as a support for arousing the enlightenment mind whereas the latter is for the purpose that, if you take refuge in it, you will be freed from evil deeds. From scripture,

> Someone who has gone for refuge to the buddha
> Will be freed from all evil deeds.

For example, it is like someone who is afraid putting himself in the care of an excellent master.

Completely afraid, I shall offer myself to Samantabhadra. And likewise To Mañjughoṣha also I shall offer this body of mine.

Also to the guardian famed as noble Avalokiteśhvara whose compassionate activity is not confused, I cry out weakly asking him to be a refuge for this evil doer.

In my search for refuge I cry out from my heart to the noble ones Ākāśhagarbha and Kṣhitigarbha, and to all the conquerors' sons, the guardians who have greater compassionate activity, seeking refuge in them.

And I also go for refuge to Vajrapāṇi, Lord of the Secret, the possessor of the vajra who upon being seen makes beings who arouse aversion in us, such as the messengers of death, flee with fear in the four directions.[67]

The reliance in terms of thought is production in the mindstream of the intent to adopt enlightenment mind. The way in which evil deeds are overcome by has already been explained in the chapter on the benefits of enlightenment mind, so will not be repeated here.

2.1.2.2.3.3.2.3 The force of thorough application of the antidote

---

[67] Maitreya, Samantabhadra, Mañjughoṣha, Avalokiteśhvara, Vajrapāṇi, Ākāśhagarbha, Kṣhitigarbha, and Nirvāraṇaviṣhkambī, were the eight bodhisatva heart sons of Buddha Śhākyamuni.

This refers to the three higher trainings for manifesting realization[68] as follows. The salve or antidote to the manifest movement of evil deeds or non-virtue is discipline. The antidotes that have such power keep mind suppressed so it does not engage in upheavals[69]. Their seeds are destroyed by prajñā which uproots them so that they are incapable of arising in the future. The buddha-word that expresses those three is what constitutes the three baskets of the teaching and their meaning is summed up in *The Sutra of Individual Emancipation* which says,

> Do not do any evil deeds and
> Act out a perfection of virtue,
> Thoroughly tame your own mind—
> This is the teaching of buddha.[70]

Before this I have transgressed your command—I have done evil deeds, I have not accomplished virtue, and I have made mind intractable by the afflictions. Now that I have seen the great fear that results from doing so and so not doing it again, I am led by your command to take refuge in you; by doing so please quickly remove the fear.

For example, if I need to comply with a physician's words when frightened by an ordinary illness, what need is there to mention the case of being perpetually struck by the illness of hundreds of wrongdoings of desire, and so on? And if just one of them—those hundreds of illnesses of wrongdoing—could—had the capacity to—destroy all the humans present on this earth and no other medicine to cure them could be found even though one travelled everywhere and searched in

---

[68] These are "the three higher trainings of śhīla (discipline), samādhi (concentration), and prajñā (correctly deciding mind), presented in that order in the three following sentences. They are trainings specifically for the purpose of manifesting the many realizations needed to attain enlightenment.

[69] ... which result in samadhi or concentration being established.

[70] The first line is explained as discipline, the second as concentration, and the third as prajñā.

all directions, then thinking as the tīrthikas do not to act in accordance with the word of the all-knowing physicians regarding that which would uproot every pain would be extremely—utterly—deluded and so worthy of denigration by the whole world.

Moreover, for those reasons it would not be all right for me to stay in a state of carelessness. If there is a need to stay attentive near even a small cliff, what need is there to mention being concerned about falling over the precipice of the hells that drops for a thousand leagues to a place where one remains for a long time?

As for how to avoid that: It is not all right to sit here happily thinking that for today at least I shall not die. The time when I will become nothing whenever it might be will arrive, there is no doubt.

Who will provide me with no fear regarding future lives? There is no one. How will I have the assurance that I will definitely be freed from this? When there is no doubt that I will be nothing, how can I remain at ease?

What remains with me of the other experiences now ended of the happiness of gods and men in the past? Nothing! However through my strong clinging to them I have gone against the words of my guru. I need to consider, "Am I not deceiving myself making the karmas of evil deeds and staying within them?"

Having discarded this occasion of being alive and similarly its relatives and friends, if I must go on all alone carrying nothing, naked, and empty-handed to places unknown, what is the use of concerning myself with having all the so-called friends and foes?

"Non-virtue is the source of unsatisfactoriness; how can I definitely be freed from that?" It is right for me to consider only this at all times, day and night. Given that not knowing is the principal cause downfalls happening, whatever evil deeds I have done in the past by unknowing delusion of the natural unmentionable acts and those associated with a vow, within the actual sight of the guardians with palms joined and with a mind fearful of unsatisfactoriness, prostrating to them again and again, I lay all of them—those wrongdoings and evil deeds—aside. I ask the guides to accept the evil deeds I have done as mistakes.

2.1.2.2.3.3.3 The last force just briefly explained

This is the force of turning away from doing wrongdoings again which some explain as "the force of restraint". If you do not have a mind of restraint that thinks, "I would rather die than do another evil deed in future", then even if you do the laying aside, the purification will not happen, therefore this force is taught to be necessary. If you have the thought that, "This evil is not good, therefore henceforth I will do it no more and afterwards will remain restrained", doing the laying aside will cause you to rise above evil deeds.

That was the second chapter of *Entering the Conduct of a Bodhisatva*, called "Laying Aside Evil".

CHAPTER THREE

Fully Adopting the Enlightenment Mind

2.1.2.3 The chapter on one of the most important topics of the main part, fully adopting the enlightenment mind

This has three parts: the preliminary part's four limbs; the main part, the ritual for truly adopting enlightenment mind; and, having gained it, being glad.

2.1.2.3.1 The preliminary part's four limbs

Adding the limbs of rejoicing, urging to turn the wheel of dharma, supplicating to not pass into nirvana, and thoroughly dedicating to the earlier offerings, prostrations, and laying aside makes the seven limbs of the seven-limbed service.

For the limb of rejoicing, there is rejoicing in virtue which is consistent with merit. **With gladness I rejoice in the** production of **virtue,** the formatives of merit, **that gives relief from the suffering of all sentient beings' bad migrations and in the** production of the formatives of unfluctuating virtue which places those having suffering in happiness.

I rejoice in the accumulated virtue that has become a cause of enlightenment—virtue which is consistent with emancipation and virtue which is consistent with definite opening[71]. I rejoice in bodied beings' definite emancipation from the suffering of samsara, the unoutflowed virtue of the śrāvaka and pratyeka noble ones.

I rejoice in the enlightenment of the protectors[72] and also in the levels of the conquerors' sons[73]. **With gladness I rejoice in the ocean of virtue of arousing the mind** that, having committed to their protection, is the cause **that makes happiness for all sentient beings and in its perfect fruition that works to benefit all sentient beings** in accordance with its commitment. By it a perfection of virtue is gained as in the story of King Prasenajit and the five hundred beggars for food.

The second one, urging, as with Brahmā urging the teacher[74]: **With palms joined I supplicate the buddhas of all directions** who have **become buddhas in the present not to let a long time go by without teaching the dharma, but to please light the lamp of dharma for sentient beings suffering and bewildered in the darkness of ignorance.**

The supplication not to pass into nirvana, like Chunda the blacksmith's son's request to the Bhagavat: **With palms joined I supplicate the conquerors as many as there are who have asserted that,** having turned **the wheel of dharma they will pass into nirvana please not to leave these migrators blind** as would happen if the teacher dies **and to remain for countless aeons.**

---

[71] "Definite opening" refers to the path of seeing.

[72] "Protectors" throughout this text means "buddhas, the givers of refuge".

[73] "First one rejoices in the true complete enlightenment of the buddha protectors, then one rejoices in all of the levels of enlightenment of the bodhisatvas on the ten levels.

[74] This is what Brahmā is reported to have said when our teacher, Śhākyamuni Buddha, had become enlightened, but had decided not to teach the dharma.

The dedication. What is to be dedicated? Having done all of these seven limbs, **may all the virtue** come from that and otherwise that I have accumulated—to what end is it dedicated?—dispel all the unsatisfactoriness of—to whom is it dedicated?—every sentient being. That is a dedication shown in summary form.

For as long as there are sick migrators—not for as long as each one is sick—and until their sicknesses are cured, may I be their medicines and physicians and their nurses as well.

May a rain of food and drink descend for the hungry and thirsty that will remove their pangs of hunger and thirst.

Then the text says, "intermediate aeon of famine" about which *Texts on the Levels* says:

> At the time when the lifespan is thirty years, an intermediate aeon of famine will occur for seven years, seven months, and seven days. And when the lifespan is twenty years, severe epidemics and infectious diseases that cannot be cured will strike during a period lasting seven months and seven days. When the lifespan is ten years, if one person sees another, an intense mind to kill will arise such that stalks of grass and the like that have been grabbed will turn into sharp weapons and they will kill each other during a period lasting for seven days.

And *The Treatise on Designation* explains:

> When the lifespan is ten years, the three intermediate aeons will arise in turn, one after another.

The intermediate aeon of famine of that sequence being without much food or drink causes hunger leading to weakness then death. And, grain seeds are inserted into the hidden warmth of their bodies which are then guarded as a treasure. And the bones at death are white because of absence of fat on their bodies. And when the bones have been boiled and the soup drunk, the bones totally devoid of bodily fat will be completely white. And, using a spoon, food is distributed each day in turns. And, then the grains are extracted from within them with a spoon and boiled in water which is then drunk, providing them with sustenance by spoon. Hungry and without strength they fall down to the ground and then, unable to arise, these emaciated creatures die. When it is like that, at the time of the intermediate aeon of famine may I become food and drink.

May I stay before those sentient beings who are poor and destitute as all the various requisites they might need.

Without any sense of loss I give up my body and likewise resources and all my virtue of—accumulated in—the three times as well in order to accomplish the aims of all sentient beings.

By giving up everything without attachment one goes to nirvana and I have a mind to accomplish non-dwelling nirvana[75] because it is in accord with my commitment. Furthermore, death is the time of giving up everything all at once and this same giving is best to do now, giving it all to sentient beings.

That being the case, because I have already given this body to all bodied beings to do with as they please now they—those sentient beings—have it forever to kill, revile and beat, and so on, whatever makes them glad.

Let them toy with this my body or mock it or ridicule it, but because this body of mine has already been given to them I think why should I treat it as something for my own use?

Given that I have done that, let them do anything with it that will not bring them harm or an evil deed. Whenever others come into contact with me, may it never be meaningless for them.

---

[75] Non-dwelling nirvana is the nirvana of true complete buddhas.

Having come into contact with me, may minds of anger or faith that are aroused in them always be a cause for the fulfilment of all their aims.

May those who speak badly of me or harm me in other ways and likewise who insult me all not accrue evil deeds through it, but have the fortune to be enlightened.

May I, having given myself to sentient beings, become a guardian for those without a guardian, a guide for travellers on the way, and a boat, ship, and bridge for those wanting to cross the waters.

May I become an island for those seeking an island, a bed for those wanting a bed, and a servant for all bodied beings wanting a servant.

May I become a wish-fulfilling jewel, an excellent vase[76], a powerful vidyamantra, great medicine, a wish-fulfilling tree, and a cow that provides the wishes of bodied beings.

He makes the prayer: May I in the same way as do the great elements—earth and the others and space—forever be a basis for the many types of necessities of life of the fathomless sentient beings. For what length of time does he pray that it will be so? Likewise, may I be a cause of the necessities of life in all circumstances in the realms of sentient beings reaching to the end of space until all have reached or obtained nirvana.[77]

---

[76] An excellent vase is one that magically provides whatever is wished for.

[77] It is not clear from the English, but the Sanskrit has a grammatical structure that indicates the two verses contained in this paragraph go together: may the first verse be the case and equally may this second verse be the case.

If you were to think, "It is not possible for a bodhisatva to turn into those material things, so such dedications are meaningless", it is not so; *The Sutra of Akṣhyamati* establishes it as in the prayer,

> With this body I definitely shall do whichever works there are to do for all sentient beings. For example, like the four great elements—the earth, water, fire, and air bases—are entirely used and fully enjoyed in various ways, various enumerations, various references, various utensils, and various resources, so I too will with this body comprised of the four great elements in a vast way support the lives of all sentient beings through various ways, various enumerations, various references, various utensils, and various resources.

The Sutra Taught by Vimalakīrti also does that in terms of water and fire, saying:

> Likewise, for earth and also wind …

Earth and the other elements can, in the end, be manifested through the power of authentic statement and concentration, though an easier way to prove it is to point to manifested field realms, and so on.

2.1.2.3.2 The main part, the ritual for truly adopting enlightenment mind

Just as the sugatas of former times first aroused the mind for unsurpassed enlightenment and progressively stayed in the stages of all the bodhisatva trainings that are to be trained in, **just so, for the benefit of migrators**—taking across those who have not been taken across, liberating those who have not been liberated, rescuing those who have not been rescued, and taking to total nirvana those who have not gone to total nirvana—**I arouse the mind** for unsurpassed **enlightenment and likewise will progressively train in all of the bodhisatva's trainings.**

"Will arouse the mind for enlightenment" is committing to the fruition and "arousing the mind to train in the trainings" is committing to the cause, so it is explained that the verse here is a two in one procedure.

CHAPTER THREE 183

Some in Tibet connect the two first examples and the two first meanings with aspiring and connect the latter two and two with engaging and this appears previously in the text when it clarifies the Buddha's intent concerning the two.[78]

And, the former is arousing enlightenment mind and the latter is taking the vows of enlightenment. I think that it is good to distinguish the two because these words in which the trainings have and have not been accepted can be a basis for confusion. Here when its says "training", the training is identified as the three disciplines: of vows, of gathering virtuous dharmas, and of performing the aims of sentient beings[79]. Some connect those three with the meaning of progressively staying in three stages, first in the path of accumulation, second in the path of connection, and then, once the bodhisatva levels have been gained[80] the last is the made into the principal thing.

In *The Ornament of Precious Emancipation*,[81] the three trainings are defined as the three higher trainings,[82] though it is considered[83] that those three and these three can mostly be conflated given that their meanings are in agreement.

The meaning of "stages" is given in our tradition as the initial arousing of the enlightenment mind, intentional conduct, and the three paths of

---

[78] This appears near the end of the first chapter when the division of the enlightenment mind into two types is clearly explained.

[79] The paramita of discipline is taught to be comprised of three disciplines the discipline of vows, and so on mentioned here.

[80] ... which happens immediately on completing the path of seeing ...

[81] Known to Westerners mainly through its mis-translated title "Jewel Ornament of Liberation".

[82] ... of śhila, samādhi, and prajñā.

[83] ... by experts who know the Buddha's intent ...

a bodhisatva;[84] it is so because of what appears in *The Descent into Laṅka Sutra*,

> The expression of the teaching itself and the bases of training coming from it are constructed in three stages in the manner of stairs set up between places ...

Then, in "just as the former sugatas ..." enlightenment mind refers to them pacifying the eight extremes of elaboration of the interdependent origination side and thus gaining peace. "Aroused" means that they made that mind manifest in their own direct perception of it.

It says in *The Heart Prajñāparamita Sutra* that the bodhisatva trainings are the conduct of the profound, Prajñāparamita. What is that? Asserting that it is to course in the conduct of the profound, Prajñāparamita, it is said to be "seeing those five aggregates to be empty of nature" and that then is to course in interdependent origination which is to follow in the tracks of the Middle Way.

The meaning of "progressively stayed in the stages of the trainings" is as follows. A beginner makes a connection with the training through prayers of aspiration and works to determine the view. Then he meditates in accordance with his determination of the view, to familiarize himself with it and in that manner gains the path of seeing. That puts him onto the path that leads on from there, the path of cultivation. Traversing that path, he journeys to the ultimate.

The commitment, "Likewise, I will do that too" is extensively set out in noble Nāgārjuna's ritual for adopting the enlightenment mind and is determined in his *Enlightenment Mind Commentary*. The determination of it in the commentary, explained here in a few words, is that "the

---

[84] Intentional conduct is bodhisatva conduct done on the paths within samsara, the paths of accumulation and connection, on which one intends to do the actual training of bodhichitta on the three paths of training which are beyond samsara—the paths of seeing, cultivation, and no more training.

system here should be understood as the uncommon system of the Middle Way".⁸⁵

In regard to the commitment, Jowo Atisha spoke of two approaches: arousing the mind of enlightenment by an intention directed at the profound and by an intention directed at the vast. The first of those is defined as the system of the profound view. The second is that there is the mind of unsurpassed enlightenment which aspires to become a buddha for the sake of all sentient beings and then there is the commitment to turn the wheel of dharma for them; and for the trainings there is commitment to the fruition in which there is the special feature that practice is done in order to join with the fruition, using manifest realizations of the path of illusoriness. There is a sequence to those manifest realizations, so there is a division into five paths, and that is posited as the system of vast conduct. The assertions of the Mind Only system are mistaken in regard to that because by this even a buddha's wisdom is, in being without nature, determined to be illusion-like and for that reason the great experts of India and Tibet distinguish the Middle Way by saying "the illusion-like Middle Way".⁸⁶

The former term is consistent with this because it is a ritual for adopting only the fictional arousing of mind, its actual referenced enlightenment being the kāya for others' sake. The uncommon system of the Middle Way that primarily adopts the superior-fact arousing of mind has the fictional one ancillary to it, its referenced enlightenment being the kāya for one's own sake. Well, *The Highest Continuum* says:

> For first ones, the first kāya;

---

[85] Generally speaking, the Tibetan tradition considers that Nāgārjuna was a champion of the tradition of enlightenment mind that was a profound system of the view and Jowo Atisha was a champion of the tradition of enlightenment mind that was a vast system of skilful means.

[86] The Mind Only schools claims that the final wisdom of a buddha is truly existent, which is not accepted by the schools of the Middle Way.

> For later ones, the two later ones.

That is saying that the dharmakāya is obtained via the family present in the dharmatā and the form kāyas are obtained through truly having taken that up. You might think, "Here, truly having taken that up contradicts the explanation of accomplishing the first", but it does not. This is because here, it is joining with the dharmatā just as it is, so it is suitable for it primarily to be a fruition of a kāya for one's own sake and then, having become buddha in the dharmakāya for one's own sake, for the form kāyas for others' sake to arise.

When the support for arousing the mind, the ritual for adopting it, has been done, one has made oneself into an uncorrupt state. If corruption of that occurs at some later point, it must be repaired. There have been differences in what the great paṇḍits and accomplished ones have asserted as the way to do the repair which has happened because of their teaching in ways that were suitable to audiences with the varying bases[87] and sense faculties of those to be tamed.

The conventions used in the explanations of each of the sūtras of the infinite sūtra section that are concerned with this are not consistent, but if they are dissected using the six limits[88], all of them can be examined to see if their meanings coincide. Gyalwang Je[89] said of this,

> The dharma languages of the various vehicles
> Are indeed true at each one's own level
> And if they coincide, that is excellent!

2.1.2.3.3 Having gained it, being glad

---

[87] "Bases" here translates "dhātu"; they are the bases from which all samsaric consciousnesses arise.

[88] The six limits are a set of six tests that can be applied to determine the actual intent of any given teaching.

[89] Gyalwang Je was the very learned and accomplished second Drukchen.

Those who with intelligence have like that taken up the most admirable enlightenment mind will also at the end in order to increase it give lofty praise for this sort of mind. A distinction is made here that this has been taught as twofold: arousing gladness in oneself and arousing gladness in others.

2.1.2.3.3.1 The ritual for arousing gladness in oneself

This has two parts: the ritual for arousing gladness and the reason for arousing gladness.

2.1.2.3.3.1.1 The ritual for arousing gladness

Today my life has been made or become fruitful for I have gained a good human existence[90]; today I have been born into the family of buddhas and because of that have become a son of the buddhas.

Now whatever happens, I will only perform the actions befitting the buddha family; I will not put a stain on or sully this faultless well-disciplined family.[91]

2.1.2.3.3.1.2 The reason for arousing gladness

This shows what happens due to having given birth to the enlightenment mind with its special good qualities. For example, just like a blind man finding something valuable such as gold in a heap of dust, by some rare coincidence this enlightenment mind difficult to be born has been born in me.[92]

---

[90] This line means "Fully adopting the enlightenment mind has given goodness to or made my ordinary human existence worthwhile".

[91] The line does not say "this family of faultless noble beings" as has sometimes been translated, but says "this faultless well-disciplined family. "Well-disciplined" means that they diligently follow the disciplines of a bodhisatva".

[92] The original says "heap of dust" not "rubbish". It was and still is
(continued ...)

Its special qualities do not end with what was said in the previous verse.

This is the supreme nectar that overcomes the lord of death of migrators. This also is the inexhaustible treasure which eliminates the poverty of migrators.

This also is the supreme medicine which completely alleviates the diseases of migrators. It is the living tree that provides rest to migrators wandering and tired on the path of becoming.

It is the palanquin which liberates all migrators from the bad migrations. It is the rising moon of mind that dispels the torment of migrators' afflictions.

It is the great sun that utterly removes the distorted vision of migrators' unknowing state. It is the buttery essence that comes from churning the milk of the holy dharma.

For the migrator guests travelling the paths of becoming and wanting to live in the enjoyment of happiness, this places them in the supreme happiness they want; it satisfies these sentient beings who are its great guests.

2.1.2.3.3.2 Arousing gladness in others

Today in sight of all the protectors I have called on all migrators to be guests in happiness until sugata-hood has been gained; gods, demi-gods, and others—all of the six migrators—be glad!

---

[92] (... continued)
common in Asia, where dusty environments abound, to sweep the dust of a room into a mound and then dispose of it. While sweeping up the dust something valuable—the text does not say a jewel but something of great value—might be swept into the pile.

That was the third chapter of *Entering the Conduct of a Bodhisatva*, called "Fully Adopting the Enlightenment Mind".

CHAPTER FOUR

Heedfulness

2.1.3 The basis for accomplishing great enlightenment, practising by following the trainings

This has three parts: advice needed for accomplishing what has been verbally declared; heedfulness that makes one very attentive to keeping the trainings; and an explanation of mindfulness and alertness, the method for guarding and purifying the training.[93]

2.1.3.1 Advice needed for accomplishing what has been verbally declared

A conquerors' son having in that way most firmly taken up the enlightenment mind shall, without wavering from it, always exert himself at not straying from the trainings which he has taken up. *The Sutra of Gayagauri* says:

> It is in regard to bodhisatvas who work at the essence of the accomplishment, it is not in regard to those who, already having enlightenment, do not do the essence of the accomplishment of enlightenment.

In general, for something undertaken rashly or not considered well, although a commitment to complete it may have been made, it is

---

[93] The first two parts comprise this chapter four and the third part comprises the next chapter five.

right to examine whether it should be done or given up. However, this is not like that; having been examined and analysed by the great prajñā of the buddhas and their sons who were witnesses and examined repeatedly by myself as well, what could there be in this that should be deferred? If having committed myself to it like that I were not to act diligently to accomplish it, I would have cheated all sentient beings. *The Sutra Petitioned by Matisāgara* says:

> The bodhisatva who, on account of taking across those who have not been taken across, liberating those who have not been liberated, rescuing those who have not been rescued, and taking to total nirvana those who have not gone to total nirvana, has heard much about rescuing all sentient beings but apart from that is not diligent at the virtues included on the side conducive to enlightenment, is a bodhisatva who cheats the world together with the gods. The divine ones who have seen the past buddhas completely denigrate that sort of thing by reviling it directly and indirectly.

And, with what was spoken of there as a cause, I should consider what sort of migrator would become in future lives? If the Buddha has said that a person who, having made up his mind to give just a small, ordinary thing, later on does not give it will become a hungry ghost type of migrator, then if I have made a strong intention to invite all migrators as guests to unsurpassed happiness then cheat them all, how could I go to a happy migration? I would not, instead my migration would be into hell.

If you think that is not true, that people who have let go of the mind of unsurpassed enlightenment can even then achieve emancipation as with Śhariputra becoming the king Chandrabhasa who, having let go of the Great Vehicle arousing of mind remained at the lesser level and became an arhat, is due to the inconceivable modes of karma so in that there is without doubt a karma that will defeat the wrong of letting go of that mind. If you say, "Show me!" then that is known only by the all-knowing one, not known by me.

That letting go of the mind of the Great Vehicle then staying in the Lesser Vehicle is the heaviest of downfalls for a bodhisatva; it is such that if it happens, it diminishes the welfare of all sentient beings. Thus, it says in *The Condensed*, "If that arousing of mind is destroyed, it is an extremely heavy thing." Please look at that!

Someone who for even just an instant hinders or obstructs a bodhisatva's merit will, because he has diminished the welfare of sentient beings, later be born in and have endless bad migrations. *The Sutra of the Miracle of Doubtless Utter Peace* says:

> Son of the family or daughter of the family, there are some who take the life of all sentient beings of this earth and take all their goods. Mañjushrī, son of the family, and daughter of the family, some others create hindrances to the virtuous mind of a bodhisatva and in the end are born as animals. If someone hinders the virtue that would arise from a bodhisatva giving a mere morsel of food, that person has created an incalculably great evil deed. Why is that? It is because of the issue[94] that has occurred of creating a hindrance to the roots of virtue which cause the arising of a buddha.

For this, if in destroying even one sentient being's happiness I become counted among those known as a degraded person, then what need is there to mention becoming a degraded person because of destroying the happiness of bodied beings infinite as the entirety of space?

If you think, "I have become degraded, but I can adopt it again and it will be all right", those who go around in samsara mixing the force of such downfalls that have arisen and the force of enlightenment mind will be hindered from attaining the bodhisatva levels of Utter Joy and the rest for a long time.

---

[94] Issue here means a wrongdoing, karmically speaking, that the Buddha would have to deal with by giving the appropriate advice.

In view of that, because there are such great disadvantages to not practising as I have committed to doing **I shall respectfully practice just as I have committed to doing.**

2.1.3.2 Heedfulness that makes one very attentive to keeping the trainings

This has three parts: advice for undertaking perseverance in the practice; now that one is endowed with a support, advice on exerting oneself at the conducive side, virtue; and advice on defeating the non-conducive side, the enemy of the afflictions.

2.1.3.2.1 Advice for undertaking perseverance in the practice

The Sutra of the King of Concentrations says,

> No matter how many dharmas are expressed as being virtuous dharmas, this heedfulness is the root of them all.

That is saying that heedfulness is necessary. Where else is that spoken about? The *Compendium of Trainings* says,

> What is this so-called "heedfulness" like? Doubts over whether corruption due to desire has arisen or non-desire has arisen comes to begin with, due to which one works industriously at being careful. It is for example, like the way that the servant of an angry and difficult to please king has to traverse a slippery flight of stairs while holding a vessel filled to the brim with vegetable oil.

And the *Compendium of Abhidharma* says:

> What is heedfulness? Through staying unattached, without anger, without delusion, and with perseverance the virtuous dharmas are cultivated and the mind is guarded against dharmas with outflows ...

Thinking about what was said there, in order to connect with the commitment I have made, I must practise out of respect. If I am not diligent from today on, I will only go into lower and lower bad migrations.

As for the fault of previously not having diligence: countless buddhas who worked to benefit all sentient beings have gone by, but because of my own faults I was not pleased by their presence, so, due to the sickness of ignorance, I did not come under their curative care.

If I continue to do the same, the same thing will happen again and again and when it does, in bad migrations I will experience sickness, bondage, being killed, my body being sliced apart, and so on.

2.1.3.2.2 Now that one is endowed with a support, advice on exerting oneself at the conducive side, virtue

If such things as the occurrence of a tathāgata, faith, obtaining a human body, and the chance to become familiar with virtue are rare, when will they be obtained? They will not!

Just now I am not sick, have food, and am free of such troubles, but life can be cheated in a moment because it can change through meeting with a suddenly occurring karmic condition; the body is like something on loan for a short while so control over it is not mine. This heedless sort of behaviour of mine should be turned into the behaviour of emancipation for such heedless behaviour will not gain me even a human body! And if a human body is not gained, in future supports in the bad destinies there will only be evil, no virtue.

At this time now, when I have the fortune needed to be virtuous but do not act virtuously, what will I be able to do when stupefied by all the sufferings of the bad destinies? Nothing!

That being the case, if I do not act virtuously but instead regularly accumulate evil deeds, then even in a thousand million aeons I will not hear even the words "good migration".

Because of that the Bhagavat said that it is extremely difficult to gain a human existence, as difficult as it is for a turtle to insert its neck into the hole on a wooden ox-yoke floating about upon a great ocean.

If even the evil done in merely an instant—such as that of the five immediates[95]—can result in an aeon spent in the hell of Unremitting Torment, then what need to mention that the evils accumulated in beginningless samsara will not result in going to the good migrations?

Moreover, having experienced just that full-ripening of karma alone does not bring complete emancipation; it is like this—while that suffering was being experienced, other evil deeds were being incessantly produced, so it is as though there is no opportunity for emancipation.

That being the case, having found such leisure as this, if I do not familiarize myself with virtue, there could be no cheating of myself by myself greater than this, there could be no stupidity greater than this.

If I realize that but through stupidity regarding karma and its effects continue to procrastinate, when the time to die comes, a tremendous misery will arise. And that is not all for if in a later life my body is burned for a long time by the hell fires so difficult to bear, there is no doubt that my mind will be tormented by the blazing fire of unbearable regret.

That being the case, having found by some coincidence this beneficial state or basis that is so extremely difficult to find, if while having

---

[95] The five immediates are five exceptionally heavy karmic actions which cause someone to die, often immediately, and fall directly into a very bad birth without the usual intervening period in the bardo.

knowledge of that—that from the causes of virtue and evil the results happiness and suffering arise[96]—I in later lives lead myself back to the hells again, it ends up that, as though stupefied by a mantric spell, I have been mindlessly wanting goodness for myself here in this world.

2.1.3.2.3 Advice on defeating the non-conducive side, the enemy of the afflictions

I do not know what is causing the stupidity; what major negativity that is making me stupid is there inside of me? If there is nothing, then it makes no sense for me to be doing actions that will cause me to harm myself!

If I consider it that way, anger, craving, and so on are enemies who do not have arms, legs, and so on, and they are not courageous or clever, but I see them as worthy of honour! How have they made me subservient to them like their slave?

While present in my mind they harm me for their enjoyment and I even tolerate it without anger, but that is inappropriate patience that will bring me down.

Even if all the gods and demi-gods were to rise up against me as enemies, they would not be able to lead me to and put me into the hot fires of the hell of Unremitting Torment. Yet this enemy of the mighty afflictions casts me in an instant into those fires of hell

---

[96] Padma Karpo explains "while having knowledge of that" as having knowledge of karmic cause and effects, which then connects this verse with what was explained in the previous few verses. However, those words can also mean that one is aware of having this very difficult to find leisure and endowment which then fits with the previous verses and the rest of this verse.

which burn up everything they meet, even Meru[97], not even leaving ashes behind. Thus, my enemy the afflictions being without beginning or end is a steady enemy that lasts for a long time; no other enemy is capable of lasting for a long time like that.

If in order to have harmony with those other enemies, I serve them with respect, they will become allies who will not harm me and will give all aid and comfort, whereas if I serve the afflictions, they will come again later and bring me down by harming me with suffering.

Thus the afflictions are a lasting and ongoing enemy, the sole cause for the increase of all that harms me; if I make a definite place for them in my heart, how could I be glad without fear in samsara?

If these guards of the prison of samsara who allow no escape from it to another place and are my killers and butchers in hell, and so on, live in a web of attachment within my mind, then, for as long as they do, how could I be happy? I could not; I would be like a creature confronted by the fangs of a murderous demon.

Thus, for as long as I have not with certainty directly seen that this enemy has been defeated, I will not put aside striving at the methods used to defeat this enemy. If proud people who have been angered by a slight harm done to them cannot sleep until their enemy has been destroyed, how should this be viewed?

You might think, "Will I be able to tolerate it if, during the destruction of the enemy, many things happen which are very difficult to bear?" For that, an exceptional ability to do so is needed. On the battlefield, a warrior facing afflicted ones whose nature is to cause suffering by death is so focussed on wanting to destroy them the opponents that, disregarding the suffering of being struck by the weapons of spears and arrows, he does not withdraw or retreat until his purpose has

---

[97] Mount Meru is a mountain of cosmic dimensions.

been achieved. If that is so, what need is there to mention that my desire for destroying, my strivings to definitely destroy the enemy whose nature is only ever the cause of all suffering might cause me hundreds of sufferings today but will not deter me or make me faint of heart.

If without real meaning the scars of frontal[98] wounds inflicted by enemies are worn on the body like ornaments with the pride of showing the marks of a warrior, then why when I am genuinely striving in order to accomplish a great meaning should I allow myself to be affected by the suffering entailed because of that? I should not.

For example, if fishermen, outcastes, butchers, farmers, and so on thinking just of their own sustenance tolerate the harms of heat and cold, and so on, then why am I not patient for the sake of migrators' happiness? I need to be patient!

To tame an enemy requires great efforts. I indeed committed myself to liberating all migrators of the ten directions reaching to the end of space from their afflictions, but at that time was not liberated from the afflictions myself. How then could I have the ability to release others from afflictions? If I did not have that ability, then declaring that commitment without knowing my own capability was madness, was it not? Thus, I will forever strive to defeat the enemy of the afflictions without turning back.

Clinging to and holding a grudge against the afflictions, I will wage war against and be victorious over them except for the type of affliction used as a destroyer of affliction. You might think that

---

[98] There is a system amongst Asian warriors that a scar on the front of the body or head indicates that the person wearing the scar is very brave; had the scar been on the side or the back, he is seen as a coward because he was apparently running away when the wound was inflicted.

afflictions of the type that war is waged against are no different from all other afflictions, but it is not so. Afflictions, when being used to destroy the mainstream afflictions, have a character contrary to the mainstream afflictions, so are not included in the afflictions to be destroyed.[99]

That being the case, for me to be chopped up—have my limbs removed—then killed[100] or have my head cut off would be relatively easy; under no circumstances will I ever bow down to the enemy of the afflictions.

Moreover, ordinary enemies might be expelled from one country but go to stay in other countries where they settle and recoup, that is, strengthen their capacities then return again to the previous country. But the way of the affliction enemy is not like that because, not having that nature of an ordinary enemy, when they have been tamed one time, they do not return again.

Thus, all afflictions are to be abandoned and, given that their root is grasping a self, they are abandoned by the eye of prajñā because that is what overcomes grasping a self. When the afflictions are removed from my mind where do they go? Where do stay in order to return to harm me? Such situations are not possible, but, weak-minded—without deep-down determination—I have ended up without the diligence needed to tame them.

Following on from that, when you look with the eye of prajñā, it is like this: if the afflictions are not present in the object, not present in the

---

[99] This way of talking comes because of the open line that says "Clinging to and holding a grudge". Both clinging and grudge-holding are afflictions. Thus he is saying the afflictions themselves can be used in the battle to overcome afflictions, in which those "destroyer" afflictions are not included in the afflictions to be destroyed.

[100] Another version of the Tibetan has "burned and killed".

sense faculties, and not in between nor somewhere other than that, then where do they reside, these ones that harm all migrators? In answer to that, they appear but cannot withstand examination so are similar to an illusion because of which I must get rid of the fear in my heart that thinks, "What could defeat this?", then attend to striving in order to take hold of prajñā! Thus, due to not getting rid of them while I have the capacity to do so, why without any meaning at all would I inflict on myself the harms of being in the hells, and so on?

Having thoroughly contemplated this topic that way, I will exert myself at accomplishing the trainings as they have been explained; if I do not listen to a physician's words, how could I be cured of a sickness which must be cured with medicines? There could be no cure!

That was the fourth chapter of *Entering the Conduct of a Bodhisatva*, called "Heedfulness".

CHAPTER FIVE

Guarding Alertness

2.1.3.3 An explanation of mindfulness and alertness, the method for guarding and purifying the training[101]

This has two parts: guarding the mind as the method for guarding the training; attending to mindfulness and alertness as the method for guarding the mind.[102]

2.1.3.3.1 Guarding the mind as the method for guarding the training

Those wanting to guard the training will closely guard the mind with mindfulness and alertness, for if they do not guard the mind, they will not be able to guard the training. The mind is like a king and body and speech are like servants, so if the mind is tamed, both body and speech are automatically tamed, and otherwise not.

---

[101] The topic of this chapter is the third part of three topics that were begun in the last chapter.

[102] The Tibetan text says that there are three parts here, the third being "advice on the two of them, mindfulness and alertness, as the principal points of practice". However, there are only two parts here, not three because later in the chapter this third heading has been turned into a subset of the second part mentioned here.

The elephant of mind when unleashed can create a connection with the harms of the hell of Unremitting Torment, whereas a drunken wild elephant—drunk on ferment—in this world cannot create such a great level of harm. Because of that, if the elephant of mind is firmly bound with the rope of total mindfulness, all feared things will become non-existent and all virtues will come to hand.

All feared things—tigers, lions, elephants, bears, snakes, enemies, the sentient beings who guard those in hell, black magic, negative forces, and likewise rākṣhasas will be bound by binding this mind alone.

The one who speaks authentically, the Buddha, taught that, "All of them will be tamed by taming this mind alone, for all feared things as well as the unfathomable sufferings come from one's own mind." He taught that in *The Cloud of the Jewels*[103] when he said,

> Mind precedes all dharmas, so, if mind is fully understood, all dharmas are fully understood.

Likewise, who is the blacksmith that intentionally made the weapons of the beings in hell? And who made the burning iron ground alive with fire? From whom—which parents—do those groups of females appearing at the top and bottom of the śhalmali trees come? These things do not come from someone else.

You might think, "Perhaps they have no cause?", but they do have a cause; the Capable One said that all such things arise from the mind of evil. In that way, in the whole three worlds there is nothing to be feared other than their creator, mind, so that is to be guarded.

For virtue too, mind is chief: generosity is completed by the mind of giving; discipline by the mind of abandonment; perseverance by the mind of enthusiasm; meditation by the mind of non-distraction; and prajñā by the mind understanding their suchness. He said in a sutra,

---

[103] ... where "Jewels" means the Three Jewels ...

Noble Shrāvakas, if you say, "Completion of the paramita of giving is the removal of the poverty of and the provision of possessions to migrators who were poor and without possessions, so is chiefly about giving material things", because there still are starving migrators, it means that the previous protectors—the buddhas—did not complete the paramita of generosity, but how could that be? It is not that they did not complete it; the completion of generosity does not depend on the external action of removing sentient beings' poverty. Thus, **the paramita of generosity is completed by having a mind to give all beings everything that one has for oneself together with the virtue accumulated as a result.**

Hence it—completing the paramita of generosity—is done by completing a state of mind of giving.

Similarly, someone might say that the completion of discipline is chiefly about material things; he would say that past buddhas completed their paramita of discipline through removing the objects of killing and so on, so that there would be no killing, and so on. However, **the paramita of discipline is not about the objects of killing—fish, and so on—and moreover the others needed as partners for sexual intercourse—women and so on**[104]—**being removed to a place where they will not be killed or be partners for sexual intercourse; it is explained in terms of achieving a mind of abandoning.**

Similarly, someone might say that completion of patience is chiefly about material things in that it is the taming of all enemies so that no harm comes to oneself or others. However, **unruly sentient beings are**

---

[104] Remember that Shāntideva was a monk who wrote this for monks. Buddhist monks have primary vows against killing, stealing, lying, and sexual intercourse which, if transgressed, result in the loss of their ordination. That is why the commentary here first mentions killing, then sexual intercourse.

as infinite as space, so they can never be entirely defeated. However, if this mind of anger alone is defeated, it will be the same as defeating all those enemies.

For example, how could I get the leather needed to cover the surface of the earth? However, wearing leather the size of my shoe soles will be the same as covering the entire surface of the earth with it.

Likewise, I cannot change the course of external things, but I can change the course of my mind, so what need is there for me to take the approach that everything else is to be changed? All those other things will go be solved by themselves.[105]

Meditative concentration also is completed by way of the mind, this time by non-distraction. Meditation produces a clarity of mind that results in birth in the worlds of Brahma, and so on—in the *Mahāparinirvāṇa Sutra* the Buddha told of a mother and her little one who were carried away in a river where the mother died while having the most unbearable compassion for her son and as a result was reborn in the world of Brahma—but even when body or speech is involved, if mind's operation is weak, that sort of result does not come.

It has been said by the one who knows of such things that all verbal recitations and bodily austerities, even though done for a long time, are meaningless when done with a mind distracted elsewhere. As scripture says:

> A distracted mind will not accomplish even my own aims, let alone the aims of others.

Prajñā too is completed by a mind which knows the factual situation. Those who do not know the supreme chief of dharmas—as *Discerning Scripture* says, "Dharmas are preceded by mind, mind is chief"—the

---

[105] This is about the paramita of perseverance: altering the course of things requires effort as does altering the course of one's mind.

secret of mind that is free of the extremes of existing and not existing, might want happiness and the destruction of suffering, but will just wander about in an ordinary, meaningless way.

Following on from that, at this point the four paramitas of method, aspiration, strength, and wisdom also are taught as chiefly about mind. As the *Trunk Design Sutra* says,

> All conducts of a bodhisatva are reliant on one's own mind.
> The ripening and the taming to be done for all sentient beings are reliant on one's own mind.

Then, the "secret of mind" is about understanding mind's suchness.

Regarding the secret of mind, *The Sutra Petitioned by Kāshyapa* says,

> Kāshyapa, if a thorough search is done for mind, it is not found and that which has not been found is not being referenced. That which is not being not referenced is beyond the three times; it is neither existent nor is it non-existent.

That being so, I should hold this mind of mine well using mindfulness as will be explained **and guard it well** with alertness. All trainings are contained within guarding the mind, therefore, **except for the yogic activity of guarding the mind, which is the chief of all yogic activities, what would be the use of many yogic activities?** They would be meaningless. That was also taught in the *Sutra that is the Compendium of the Dharma*,

> Viśhkambhanamati bodhisatva requested, "What is a dharma, a phenomenon which will be called a 'dharma', is not present in some country and is not present in some direction; a dharma only happens in relation to one's own mind and that being the case I should hold my own mind to the utmost, keep it happy, go to its very limits, utterly tame it, undertake thoroughly smoothing it out, and thoroughly annihilate it.

> Why is that? It is because I think, 'Where there is mind, there are good and bad qualities, whereas where there is no mind, there are no good and bad qualities.' Therefore, a bodhisatva turns his mind away from bad qualities and engages in good qualities. Hence it has been said: 'Dharma happens in relation to mind. Enlightenment happens in relation to dharma'."

An example of how to guard that mind is shown. Here, there is a single phrase in the Sanskrit original "capala" which was translated into Tibetan with two terms in order to capture two principal connotations in the term. The Tibetan terms come out to being "pushy" and "uncontrolled". **Just as I would be very protective of a wound on the body when in a jostling uncontrolled crowd out of concern that it might be hurt, so I should always guard this wound of a mind when staying amongst bad people.** If you think, "If a wound is hurt it causes suffering, but it is not like that for mind", then consider this. **If I am careful of a wound for fear of the small suffering that goes with it, why would I not guard the wound of mind for fear of being crushed by the big iron mountains of Crushing Hell?** In other words, I must guard it.

If I stay within this sort of behaviour of guarding my mind, then whether I stay amongst bad people who are behaving in inappropriate ways **or amongst women** who have both the eight abilities to charm, cunning and deceit, and so forth, **the steady effort to keep my vows will not—due to not being angry or desirous—deteriorate** because I will not have fallen under the influence of the afflictions. If you think, "If I were to stay like that, my material acquisitions would deteriorate", then **it would be better for my gains and honours, my body and sustenance of life, and my other virtues also to deteriorate than ever to let the virtues of mind deteriorate!** The *Verses of the Nāga King Drum Sound* says,

> I will give up my wealth, but guard my body.
> I will give up wealth and body, but guard my life.

> I will give up wealth, body, and likewise life, and
> Having given up everything, in this life will guard the
> dharma.

That, which says that dharma is more important than those three things, fits with what my divine guru has said. Moreover, among virtues the enlightenment mind must be most treasured for if that does not deteriorate, even though your other virtues deteriorate, you will not lose the name of a bodhisatva, similar to a tree trunk remaining unimpaired though its branches and leaves have been cut away.

2.1.3.3.2 Attending to mindfulness and alertness as the method for guarding the mind

This has three parts: advice on guarding mindfulness and alertness; guarding mindfulness; and guarding alertness.

2.1.3.3.2.1 Advice on guarding mindfulness and alertness

Most important is guarding the mind. Guarding it from what? Guarding it from desires. Guarding it with what? Guarding it with mindfulness and alertness. Guarding it how? Guarding it even at the cost of life. Therefore, he advises others in these words: **with palms pressed together I say to those wanting to guard the mind, "Guard it with mindfulness and alertness with all your might!"**

Here, mindfulness means knowing prescriptions and proscriptions as prescriptions and proscriptions then not forgetting them. The *Jewel at the Crown Sutra*[106] says,

> Mindfulness by which none of the afflictions are allowed to arise; mindfulness by which no opportunity is given to any of māra's activities; mindfulness by which one does not commit bad actions or go astray from the path; mindfulness like an order by which no opportunity is given to non-virtuous

---

[106] *Ratnachūḍa Sutra.*

dharmas of mind and mental events—this is called "right mindfulness".

Alertness means individually examining then genuinely the situations of body and mind; this is so because the *Prajñāparamita* says:

> It is to utterly know when I am acting, "Truly I am acting".
> It is to utterly know when I am standing, "Truly I am standing" ...

If mindfulness and alertness are absent, then for example, the bodies of people who are disturbed by sickness have no strength to do anything. Similarly minds disturbed by stupidity have no power to do any virtuous activities.[107]

With a mind lacking alertness, any hearing, contemplating, and meditating that is done will, like water leaking out of a cracked vase, not stay in memory.

If there is an absence of alertness, which is the meaning of "due to forgetting it, one does not proceed without haste", discipline will not be perfected. There are those of much hearing, faith, and diligence, but if they develop the fault of not having alertness, they will come to have the muck of downfalls. This is because not being aware is the door to the occurrence of downfalls.

The thieves and robbers of the afflictions that come with not having alertness follow along from the deterioration of mindfulness and like robbers steal away the merits that are causes of good that I have so carefully accumulated and with them gone I go to the bad migrations.

---

[107] Where stupidity means the lack of knowing that comes with the absence of mindfulness and alertness.

If mindfulness and alertness are absent, the result of birth in the happy migrations is prevented too. **This gang of thieves and robbers, the afflictions, is seeking an opportunity** wherever they can find one **and having found one will steal away my virtue and destroy lives in the happy migrations too** as in the case of Māndhātṛi,[108] who produced a bad mind towards Kauśhika.[109]

2.1.3.3.2.2 Guarding mindfulness

This has three parts: the way to guard mindfulness; the cause of mindfulness together with its benefits; and the abandoning of meaningless conduct by mindfulness.

2.1.3.3.2.2.1 The way to guard mindfulness

Therefore I shall never let mindfulness, which is like the doorkeeper of mind, depart from the door of mind. If having found it difficult to hold its place, **it does go away, I shall remember the harms of the bad migrations then bring it back** and firmly place it there **at that door once more.**

2.1.3.3.2.2.2 The cause of mindfulness together with its benefits

Due to keeping company with the guru, staying under the influence of the preceptor, and fearing being ashamed in front of the holy beings with whom one keeps company, **the fortunate ones who show respect** for the guru **and companions whose conduct is equivalent to that of Brahma**[110] **will easily have mindfulness arise.**

---

[108] Tib. nga las nu. Literally meaning "Suckle From Me", this is the name of a chakravartin emperor who was a previous incarnation of Shākyamuni Buddha.

[109] One of the names of the god Indra.

[110] This is a play on the word "brahmacharya" literally meaning the conduct of Brahma which is a "conduct of purity". Here it means the "celibacy" of the monastics who are one's peers.

Furthermore, **Due to thinking, "The buddhas and bodhisatvas possessing unhindered sight of all, I am always in the sight of all of them", I come to have embarrassment, respect, and fear.** In regard to this the *Narratives of Former Lives* says:

> How could those who unseen do evil,
> Which is like eating poison, be happy?
> It is impossible for them not to be seen by
> The completely pure eyes of the gods and humans with yogic attainments.

And having done that, the recollection of buddha will also arise in me again and again.

When mindfulness has been stationed at the door of mind for the purpose of guarding it, then alertness will come about and the mindfulnesses that had gone away before will return again.

2.1.3.3.2.2.3 Abandoning meaningless conduct by mindfulness

Having become aware in the first moment before acting that there is a very faulty sort of mind that, like wanting to drink poison, is intending to do some unvirtuous act, **I will hold myself like a piece of wood, not moving in the direction of non-virtue but remaining capable of withstanding it.**[111]

---

[111] When, at the commencement of any activity of the two doors of speech and body, I see that the motive in this mind of mine for the impending action is of the sort discussed above, that is, non-virtue, and understand that, as though wanting to poison itself, it has become tainted with a fault, then right at that time I am to withstand the impulse that has come up and have the strength to be able to hold the mind unmoving, like a piece of wood, so that it does not proceed on towards actually doing the non-virtue. The meaning behind this is the meaning of any karmic action having four parts; at the commencement of the action there is the intention which is the motive for the action and the remaining three parts are connected with the actual performance and completion of the action.

Then, for how to restrain the senses, I will never look around with eyes distractedly for no purpose, but with an ascertaining mind or alertness will always keep my eyes looking down at the ground. In order to rest up from the weariness of looking that way for a long time I will sometimes look about—though doing so has meaning so does not contradict what I have just said.

If someone appears in my field of view, I will look at him then say, "Hello". And furthermore, in order to check for dangers on the path and so on, I will look again and again in the four directions.

And, on resting, I should look ahead then look behind to see, "Are there no enemies or the like?" Having examined ahead and behind, I should proceed either to go forward or go back.

Having understood the need for that in all circumstances of hearing sounds, smelling smells, tasting tastes, and knowing bodily contacts, that is how I will conduct myself.

Here, Śhāntideva has spoken about "restraint of mindfulness" and "restraint of the senses". However, he has defined restraint only as using mindfulness to stop mind from engaging in non-virtue and using the senses to stop body and speech from meeting with unvirtuous spiritual friends.

2.1.3.3.2.3 Guarding alertness

This has three parts: a synopsis made from the perspective of guarding alertness; an extensive explanation from the perspective of guarding and purifying the body using alertness; and concluding by showing the characteristic of alertness.

2.1.3.3.2.3.1 A synopsis made from the perspective of guarding alertness

This has two parts: the ways of individually examining the body and the mind.

2.1.3.3.2.3.1.1 The way of individually examining the body

For any of the four types of conduct, Having prepared for an action with the knowledge, "My body will remain like this", once the action has been undertaken I should periodically look to see, "How is it situated?" If it is not situated as it was originally placed, I will correct it.

2.1.3.3.2.3.1.2 The way of individually examining the mind

I should make every effort to examine the drunken elephant of mind that before this was drunk on the ferment of heedlessness and now has been bound to the great pillar of minding the dharma—the great pillar of the nine ways of placing the mind—to see how it is bound and to ensure that it has not escaped from the rope of mindfulness and alertness and wandered off elsewhere to some other point of reference.

When striving by whichever means at the concentration of meditative concentration, in order not to wander off for even an instant I must individually examine my mind thinking, "Whereabouts is my mind focussed? Is it still on its reference or has it gone somewhere else from that?" That is individually examining prajñā that is keeping mind properly focussed.

How should beginners who are not capable of maintaining that concentration in all situations behave after they come out of the concentration? If someone is not able to practice this in the circumstances of being frightened by enemies, involved in festive activities, and so on, then he should do what is comfortable for him. It is like the Buddha's teaching that at the times of giving—training in generosity—one could be indifferent to the disciplines[112] such as not to touch gold, and so on.

---

[112] Discipline here means the disciplines of personal emancipation, such as are upheld by lay people or by the various degrees of monks and nuns.

If I am able, then I should undertake what I have thought of and not think of anything else. Once I have undertaken it, with mind focussed on that task, I should set about accomplishing it for the time being.

If that approach is taken, all will turn out well. If something else is also undertaken, then neither of the two will turn out well. The two things mentioned here are as follows. If one is unable to train oneself continuously in a prior training, then even if it is deferred, there is no fault. If that is not the case and a new training is started without finishing the prior one, it becomes an obstacle to finishing that training. If one acts in that way, the subsidiary afflictions that are categorized as factors of ignorance that are not alertness will not grow.

It is not just that there will be no accomplishment of both, but because of the unsteady engagement the afflictions that are not alertness will moreover be entered and when they have been entered, they will increase.

Therefore, although it has been permitted that in regard to the activities of festivities, and so on one can do what is comfortable for oneself, there is still a need to guard the mind against activities that will have a bad fruition. In terms of that need, I must abandon attachment to conversations filled with baseless stories and to being entertained by many kinds of wondrous spectacles.

If I do meaningless things like digging at the earth, picking at grass, drawing patterns on the ground, and so on, I should remember the trainings spoken by the Sugata then out of fear immediately stop.

2.1.3.3.2.3.2 An extensive explanation from the perspective of guarding and purifying the body using alertness

This consists of three parts: individually examining the situations of body and mind; training in conduct gripped by alertness; and an explanation of repairing the alertness if it has deteriorated.

2.1.3.3.2.3.2.1 Individually examining the situations of body and mind

This is divided into two parts: individually examining the situations of the mind and of the body.

2.1.3.3.2.3.2.1.1 Individually examining the situation of the mind

When I want to move or want to speak, I should first examine my mind to see whether it is virtuous, unvirtuous, or unspecified, then if it is classed as virtuous, should proceed with composure to do what is right.

When I see that my mind is attached or angry, I should not act with body nor speak, but should remain unmoving, like a piece of wood.

When I am agitated and about to laugh derisively or if am puffed up with pride, and about to reveal others' hidden faults, or am about to deceptively claim faults in others while making every effort to praise myself, or am about to revile and criticise then quarrel with others, then at such times I should remain like a piece of wood.

When I want gain, honour, and fame, or seek a circle of assistants, or have a mind wanting to be venerated, at that time too I should remain like a piece of wood.

When a mind arises that wants to speak out about my wishes to forsake others' aims and look after my own aims, then I should remain like a piece of wood.

When minds of attachment to my side arise of impatience, laziness, cowardice, and likewise impudence and speaking without shame, then I should remain like a piece of wood.

Having examined his mind in that way for afflictions and meaningless undertakings whose virtue or not has not been specified, the hero[113] should then hold his mind steady using the antidotes for abandoning bad conduct.

Those verses have explained how to conceive of the afflictions to be abandoned. Now the next three verses starting with "I should be extremely certain" nicely explain how conceive of their antidotes and the three verses are divided into four topics.

I should be extremely certain about what to reject and what to adopt, **utterly faithful, steadfast with the antidotes, defeating the despicable acts through being respectful and deferential in body and speech** toward the objects of worship, **having a sense of shame and fear** in relation to the full-ripening of bad conduct, **and having tamed the senses, pacified**; residing in these eight dharmas of respect is the first topic. I should deliberately **strive to make others happy**; that is the second topic.

I should not be disheartened by the wishes of the childish when they are in disagreement and when afflictions have arisen for them; with love I will think, "These are produced by the mind". That is the expression of love and compassion towards the mistaken practices of loved ones; it is the third topic.

And in doing the things that are not the despicable acts, I will always hold this mind to taking the standpoint of myself and sentient beings and acting like an apparition which is without a sense of "I". This teaches the absence of conceit while doing the deeds, which is the fourth topic.

Having contemplated again and again that I have gained supreme freedom after being in samsara for a long time, I should hold as unmoving as Mt. Meru that kind of mind which accomplishes a great

---

[113] "Hero" here is an abbreviation of bodhisatva, meaning "enlightenment hero".

purpose. When that is done, discipline and concentration will mutually make each other grow. Those verses teach the conduct of training the mind.

2.1.3.3.2.3.2.1.2 Individually examining the situation of the body

If you, mind, will not be happy when the body is being torn apart, dragged about, and carried away by vultures greedy for flesh, then why do you counsel that it should be guarded now?

If you think, "It is due to grasping this body as mine", then you must ask, "Why mind do you guard this body?" for it is not reasonable to protect it. And why is that? "If you and it are two separate things, then what use can it be to you?"

Why stupid mind, if you think you need a support, do you not grasp at a clean form made of wood? This machinery that is a mass of impurity is rotten by nature, so what point is there in guarding it?

To begin with, mentally separate off the outer layer of skin from the flesh. Then with the scalpel of prajñā separate the flesh from the skeleton of bones.

Separate the bones as well into individual bones, then look into them down to the marrow, and examine yourself asking, "Does this body have an essence?"

If you exert yourself at searching like that but do not see an essence in it, the body, why are you still guarding this body out of attachment?

Furthermore, if your excrement coming down from your body is not fit to eat, your blood is not fit to drink, and your intestines not fit to be sucked, then what use is this body to you, mind?

As a second-best proposition, could it be reasonable to guard it for the purpose of making food for the jackals and vultures? This human body of ours is something to be employed only for virtue; it is not right to consider it as something to be tossed away.

It is like this: you may have guarded it, but if the merciless Lord of Death steals it away and gives it to the birds and dogs, what will you be able to do?

If people are not given clothing and so on when they will not be able to serve—be employed together—with the other menials, why do you exhaust yourself in order to sustain this bag of meat broth when even though you hand-feed it, in the long run it will go elsewhere?

Alternatively, having paid my body its wages for doing virtue, now let me put it to work for my sake! If it does not do that and is of no benefit, I will not give it anything.

Moreover, I will regard the body as a boat, simply a support for coming and going across the great river of samsara, or, in order to accomplish sentient beings' aims, I will transform it into a wish-fulfilling jewel of a body. Having given myself control of myself like that, I shall guard myself as will be explained.

2.1.3.3.2.3.2.2 Training in conduct gripped by alertness

Having control of myself like that, I must always show a smiling face! I must completely give up frowning and scowling and be a friend and counsellor to migrators.

I will not be noisy whilst taking a seat on chairs and the like. When departing, I will not open doors with un-necessary force; I will always take joy in humility.[114]

---

[114] This is saying the following. "When I come into a room and take my
(continued ...)

By moving stealthily without a sound, the stork, cat, and thief all accomplish what they desire to do, so the Capable Ones always conduct themselves in the same way,[115] keeping their conduct of body, speech, and mind as a whole in the conduct of humility, and so on.

When someone says something for my benefit that admonishes or advises me wisely and without confusion, I should accept those words with high respect; in general I should always be a student of all.[116]

To all those who speak well I should say, "Well said!" for the sake of pleasing them. If I see others creating merit, I should cheer them on by praising them.

If others have good qualities that are not apparent, I should express them, and if another's good qualities have been expressed by someone else, then I should follow along and express them too. If others express my own good qualities while I am present, then, thinking, "I do have those good qualities", I should simply be aware of them.

---

[114] (... continued)
seat, I should do it without drawing attention to myself by not making a lot of noise as I do. And when leaving, I should gently open the door, again without drawing attention to myself this time by not opening the door forcefully. In these two cases and others like them, I should act without drawing attention to myself, because of taking joy in absence of self-importance.

[115] Here "capable ones" means practitioners in general, the ones who can withstand the rigours of the dharma path. In the current context, it means the bodhisatvas who are capable of withstanding ...

[116] The text actually says, "respectively accept the words at the crown of my head". In Indian culture, the way to show the highest respect to something was to elevate it to the crown of your head, which is the meaning intended here.

The reason for needing to do that is that all the undertakings of enlightenment mind are because of others' joy, a joy that would be rare even if it could be bought with money. Therefore, I should live in the happiness of finding joy in the good qualities made by others.

By doing so, in this life I will suffer no loss of things such as food and wealth and by it in future ones too, there will be—I will gain—a greater degree of happiness. On the other hand, the fault of disliking their good qualities and being jealous of them will cause me not to be joyful and to suffer in this life and to have a greater degree of suffering in future ones too.

That being so, in order to please sentient beings: when I speak, what I say should be pleasing to others because of inspiring trust and being clear in meaning; it should be free of the expressions of desire and anger; and it should be gentle and in moderate tones.

And when I am looking at sentient beings with my eyes, thinking, "I will become a buddha in dependence on these very beings", I should look at them with sincerity and loving kindness.

Because of always being motivated by great aspiration or by the antidotes—non-attachment, and so on—the virtues made in the field of good qualities—the Three Jewels, the field of beneficial providers—mother and father, and so on, and the field of suffering—those who are ill, and so on will be very strong.

And in particular, because of training in the conduct of the paramitas, I will always do the activities of the six paramitas having equipped myself with expertise and joy. All of those activities will be done without relying on anyone else.

The six paramitas of generosity and the rest are carried out in an upward progression, with each one more distinguished than the last, like discipline is a step up from generosity. It is said that one of greater meaning should not be put aside for the sake of one of lesser meaning and also that one of lesser meaning should be put aside for the sake of one of greater meaning. However, one should consider other's sakes as most important.

When that has been understood, I should remain diligently working for the sake of others. Those of compassionate activity, the buddhas, having looked on from afar, have prohibited some actions—the seven non-virtues of body and speech prohibited in the teachings on personal emancipation—but allowed them for the bodhisatvas. In a sutra, the Buddha says, "I pronounce that even if a bodhisatva with full ordination were to break all four root downfalls of the ordination, the bodhisatva would not accrue the downfalls because he would dispel such faults through his expertise in the methods of a bodhisatva". Now, in regard to someone who has full ordination alone, *The Compendium of Trainings* says,

> If in turning into something done for the sake of sentient beings it is seen as special, then the training is lacking. Of those two types, the former is, in general, special though such a person who is on the bodhisatva levels of purification and has been fully ordained does not destroy the Shrāvaka's teaching but guards it and therefore does not get involved with any of the non-brahmacharya[117] types of conduct.

What that says is saying that the bodhisatva protects the teaching of the Shrāvakas and stays under the influence of the preceptors and the like. *The Compendium of Trainings* also says,

> This has to be thought about in regard to someone who has attained the bodhisatva levels and has carried out the six paramitas, not in regard to anyone else.

However, that has to be given consideration.

---

[117] Brahmacharya refers to the celibate life of purity that is undertaken by ordained monks and nuns.

When a bodhisatva who is fully ordained has gone out begging, he must be mindful of the trainings to be followed while on begging rounds and then, having returned from, should proceed as follows. Having divided food received into four parts, a bodhisatva must share three parts among those who have fallen into the bad migrations, those who are without a guardian, meaning paupers, and those who are staying in the yogic discipline of the pure conduct of brahmacharya. Then he should eat moderately because if he eats less than that, he will become very weak and so unable to practice virtue, and if he eats more than that, he will become heavy then overcome with sleep.

When eating, he does so while contemplating, "May the various organisms within my body that have gathered together now because of material things gather together in the future because of dharma". Using that as an illustration, everything we have for our own use is blessed into being for others' sakes and then we must actually carry it out. Otherwise, if we act out of attachment to ourselves, we will have downfalls with affliction.

Having eaten, he goes to work on virtuous things; if not, the substances provided by the faithful will turn into poison. *The Heap of Jewels Sutra* says,

> An offering was made out of faith to two monks. Who were the two? They were ldan pa and grol ba. Monks! monk ldan pa was a practitioner who having entered my teaching saw all compounds as impermanent, saw all compounds as duḥkha, saw all dharmas as without self, and understood that nirvana is peace because of which even though he used the resource of a mountain of food given him by the faithful, his good qualities became completely purified.

And in a sutra of the Buddha's sutras it says,

> Śhāriputra having become hungry thought that there might be something better than eating the flesh of his own thigh or breast. Unaware of the disadvantages involved, he used what

was given him by a faithful person as a resource for himself. That is not the way.

For someone who is fully ordained: all of my articles except for the three robes, can be given away. In the case of a beginner, this body that is being used to carry out the holy dharma should not be harmed on account of something of little meaning. Taking that approach of guarding this support of leisure and endowment the intentions of all sentient beings are quickly fulfilled. Because such a chance exists, at the time of being an ordinary being when the mind of compassion is impure, this body should not be given away. The master himself—Śhāntideva—said,

> For example, a medicinal tree lovely to see
> Whose roots and so on are suitable to use and
> Whose seeds should ever have their lustre guarded—
> The complete buddha is like that medicine tree.

Later, when a pure special intention has been attained, by all means the body should in this and future lives be given over to becoming the cause of accomplishing a great purpose.

Generosity of dharma: The dharma should not be explained to those who do not respect it, for if it is explained to them, that will cause it to become corrupted, nor to those who, like a sick man, have wrapped a cloth around the head[118], nor to those carrying an umbrella, mendicant's staff, or weapon, nor to those wearing a covering on the head[119].

The profound and vast Great Vehicle should not be explained to followers of the Lesser Vehicle and not to a woman by herself, unaccompanied by a man. I should in every way respect the lesser

---

[118] This refers to wearing a turban or similar device, which denotes a certain level of pride of lineage.

[119] A covering on the head means any head covering, such as a hat.

and supreme dharmas as equal, not conceiving of them as bad and good.

Also, I should not connect those who are vessels for the very vast dharma, the ones who belong to the Great Vehicle family, with the lesser dharma of the Lesser Vehicle. I should not completely cast aside the bodhisatva trainings. And if I have done so, even then I should not seduce others by means of the sutras and tantras, telling them that "reciting sutras and mantras" is superior to keeping the bodhisatva trainings.

In regard to improper behaviour that would be done during the day, there is the following. When I spit or discard a tooth-cleaning stick, I should cover it up. To urinate and so on in water or on land that is used by others is condemned so I will not do that.

When eating I should not stuff my mouth, eat noisily, nor eat with my mouth open. I should not sit with my legs outstretched nor should I rub my hands together.

I should not stay in vehicles, on beds, or in isolated places together with the women of others. In brief, having observed for myself and inquired of knowledgeable people as to everything that the world finds improper, I will abandon all such behaviour.

I should not give directions with one finger, but instead indicate the way respectfully with my right arm with all my fingers fully outstretched.

Nor should I wave my arms about, but should communicate with slight gestures and a little sound, such as with a snap of the fingers, and so on, otherwise I shall become unrestrained.

Then, as for the nighttime, there is guarding the body when going to sleep. Like the Guardian, meaning the Buddha, lying down to pass into nirvana, I should in the desired direction and with alertness first of all make a firm decision to quickly arise from that sleep.

2.1.3.3.2.3.2.3 An explanation of repairing the alertness if it has deteriorated

In scripture it says that, **the conducts of a bodhisatva are immeasurable, so for the ones I am unable to train in, I must carry out the conduct of cleansing the mind until it is certain that the stains of mind have been purified.**

If downfalls occur while purifying the mind, they must be laid aside. The downfalls of a bodhisatva that must be laid aside arise exclusively from deterioration of the mind for others' sakes. Moreover, *The Compendium of Trainings* says,

> Four general categories are explained: "downfalls and seeming downfalls and non-downfalls and seeming non-downfalls" of which only the first and last are to be laid aside given that the other two are not wrongs.

The way to lay them aside is as follows. Having seen the results of non-virtuous karmas, great regret for evil deeds that have been done arises because of which one will recite *The Sutra of the Three Heaps* three times during the day and three times at night. *The Compendium of Trainings* explains that the three of laying aside evil deeds, rejoicing, and urging oneself on are the three heaps. *The Sutra Petitioned by Upāli* says,

> In regard to this, if a bodhisatva who is genuinely seated in the Great Vehicle has a downfall in morning but in the afternoon remains inseparable from the mind of all-knowing, then in view of that, the heap of discipline of the bodhisatva who is truly seated in the Great Vehicle is without limit ...

It also speaks in that sutra of modes of laying aside heavy and light downfalls. Then, for downfalls other than that, there is "laying aside that is done day and night only in relation to the thirty-five buddha bhagavats", in which case the laying aside of downfalls is done with the three heaps of prostrations, laying aside, and dedication and, having done them, one produces a restrained mind which will not do the downfalls henceforth.

I will recite *The Sutra of the Three Heaps* three times during the day and three times at night, for by relying upon the conquerors and bodhisatvas my remaining downfalls will be alleviated.

Those situations fall under the discipline of vows[120]. Now, whatever I am doing in any particular situation of those ways of working for the sake of sentient beings, whether it is for myself or the gathering of virtuous dharmas for others, I will exert myself and train in whatever training has been taught for that situation.

That is more extensively explained: There is not anything that is not learned by the conquerors' sons for the purpose of all-knowing[121] because of which they learn or teach the Lesser Vehicle which is done for the purpose of learning all that is knowable, not for the purpose of manifesting it; for someone who is skilled at living like that there is no such thing as merits not arising.

I should not do anything, either directly or indirectly, other than for the sake of sentient beings and should dedicate all conduct I do exclusively for the sake of sentient beings attaining great enlightenment.

The way those trainings are to be known is through attending a virtuous spiritual friend, so I will always attend a virtuous spiritual friend and, the one who I will attend is expert in the meaning of the

---

[120] There are three main aspects of the paramita of discipline: the discipline of vows, the discipline of working for the sake of sentient beings, and the discipline of gathering virtuous dharmas.

[121] All-knowledge is the all-knowing wisdom of a Buddha.

Great Vehicle and possesses the supreme yogic conduct of the bodhisatva, and even at the cost of my life will not abandon him.

I will train in how to attend the guru according to the extensive explanations found in *The Emancipation Story of Shri Saṃbhava*. In summary it says,[122]

> Son of the family, you must generate the perception of yourself as a sick man. You must generate the perception of your virtuous spiritual friend as a doctor. You must generate the perception of following the teaching as medicine given and the perception of recovering from the sickness as assiduously gaining experience in that teaching …

I should know this and other instructions given by the Buddha that are not mentioned here through reading the sutras. The trainings appear extensively in the sutras, therefore I will read them. To begin with I should look at *The Sutra of Ākāśhagarbha*. Why? Because in it the conduct that is to be constantly carried out is very extensively shown. In it, the root downfalls that cause destruction of the vows—the five of kings, five of ministers, and eight of beginning bodhisatvas making eighteen in all—are shown. What repairs them—expressing the name of bodhisatva Ākāśhagarbha or "Space Essence" with prostrations and supplications and undertaking the laying aside of the downfalls with him shown in his own form or as a brahman, and so on—is shown. And it is also shows through him what a person who is knowledgeable in the means of the Great Vehicle is like and it shows how being knowledgeable in the means of the Great Vehicle serves to make the beginning bodhisatva achieve the "samadhi that does not forget enlightenment mind", and so on.

As explained in *The Bodhisatva Levels*[123], these downfalls condense into four: the downfalls of king and minister, the third, a schism of the

---

[122] This was said by the Buddha in one of his discourses.

[123] The *Bodhisatvabhūmi* by Asaṅga.

sangha, and the remaining seventh and eighth downfalls of a beginner come together under not giving wealth because of avarice, abandoning shamatha comes under not giving dharma, the second of the fifth and first of the eight are brought together under abandoning the Great Vehicle, the second of the eight and wrong views come together under appearing as teaching that appears to be like the holy dharma, the third, fifth, and sixth are brought together under praising oneself and belittling others, the third of the five and the remainder of the four are brought together under destruction of villages and the like. These are explained to be the intent of the Capable One.

Apart from that, I definitely should look again and again at the extensive *The Compendium of Trainings* which I also composed, because its explanations primarily elucidate the activities of a beginner. Alternatively, if I cannot manage that much, I should look at something more condensed, such as *The Compendium of Sutras*. Furthermore, I should also make an effort to look at the two works—*The Compendium of Trainings* and *The Compendium of Sutras*—by noble Nāgārjuna.

In short, I should carry out whatever conduct is not forbidden in those works and proceed in accord with what has been prescribed. However, when I see a training that has been forbidden but permitted to be done in some circumstances in order to guard worldly beings' minds, it will be all right to truly undertake it in that circumstance that needs it and I should have no regrets over doing so.

2.1.3.3.2.3.3 Concluding by showing the characteristic of alertness

I shall examine again and again the situations of both body and mind. When that is summarised, it has the characteristic of guarding alertness.

It is necessary that I shall use my body, speech, and mind to put these conducts into practice, otherwise, what would be accomplished merely by talking about it? Will a sick man be benefited merely by reading medical texts?

That was the fifth chapter of *Entering the Conduct of a Bodhisatva*, called "Guarding Alertness".

CHAPTER SIX

Patience

2.2 Performing the conduct that goes with accomplishing enlightenment mind, the conduct of the paramitas

This has three parts: a general explanation that distinguishes the main road taken by the conquerors; an in-depth review of it that seeks the company of those who know the way; and how it is traversed in association with the three higher trainings.

2.2.1 A general explanation that distinguishes the main road taken by the conquerors

The *Condensed* says,

> The path of all the conquerors passed, not come, and seated
>   in the ten directions
> Is this paramita, not some other path.

That is saying that the path called "paramita" is the main road by which all buddhas arrive at buddhahood. Thus, the commitment to enlightenment that is made when the mind for enlightenment is aroused is accomplished in dependence on the paramitas. As *The Mother* says,

> Those wanting to train in the buddha-knowing that knows
>   all superficies
> Will have to train in Prajñāparamita.

The purpose of the paramitas is, moreover, to utterly pacify the referencing of the three spheres[124], but that does not happen until the level called Utter Joy[125] has been attained, so, prior to that the virtues of generosity, and so on are wholly dedicated to performing the conduct until unsurpassed enlightenment has been reached. In view of that, the actual paramita is prajñā—it realizes superior fact to start with, which is the paramita of going to the other shore, and after that it becomes expert in the method of fiction which is the paramita of having gone to the other shore. It is like the way that a drop of water put into an ocean does not dry out for as long as the ocean has not dried out.

In terms of the divisions of that sort of paramita, *The Mother* says that "the mind that knowing all superficies carries out the conduct of the six paramitas will quickly become a manifest complete buddha". The six paramitas are those of generosity, discipline, patience, perseverance, meditative concentration, and prajñā. After those six come the four paramitas of method, strength, prayers, and wisdom making ten in all. The Buddha spoke of many divisions of paramita in the sutras, such as the one hundred and eight paramitas mentioned in *The Sutra of the Good Kalpa*, and other places, though all of these paramitas come together in a group of six in the same way that the smaller rivers of Jambudvipa come together in the Ganges and Sindhura rivers.

2.2.2 A in-depth review of it that seeks the company of those who know the way

By generosity one obtains a perfection of resources, by discipline a perfection of body, and by patience a perfection of retinue. By the last two of the six one does not fall under the control of the afflictions and in activities there is no mistaken accomplishment, so the earlier three make a strong connection with rebirth in the higher levels, the last two bring the definite goodness of nirvana, and perseverance will accompany all of them.

---

[124] The agent, action, and doing of the action.

[125] Utter Joy is the first level of bodhisatva who has passed beyond samsara.

In that way there is a sequence: the first three paramitas are included in the higher training of discipline, perseverance is included in all three higher trainings, and the last two are included in the higher training of mind[126] and the higher training of prajñā respectively; as the *Ornament of the Sutras* says,

> The conqueror explained the six paramitas
> At length, including the first three in the first,
> The last two as two separate types,
> And one in all three.

The first three paramitas are counted as the accumulation of merit and recommended as most important for householders. The last two are counted as the accumulation of wisdom and recommended as most important for the ordained. The first three accomplish others' aims and the last three accomplish one's own aims, so a count of six is ascertained. The *Ornament of the Sutras* states that they arise in a succession of inferior and superior or of coarse and subtle.

If you think, "The presentation at this point in the text of the paramitas being divided into six does not fit with the way the text has presented them so far, does it?" That is indeed true, but the giving away of all of body, resources, and virtue was shown in the chapter on fully adopting the enlightenment mind and the giving of material things, the body, and dharma was taught in chapter five, so it was not necessary for Śhāntideva to speak about generosity in a chapter named for it. And discipline, having been set as the primary topic of the fifth chapter was explained extensively there, even though the chapter was not named after it.

---

[126] The higher training of mind is another name for the higher training of samadhi, because the development of samadhi or concentration is primarily a training of mind.

In regard to the guarding of discipline, in scripture the Buddha speaks of four teachings to be carried out by trainees in virtue:[127] though criticised, do not be critical in return; though anger is expressed, do not be angry in return; and so on. That being about patience, it is included in the first higher training.

2.2.3 How it is traversed in association with the three higher trainings

From here, these three are to be thoroughly explained: patience relates to higher discipline; perseverance relates to all three higher trainings; and the last two trainings relate to the higher trainings of meditative concentration and prajñā respectively.

2.2.3.1 Patience relates to higher discipline

This has three parts: donning the armour of forbearance; defeating the army of anger; and taking the capital city of patience.

2.2.3.1.1 Donning the armour of forbearance

One moment of anger destroys all the good conduct of guarding the disciplines of **generosity, offering to the sugatas, and hearing, contemplating, and cultivating, and so on** that has been accumulated over the course of **a hundred thousand aeons**. A sutra from the bodhisatva's section of sutras says,

> The anger referred to as "anger" destroys the roots of virtue accomplished in one hundred thousand aeons …

And *The Play of Mañjuśhrī Sutra* says,

> The anger referred to as "anger" destroys the roots of virtue accumulated in one hundred thousand aeons …

---

[127] "Trainees in virtue" is a name coined by the Buddha for his followers in order to distinguish them from spiritual seekers of other traditions of the time.

In regard to this, some great Tibetan teachers have said, "Well then, if that is the case, it means that ordinary beings might make a few roots of virtue but that would be meaningless because for that sort of being not to give rise to anger just once during a thousand aeons is not possible". In reply to that, there are three distinctions to be made. First is a distinction concerning what is destroyed: it refers to virtue that is the same sort of thing as merit, but not to virtue that is the same sort of thing as emancipation. Second is a distinction concerning what does the destruction: in the case of having given rise to strong anger towards a distinguished object such as a guru or buddha or bodhisatva and so on, and having done so without an antidote there is destruction, but not in the case of mere anger. Third is a distinction concerning the mode of destruction: the potency of virtue has been temporarily suppressed, but not absolutely eliminated; for example, someone who has the virtuous karma to be reborn as a god or human in a future life gives rise at the verge of death to a strong anger which causes the virtue for birth as a god or human to be suppressed and the person to be born in a bad destiny, where he would have been born before.

The great master Śhāntipa said that from the perspective of the support, enlightenment mind, if one gives rise to anger and sentient beings are wholly rejected, that will sever the roots of virtue of the vows; because of that, when the bodhisatva Jinamati became angry at a leading dharma teacher of Utter Joy, it caused him to fall into the hells. Hence, **there is no evil like anger.**

If you think, "Anger and hatred are different in that the former is a root affliction whereas the latter is a secondary affliction, so it is not all right to use "hatred" here as in, 'There is no evil like hatred'", then consider this. The coarse mind of malicious mind[128] is a form of anger and the engagement in actions such as wielding a stick that come from it is hatred. Both are to be abandoned by patience, so here both words are shown in the use of a single term.

---

[128] Malicious mind is the eighth of the ten non-virtues.

Just as there is no greater evil than either of the two, there is no greater fortitude, no greater antidote to them than patience. Thus, **there is no fortitude like patience.** The patience that is a holy kind of fortitude is, the conqueror said, "supreme to nirvana".

Therefore, I should work assiduously at cultivating patience in various ways—seeing the disadvantages of hatred, seeing the advantages of patience, seeing that it is a condition conducive to harm and suffering, having compassion for those who cause harm, and seeing that it has no nature.

If I hold onto painful thoughts of anger, it being like a poison arrow that has penetrated me, **mind will not experience peace and, not finding joy and happiness, sleep will not come and I will be unsettled.**

Even those who have come to depend on a person of high position because out of great kindness he has in the past provided them with funds and considerate treatment, will try to kill him if he has become filled with anger.

By it, close ones and friends and associates **too become disheartened and, although they are drawn in to my circle of close ones and friends by my generosity, they will not trust me. In short, be it myself or others, no-one stays happily with someone who has hatred.**

Hence the enemy, hatred, will be the creator of sufferings such as those, whereas someone who persistently overcomes hatred will be happy in this life and others in the future.

2.2.3.1.2 Defeating the army of anger

Having found its sustenance—a mind unhappy at **having to do what I do not want to do and being prevented from doing what I do want to do—and consumed it, the body of anger grows in size and then destroys me.**

Therefore, I will completely destroy the sustenance that makes my enemy, anger, grow. This is how it is: this enemy has no function other than to do me harm.

Thus, whatever happens, I will not allow my happy state of mind to be disturbed, which I will do by preventing unhappy states of mind from arising. I could make myself unhappy over something, but then my wishes would not be accomplished and my virtues would deteriorate.

If something that happens that is the cause of an unhappy state of mind arising can be remedied, what is there to be unhappy about given that there is a remedy for it? And if it cannot be remedied, what benefit will come from making myself unhappy over it when nothing can be done about it?

I do not want any of the four things called "maker of suffering, contempt, harsh words, and unpleasant words" for myself or my close friends, but want the four of happiness, and so on for myself and them making four times two times two items, a total of sixteen. But for my enemies it is the opposite—for them I want the four of suffering, and so on and do not want the four of acquisition, and so on, making eight items, which added to the sixteen items makes twenty-four, which is how people in past generations have explained it. The above does not include an account of the friends of enemies because, if they harm me, they are included in being an enemy and if they do not, then they are not objects of my attachment and aversion.

The causes of happiness—which fall on the side of what is wanted—only sometimes arise, but the causes for what is not wanted, suffering, and so on, are very many.

2.2.3.1.3 Taking the capital city of patience

This has three parts: the patience of willingly accepting suffering; cultivating the patience of a mind that ascertains dharma; and the patience of not being bothered by being harmed.

2.2.3.1.3.1 The patience of willingly accepting suffering

Without suffering no-one would find meaning in emancipation and, not finding meaning in that, **there would be no renunciation that would lead to the attainment of nirvana. Therefore, due to disenchantment with suffering, one seeks renunciation, and because of that when there is suffering, you mind,** rather than not wanting it, **should have a firm resolve** to be strong in patience.

For the great Īshvara[129] who dwells in the completed fortitude of withstanding difficulties, all gods manifest as his consort Parvati then, because they work to develop the ability to turn back from difficulties by withstanding difficulties, they become known those who are "turning back from difficulties". **If the ascetics who put faith in the turning back of Īshvara and the people of the southern Indian land Karṇāṭa who at the time of the lunar eclipse tolerate the pains of burning** their own bodies, **cutting** each other **with weapons, and so on because of their desire for emancipation exercise patience for the sake of that sort of thing that has no meaning, then why do I not have the armour of courage for emancipation which is meaningful? It is not all right for me not to be patient with suffering!**

If I think, "Duḥkha is difficult to bear", then it has to be said that there is nothing anywhere that will not become easier through familiarization. Therefore, if I familiarize myself with small harms now, I will be able to exercise patience without difficulty with great harms later on.

---

[129] Īshvara is one of several names for the Hindu god Śhiva. Śhiva is known to Hindu followers as the great god among other gods, the one who has gained supreme realization. Part of gaining that realization is that he had to withstand all difficulties of the journey, so he is known as a "withstander of difficulties". His followers put great emphasis on developing the same quality in themselves.

If I think, "How could I exercise patience with small things?", then it has to be asked, "Who has not seen a need to do this—to exercise patience—with the meaningless sufferings caused by snakes and flies, sensations of hunger and thirst, and so on and with itchy rashes and the like?"

If a need has been seen, then because it does have meaning, I should not lose patience easily with—meaning have only a limited ability to withstand—heat and cold, wind and rain, and so on, nor with sickness, bondage, and beatings, and so on because if I do, it will only serve to increase the harm caused.

At the time of a fight, some become extra brave when they see their own blood coming from a bodily wound and develop a stronger determination to defeat their opponent. Some do not need to see blood coming from themselves, but faint and fall unconscious when they see the blood of others. These reactions come from mind being either steadfast or timid respectively. It is not all right for the mind to be timid, therefore, when something harmful occurs, I must dismiss it and remain un-affected by the suffering!

When those who are expert meet with suffering, even then they keep their minds lucid and un-defiled by turbulence and unhappiness; that is how they are as they do battle with the afflictions, for during the battle much harm which is difficult to bear can be inflicted. However, it is those who have defeated the enemies of hatred and so on by persisting in the face of difficulty and dismissing all suffering that are the warriors who have been victorious over the enemy. The rest, because they subjugate only the external enemy, are like slayers who kill corpses by striking their weapons into them.

Now, having it explained it at length like that, the meaning is distilled. Furthermore, suffering has good qualities that come with its being in accord with the path of developing familiarization: being disheartened by it after it has arisen dispels haughtiness over physical appearance, resources, learning, and so on; it rouses compassion for those tormented by suffering in samsaric existence; and it results in avoiding evil because evil is the cause of suffering yet to come and taking joy in virtue which, like a medicine for curing disease, will bring emancipation from the suffering.

2.2.3.1.3.2 Cultivating the patience of a mind that ascertains dharma

This has three parts: showing that what does harm is not independent; negating the assertion of a self and primal substance having independence; and explaining the demeanour of that patience.

2.2.3.1.3.2.1 Showing that what does harm is not independent

I do not become angry at the greater sources of suffering, sicknesses such as jaundice—a sickness that arises when the phlegm and wind come together in a way that leaves them out of balance, and so on because of thinking, "Those illnesses do not create duḥkha because of having a mind to do so, rather, it is a being's collection of causes that disturbs the constituents", so why should I be angry with those who do have a mind, saying "They harm me"? If I think, "They harm me due to having a mind to do it for their own purposes", then that is not the case. I should not be angry with them when all of them are pressed on by conditions of karma and affliction, so are interdependent too.

For example, in the same way as this sickness will arise although it is unwanted, likewise these afflictions of anger, and so on will persistently arise even though they are unwanted.

Therefore, if we think this through ahead of time, beings do not deliberately think, "I will get angry", but just become angry. Likewise anger without deliberately thinking, "I will produce myself", is just produced.[130]

---

[130] The point here and in subsequent verses is that neither the person who
(continued ...)

Hence all wrong behaviour as much as there is and all the various types of evil arise through the force of one's own causes and conditions, so it is not that they exist independently. It is, for example, like a mask changing the facial appearance into something unattractive.

These conditions that assemble together do not have a mind that is thinking "I will produce hatred, and so on" and neither does what is produced by them—the hatred, and so on—have a mind thinking, "I will be generated by the causes and conditions". Because all dharmas have in that way not been made, it follows that because this exists that arises and because this has been produced, that is produced. Hence, except for being mere interdependent arisings, they are not something that is independent.

2.2.3.1.3.2.2 Negating the assertion of a self and primal substance having independence

The Sāṃkhya school says, "The primal substance having independence which is the doer or creator of everything and the self having independence that comes together with an heroic being are what does harm". The Nyāya school adds, "self, space, and so on also have independence". A refutation of their positions follows[131][132]. [133]

---

[130] (... continued)
gets angry does it deliberately nor the anger which is produced produces itself deliberately. In all cases the anger is and interdependent arising.

[131] The Sāṃkhya school, meaning the school of Enumerators, and the Nyāya school, meaning the school of logicians, were two of the main Hindu schools present at the time of the Buddha. Arguments against their assertions of a self are presented in this section and at length in several sections in the ninth chapter. The reader is advised to look at the section here and the sections in the ninth chapter in conjunction with each other.

[132] The Sāṃkhya or school of Enumerators was founded in ancient India by the Rishi Kapila. They received the name "Enumerators" because of their claim that everything in existence can be enumerated as belonging to one

(continued ...)

That which is asserted as "the primal substance" whose nature is that it has the three factors of sattva, rajas, and tamas in equal parts **and that which is designated as "the self"** which possesses the specific qualities of being the eater, and so on **do not arise having deliberately thought, "I will arise** in order to do harm to other", because they have been defined as permanent.

If you are thinking, "The self being permanent is without production", then if, like a rabbit's horn, **in not having been produced the self does not exist, any wish it might have to be produced also would be non-existent** which does not in agreement with their being produced as that which does harm. If they were produced, it would be in relation to a cause, which undermines the assertion that they have independence.

In regard to the characteristics of the self, "the eater" meaning something that "consumes resources" is refuted as follows. **The self would be permanently involved with apprehending the eaten objects, hence**

---

[132] (... continued)
of twenty-five categories. One of their key claims is that there is a primal or principal substance and a self, each having self-control or independence. This section refutes those assertions of a self.

[133] The followers of this system believe that all phenomena—except the permanent and unchanging self—are created from an all-pervading primal or principal substance which consists of three factors in a balanced state of three equal amounts. When the three change to being in an imbalanced state, the animate and inanimate worlds become manifest and what was called the primal substance is now called "what creates the world". When the self comes into contact with the primal substance, a series of manifestations such as the intellect, the sense faculties, and the sense objects issue forth from it and are then experienced by the self. Thus the primal substance is a permanent, partless, universal, non-appearing substance that creates and is the nature of phenomena in the experienced world. The self is the unchanging consciousness principle that becomes bound to the world through its false identification with the manifestations of the primal substance.

would not cease doing so. If it were to cease, it would have gone to being impermanent and if it were not to cease, that would be a plain contradiction.

That the self is the doer or creator is refuted as follows. **If that self were permanent, it would clearly be devoid of action, like space.** They reply: "It is permanent but 'has with it a condition for doing', and 'has effort, and so on which are acting in close connection with it'". To that, we say that **even if it met with other conditions, because of being changeless**—because that self has the permanence of being changeless—**what effect could be apparent**, given that it cannot undergo any transformation?

If, even when there is a condition that has become present **for it to do something, it remains as it was before**—as it was when there was no condition for its doing something, **then what effect could its doing something have had on it**, that self? It would not have had any at all, so the self would not become the doer.

If you say, "Because the condition has brought about a change from being the self to having another meaning, it is acceptable for the self to be a doer and a permanent thing", then we say: **How could saying, "This is its—**that self's**—doer" make them**—the two, self and doer—**causally related**? Thereby, in the functioning of a permanent self and an impermanent doer there is no affected and effector for the permanent self, so it has been shown that is no relationship between the two.

2.2.3.1.3.2.3 Explaining the demeanour of that patience

Thus all things outer and inner are dependent on something else and due to that whatever arises from them arises without independence. If I have that sort of understanding, I will not become angry with any of these apparition-like things.

And then there is the question, "If everything is an apparition without truth like that, then **what antidote will turn away which anger**?" to which one person says, "It would not be all right to turn away anger because it is equivalent to buddha-knowing[134]!" However, there is nothing not all right with doing so because it is asserted that in dependence upon doing so the sufferings will have their continuity cut. The force of fundamental ignorance which maintains that "this has been produced" leads to involvement in the formatives, and so on—all the aspects of samsaric mind—causing the duḥkha of samsara to continue on, but if the precursor ignorance is reversed, all of the subsequent sufferings will have their continuity cut, so there is nothing about turning away anger that is not all right.

If I see someone, whether enemy or friend, who because of that situation of not having independence is doing something harmful that is not all right, I must reflect that "this has happened without independence due to some sort of condition" and not make my mind unhappy but take up a happy frame of mind!

If things came about by choice—merely by one's wanting them, without cause, then since no one wants to suffer, suffering would not arise for any of the bodied beings.

Being heedless some people—the Tīrthikas—harm themselves with laying down amongst thorns, jumping onto the sharp points of a triśhūl[135], and other such things. Some ordinary people become obsessed and stop eating, and so on because of trying to obtain a woman, and other such things and so exhaust themselves physically and mentally.

And there are some who harm themselves by hanging themselves, leaping from cliffs, eating poison or unhealthy foods, and doing other such merit-less deeds.

---

[134] Skt. vidya, Tib. rigpa. The opposite of buddha-knowing is usually translated as ignorance as will be seen just a little further on.

[135] A triśhūl is a type of trident carried by Hindu gods and their human followers.

When they have fallen under control of the afflictions, people will not hold themselves in esteem but will see themselves as worthless and even kill themselves. At such time, how could they be expected not to harm the bodies of others?

If I cannot give rise to compassion for such people who have set out to kill me and the like because their afflictions have been aroused, the last thing I should do is become angry with them for that is not the right approach.

Just as the nature of fire is to burn but it is not right to be angry with it, so the nature of these childish ordinary beings might be to injure others, but it is still not right to be angry with them.

Well, if that fault of injuring another was a temporary occurrence, like a negative force suddenly causing havoc, and if sentient beings' nature has been ascertained as not injurious[136], it is not right to be angry, for that would be like begrudging space for allowing smoke to arise in it.

In the case of a stick or the like that is actually used to harm me, if I become angry with the wielder, since the wielder in turn was incited by anger, further examination will show that it would be correct to be angry at the hatred not at the person involved.

Before now I must have done this sort of injury to other sentient beings. Therefore it is right that this harm comes back to me, the one who has injured other sentient beings, like when one cries out to rocky mountains, a reply comes back from them.

---

[136] The meaning here is that sentient beings in general are ascertained to have a nature of basic goodness.

Both the weapon of that harmful one and my body are causes of my suffering. Since he came up with the weapon and I came up with the body, with whom should I be angry? Both are equally at fault!

If, blinded by the attachment of craving for this body of mine abscess of a human form that cannot bear to be touched and suffers in many ways, I grasp at it being mine, then with whom else should I be angry in response to this body that cannot bear being hurt?

The childish ordinary beings do not want suffering yet are greatly attached to its causes, so like moths flying into a flame, it is their own fault that they are harmed. In that case why should I bear a grudge towards others?

For example, as with the sentient beings who are guards of the hells and the forest of sword-like leaves this was created by my own karmic actions, so with whom should I be angry?

Brought on by my own karmic actions of the past these ones who harm me now arise and if their actions now send them on to becoming hell beings later on, I will be the one who has brought them such loss, will I not?

These ones whose actions have caused me harm have become a basis for cultivating patience through which many of my evils will be cleared away, but based on the harms they have done to me, they will be sent on to the hells where they will suffer for a long time.

I am causing them harm and they are benefiting me. Hence it would be correct to be filled with regret at having harmed them and filled with joy at having received benefit for myself. Why then unruly mind, do you become angry in such a mistaken manner at these ones who are doing harm?

If the harm done by them has the effect of benefiting me and I think, "To repay their kindness it is right that I should harm them", then that is incorrect. If I have a good attitude of love for those who harm me, I will not go to hell because of it. In that case I have protected myself by being expert in method like this, but how could the same happen for them, the ones who have harmed me? It could not.

However, if I were to harm them in return, it would not protect them and it would degrade my conduct, with the result that my capacity for withstanding difficulty—my patience—would fail.

Moreover, if I examine that harm to find out where, in body or mind, it is, mind does not have a physical body, so cannot be destroyed in any way by anyone. However, it does cling strongly to the physical body, so the body is harmed by sufferings.

If I think, "That is reason to become angry", if abusive speech, harsh speech, and unpleasant words will not result in harm to my body, why, mind, do you become so angry at them—these three things?

If I think, "The ones who do those three things to me do not like me, so I will not be patient with them", then if those others not liking me will not devour me—meaning will not harm me—in this or another life, why do I not want it?

I may not want these three things of abusive speech and the rest because they will create an obstacle to my having material gains in this life. However, it has to be said that want them or not at the time of death, I will have to leave my material gains of this life behind, whereas my evils will remain firmly in place and follow me into the next world.

Therefore, on account of all the above, it is not all right to become angry.

If I think, "If I have no material gains, I will not survive", it would be better that I die today than live long with bad livelihood. Someone like me might stay long in this world, but the suffering of death cannot be avoided and when it does happen, happiness will not follow but suffering will.

Suppose someone wakes up from a dream in which happiness was experienced for one hundred years and someone else wakes up from a dream in which happiness was experienced for a short while. For both of them, that happiness will never return. Similarly, in both cases, whether the lives are long or short, at the time of death it will end up like that.

Although I might, like the wheel-turning emperors, have had many material gains and lived happily for a long time, at the time of death I will go on empty-handed, like having been robbed by bandits.

I may say, "If material gains enable me to live for a long time and practice dharma, I will be able to end evil deeds and make merit". However, if I become angry on account of material gains, will not my merits be ended and evil deeds increase?

That being so, if the purpose of my life lies in the hope to accumulate merit but that is undermined by anger and only evil deeds are done, what meaning would such a life serve? It would be meaningless!

If I say, "I should be angry with those who say things unpleasant to hear—the three things of abusive speech and so on—that cause other sentient beings' liking for me to be undermined", then why is it, mind, that you are not also angry with those who express unpleasant things to others?" The reasoning regarding others' liking oneself is the same as for others' liking others.

If you, mind, can be patient with this loss of faith due to the expression of things unpleasant to hear in someone else, why can't you be patient with someone who says unpleasant things about me because of afflictions that have been aroused in him? It is right that you be patient!

Others might speak irreverently about or with their bodies destroy statues, stupas, or the texts of the holy dharma, but even then it is not right to be angry about it because the buddhas, and so on cannot be harmed.

I will also turn back anger towards those who do harm to gurus, their relatives, and so on and to close ones, due to seeing in the manner shown before this that their harmful behaviour happens in relation to other; their actions have come about through afflictions that have arisen, without independence, from conditions. As *Letter to a Friend* says,

> You must not do evil on account of
> Monks, brahmins, gods,
> Guests, husbands and wives, nuns, or retinue for
> There will be nothing good about your share of the full-
>   ripened result, the hells.

If bodied beings are injured both by beings with a mind and things without a mind, why single out beings with a mind and be hostile towards them? It follows that I must be patient with all harm!

If someone out of stupidity does wrong to another and the other stupidly becomes angry in return, which one of the two—the original one who did harm and the one who replied with anger—would be without fault? Which one would be with fault? If I think it through, they are, as though weighed on a beam balance, equally at fault.

Why did I previously do those karmic actions because of which others now do me harm? If everything in the end depends on my karmic actions, why should I have hostility towards these harmful beings?

Having seen that to be so—that it is not all right to be angry—I see that a mind of mutual loving kindness is needed for everyone, so I will conscientiously make the merits for that to happen.

For example, if a fire burning in one house has spread to another house, flammable matter like straw should be removed from the other house out of concern that that it might catch fire and burn the things in the other house. Similarly, when the fire of anger spreads to whatever my mind is attached to, I should immediately get rid of it out of concern that my merit will be burned.

2.2.3.1.3.3 The patience of not being bothered by being harmed

This has three parts: showing that small suffering can dispel great suffering; cultivating joy at others' good qualities; and showing that adoption and rejection are equally to be known.

2.2.3.1.3.3.1 Showing that small suffering can dispel great suffering

What about it is not fortunate if a man condemned to death is released after merely having his hand cut off? One has to think, "For having the patience to bear merely having his hand cut off he saved himself from death. It is fortunate". What about it is not fortunate if my human suffering will be enough to stand in for and subsequently free me from birth in hell? It is fortunate.

If thinking to myself, "This is suffering", I am unable to be patient with this relatively minor suffering of the present, then how could I possibly be patient when faced with the sufferings of the hells and why do I not turn away from anger, the cause of the enormous suffering of the hells?

For the sake of my desires I have experienced being burned, and so on many thousands of times in hell, but apart from suffering myself no meaning at all has come from it. In doing so, I have accomplished nothing of my own or others' sakes.

Only gladness for this suffering is appropriate here, for this suffering of austerity undertaken for the sake of dharma does not involve even a fraction of that much harm, but very meaningful things will be accomplished through it that will dispel the harms of migrators who have gone to the bad migrations.

2.2.3.1.3.3.2 Cultivating joy at others' good qualities

If a person who praises another with good qualities saying, "He has good qualities", gains the happiness of a joyful mind, why, mind, do you not praise him for his good qualities and make yourself joyful too?

This joyful happiness of yours, mind, that has come from rejoicing in the good qualities of others and praising others would be a source of happiness in a later life and would result in an absence of wrong-doings in this life that would be done out of jealousy. Permitted by those having good qualities, such commendation of another is also a supreme means for gathering disciples, for bringing them into one's own retinue.

It is said that others will be made happy like that. However, if you do not want them to be happy, you could do things such as stop paying their wages, though if you do that, there will be results both seen and unseen that will cause you to degenerate.

It is said that others will be made happy like that. However, if out of jealousy you, mind, do not want them to be happy, you could do such things as stop paying their wages, and so on, though if you do that, but there will be results both seen in this life and unseen until future lives that will cause you to degenerate.

When people speak of my own good qualities, I want others to be happy too, but when they express the good qualities of others, out of jealousy I do not want happiness even for myself. There is that not wanting to be happy even for myself and there is wanting all sentient beings to be happy due to which the mind for enlightenment has been aroused. Having aroused that mind, why am I angered by sentient beings finding just a little happiness for themselves? It is contradictory.

If I have committed at the time of arousing enlightenment mind to the want sentient beings to become buddhas who are worshipped by the three worlds, why are you, mind, now tormented on seeing them receive the most basic service and respect?

Moreover, if a relative who you certainly must support and provide for has been able to find his own livelihood so that you no longer need to provide for him, wouldn't you take joy in this, rather than becoming angry?

With the thought, "The happiness that comes with the commitment to set others in buddhahood is not a commitment to someone else accomplishing it", if I do not wish for migrators to have even that little bit of the happiness of this world, what meaning is there in my wishing that they become enlightened? The final word on this is that it is "completely wrong". Therefore, how could there be enlightenment mind that wishes to set others in benefit and ease in someone who becomes angry when others receive something?

Whether a donor gives a recipient something or does not and it remains in the donor's house, because you will never have ownership of it, it makes no difference whether it is given to the recipient or not. What use is the envy involved given that it will never benefit me?

There are three causes of gaining material things: the power of merits made in a previous life; the faith others have in me in this life; and my own good qualities of discipline, hearing, and so on. Why do I throw away the three things of my merits, the faith of others, and my good qualities by becoming angry? By throwing them away I am not keeping what will turn into material gains, so tell me, why am I not angry with myself, the one who throws them away?

Not only do you not despair over the evils that you have done, but you want to compete with others who have done meritorious deeds?

The second bundle starts here.

If an enemy becomes unhappy, what cause is there for you, mind, to be glad about it given that it is not of the slightest benefit to you? You might think, "If the enemy is brought to ruin by it, what is wrong with that?" However, your simply wishing for that will not cause your enemy to be harmed but will turn into a cause for you to be harmed.

And even if he suffers ruin as you had wished, what cause is there for you to be glad about it? There is none. If you say, "I will be satisfied by it if the enemy comes to ruin", what will come of that is ruin for you and what else?

The fishing line cast by the fisherman of the malicious mind of the afflictions has an unbearably sharp hook; having been caught on it without escape possible, it is certain that I will be cooked by the guards of hell together with other sentient beings in the cauldrons of hell.

2.2.3.1.3.3.3 Showing that adoption and rejection are equally to be known

There are five aspects to seeking meaning in the world: increase of merit and life; increase of strength; absence of illness; and physical well-being. The honours of praise and fame will not turn into merit in later lives, nor lead to a longer life in this life. They will not give me greater strength, will not bring absence of illness, and will not provide physical well-being.

That being so, if I knew what would be meaningful for me, what value would I find in these things of praise and fame, and so on? In thinking, "It would create a little mental happiness", if all I want is mental happiness, I must apply myself to its causes—gambling, and so on and liquor, too, but then that would only propel me towards what I do not want.

If for the sake of becoming renowned as someone who is "very generous" I lose my wealth to others or for the sake of being "a hero" get myself killed with a weapon, such fame would end up as empty words, what use would those words be then? Once I have died, who will they make happy? In Jambudvipa, the words of commendation "there is none like him" go on continuously, but when the person dies, the need for them is gone and those words turn into empty statements, such as the sounds of wailing.

For example, when their sandcastles made for play collapse, children cry and cry in despair. Likewise when my praise and fame decline, my mind becomes upset like that of a child.

Short-lived sounds have no mind—they are no more than audible sounds—therefore they cannot possibly have a mind that thinks to praise me. However, the audible sound "he is liked by others" is counted as a cause of joy, so it makes the person doing the praising happy and makes me happy too.

What benefit does the other's joy, the one doing the praising, bring me, the one being praised? That happiness of joy belongs to him—to the mind of the one doing the praising, so I will not get even a part of it.

And, if his happiness—the one doing the praising makes me happy, then I need to have that approach with everyone else as well and if that is so, how could I be unhappy when others such as an enemy are made happy by what brings them joy? It would not be all right.

In the same way, my own mental joy produced from thinking, "I am being praised", also is not acceptable and ends up being nothing else than the behaviour of a child.

That being so, praise and so on distract me. They destroy my disenchantment with samsara. They make me envious of others who have good qualities, my mindstream being burned by the blazing fire of envy. They uproot and destroy the fruitions of a perfection of virtue.

Therefore, I should be aware, "Those who are closely involved with finding ways of tearing down the joy that comes from my praise and the like are also here in order to guard me from falling into the bad destinies, are they not?"

For I who seek liberation, being bound by material gains and honour is unnecessary. How then could I be angry with those who have in the past liberated me from being bound by them material gains and honour?

And furthermore, if I am patient, how could I be angry with those who want me to suffer when, like buddhas giving a blessing, they close the door that leads to suffering?

I might recognize someone—who has avarice and the like—as an "obstructor who prevents the creation of merit", but it still would not be right to be angry with such a person. If there is no fortitude that withstands such difficulties as patience, I should dwell in it, should I not?

If due to my own faults of being short-tempered, and so on, I am not patient with this person, it will end up that I have made not being patient with this cause of merit who is present right in front of me into an obstructor of merit, which is like spitting out food that is very tasty.

If there is none at all of what is called "a cause", a result will not arise and if there is, it will. If as with seed and sprout one thing is considered to be the cause of another, how could I say that it—the causal thing—is "obstructive"?[137]

For example, at the time of wanting to engage in giving, a beggar is not considered to be an obstructor of generosity and it does not work to call those preceptors and disciples who participate in an ordination "obstructors of ordination". The meaning here is that in the first case avarice and in the latter case lax discipline are being referred to as "obstructors".

In the case of giving, there are indeed beggars in this world but those who would harm me are scarce, for if I have not harmed others, none will harm me.

Therefore, I should be glad to have an enemy for, like a treasure that has come forth in my house without need of tiring effort, he assists me in my enlightenment conduct. Being glad here is about having an attitude of gratitude.

"What is the cause of being glad to have an enemy?" you ask. I accomplish patience in concert with this enemy, therefore he is worthy of being given the fruits of the patience first. It is so because he has become the cause of my patience.

"If this enemy does not have the thought that I must accomplish patience, he is not to be worshipped", you say. Then why would I worship the holy dharma given that it too is fit to be a cause for accomplishment and moreover has no thought to benefit me?

---

[137] This is the literal translation of what appears in the text. The cause has to be understood as the person or thing which is creating harm—an enemy—and its result has to be understood as the production of merit. If the cause of merit is defined as a cause of something being produced from it, then it cannot be considered to be something that prevents that result.

"If this enemy has the thought that I should be harmed, he is not to be worshipped", you say. Then how would my patience be accomplished if others, like physicians, always strove to do me good? In that case there would be no need for patience.

Therefore, since patience is produced in me in dependence on another who has a very aggressive mind, that person having become a cause of patience is, like the holy dharma, worthy of worship.

Because of that the Capable One spoke of "the field of sentient beings and the field of conquerors"[138]. *The Sutra that Authentically Condenses Dharma* says,

> The field of sentient beings is the bodhisatva's field of buddhas, a field of buddhas from which the buddha qualities can be obtained, so it would not be right to accomplish the wrong way in relation to that field.

By seeing that these sentient beings are to be pleased, many have gone to the other shore of gaining perfection of their own and others' sakes.

Thus the buddha qualities are accomplished through depending on sentient beings and the conquerors and since it is that way, how is it that do I not respect sentient beings in the same way that I respect the conquerors?

I might think, "It is because buddhas possess immeasurable good qualities whereas sentient beings have many faults". However, this is not about the good qualities of their intentions being equivalent, but about their results being equivalent—just as enlightenment is gained by having faith in the buddhas and worshipping them, so buddhahood is gained by having love and loving kindness for sentient

---

[138] This is the wording of the text, though as the following quote shows, it means that the Buddha spoke of "the field of sentient beings" and how that field of sentient beings is equivalent to being a field of buddhas.

beings. Because of that equivalence, sentient beings are understood to have good qualities, too. *The Sutra of Famed as Stainless* says,

> For the sake of being born into the wholly pure buddha field, sentient beings are to be viewed as being the same as the teacher.

That being the case, the merit that comes from worshipping someone having the enlightenment mind[139] has a character of greater merit and is due to the greatness of the object referenced being sentient beings, and similarly the greater merit that comes from having faith in the Buddha is due to the greatness of the object referenced being a buddha.

If both buddhas and sentient beings are depended on, they each have a share in being the causes for accomplishing the buddha qualities, therefore they—buddhas and sentient beings—are asserted to be equal. However, none are equal to the buddhas who are limitless oceans of good qualities.

Their collection of supreme good qualities is unrivalled, because it is that of the buddhas alone. And for those few in whom a mere portion of their good qualities appears, if for the sake of worshipping them the entire three realms were offered, it would be insufficient for the task.

Sentient beings have in their own mindstreams a share in giving birth to the supreme buddha qualities, therefore, in conformance with just that much of a share, it is correct to worship sentient beings.

---

[139] Some other editions have "loving kindness" rather than "enlightenment mind". The point is that sentient beings are equivalent to the buddhas because both can be responsible for the creation of merit.

Furthermore, I think to myself, what else except for pleasing sentient beings will repay the kindness of those—the buddhas—who befriend us without deceit and provide us with unfathomable assistance?

Benefiting them—those sentient beings—will repay the kindness of those buddhas, the ones who have in the past even given their bodies and even done such things as having entered the hell of Unremitting Torment like swans coming to a lake of lotuses for the sake of sentient beings. Hence I will assist in the accomplishment of those activities so difficult to do and because of that I will behave impeccably in everything that I do, benefiting sentient beings with all of body, speech, and mind even if these sentient beings do me great harm because of it.

When those who have now become my lords—the buddhas—have no regard even for their own bodies but work for sentient beings' sake, how is it that I, so stupid, act towards them with pride and through bloated self-importance do not act as a chattel, their servant? I must do so!

The leaders among capable ones are gladdened by sentient beings' happiness and made unhappy by their being harmed. Thus, by making sentient beings glad I make all of the leaders among capable ones glad and by harming them I harm all the leaders among capable ones like the way that when an only child is harmed the mother is harmed.

If my body were totally ablaze with fire, my mind would not be happy even if all desirable sense-objects were piled up before it. Likewise if sentient beings are harmed, there is no way that the greatly compassionate ones could be glad.

Therefore, since before this I have done harm to migrators, today I individually lay aside whatever evils I have done that have not gladdened the compassionate ones. Please forgive me, compassionate ones, for the unhappiness I have caused you.

In order to gladden the tathāgatas, from today onward I shall definitely tame myself and be a servant of the world. Though many migrators stamp upon my head or even try to kill me, I will not retaliate against those sentient beings. Thereby may I gladden the guardians of the world!

There is no doubt that the buddhas, whose nature is compassion, regard all of these migrators as themselves. And they directly see sentient beings' entity, which is the hidden-from-view guardian that is none other than the buddha's enlightened mind. Why then would I not respect the functioning of their buddha nature?[140]

This pleasing of sentient beings is what pleases the tathāgatas. Just this is also what truly accomplishes my own aims. Just this is also what dispels the suffering of the world. This being so, I should always do just that.

For example, if some of the king's men were to harm many people, farsighted men after examining the future outcome to see whether it would be good or bad, would not return the harm even if they could do so, for they would see that the men were not acting alone but were a force representing the entire might of the king. Similarly, I should not underestimate a few weak beings who do me harm, for they are a force representing the guards of the hells and the compassionate ones. Proceeding like the subjects of that fierce king and recognizing the situation for what it is, I shall please all sentient beings.

---

[140] The first point is that because of compassion, the buddhas see sentient beings as themselves, so we should do the same. The second point is that the buddhas directly know that sentient beings' entity, even if it is hidden from ordinary people's view, is the buddha nature, so we should respect sentient beings as buddhas, no matter how their buddha nature functions as the activity of sentient beings.

If someone such as a king were to become angry, and even if he set down a law, could he make me experience the harms of falling into hell that will be experienced because of not pleasing sentient beings? He could not.

And if someone such as a king were to be pleased, he could not possibly grant me the buddhahood that will be obtained by pleasing sentient beings.

Why do I not see that, putting aside the fact that the future attainment of buddhahood comes from pleasing sentient beings, in this very life great glory and fame and happiness all come from the same? This must be seen!

The benefits of patience are that while circling in cyclic existence, it brings a beautiful body and so on, absence of sickness, renown, an extremely long life, and the vast happiness of a wheel-turning emperor.

That was the sixth chapter of *Entering the Conduct of a Bodhisatva*, called "Patience".

CHAPTER SEVEN

Perseverance

2.2.3.2 Perseverance relates to all three higher trainings

This has three parts: the way in which a persevering person has enlightenment; a synopsis of perseverance together with its non-conducive side; and the second part extensively explained.

2.2.3.2.1 The way in which a persevering person has enlightenment

Having become patient with harms and sufferings like that, perseverance at the virtuous karmas must be undertaken given that enlightenment is present in those who have perseverance. Just as there is no movement of trees and so on without wind, the cause of enlightenment, the two accumulations of merit and wisdom are something that does not arise without perseverance and without those two there is no enlightenment.

2.2.3.2.2 A synopsis of perseverance together with its non-conducive side

What is perseverance? It is delighting in virtue. Its non-conducive side is explained to be laziness, which comes from clinging to what is bad, procrastination, and low self-esteem.[141]

---

[141] The definition of vira, the Sanskrit term translated here as perseverance,
(continued ...)

Because of experiencing the pleasurable taste of idleness and deterioration of virtue and because of craving for sleep, there is no disenchantment with the suffering of samsara and laziness grows strong.[142]

2.2.3.2.3 The second part extensively explained

This has three parts: the way to dispel the adverse side; the way to create a force of antidotes; and drawing a conclusion.

2.2.3.2.3.1 The way to dispel the adverse side

The creature of mind having been caught in the trap of the afflictions, I have been driven towards and entered the trap of birth and gone into the mouth of the lord of death. How is it that I am still not aware of that? If I were aware of it, I would know that laziness is not the right approach!

In this world, the lord of death is systematically slaughtering our species, but you do not see it! Nevertheless, those who prefer to sleep are like buffaloes to be slaughtered facing a butcher, the slaughterer.

Having blocked off every path of escape the lord of death is looking right now to kill, so how can you enjoy eating and how can you enjoy sleep?

---

[141] (... continued)
is that one both puts out energy to accomplish something and that one takes delight in it, or you could say, one is enthusiastic about doing that particular task. We do not have a single word in English with these two connotations, so the reader should bear this in mind. Some Tibetan texts say that perseverance means being delighted in the buddha's dharma, but that is just a specific case of the more general meaning of perseverance.

[142] A lack of self-esteem leads to thinking that one is worthless and incapable of accomplishing anything.

Death will be here quickly, but for as long as it is not, it is right that I will gather the accumulations. As it says in the *Sutra of Excellent Night*,

> I could die tomorrow or who knows when.
> It could be today, I cannot say.
> The lord of death and his minions
> Are no friends of mine.

If I think, "When I am on the verge of death, it will be appropriate to make efforts at virtue", I might attempt to abandon laziness when death arrives, but it is not the time for making virtue nor is there the chance to do it, so what will be the use?

When something that was planned to be done has not been undertaken and I have the thought, "Now I must have the patience needed to get this done", or has been started, or is only half finished, the lord of death will suddenly come while there is still more to do. I will think, "My human life has been meaningless" and will feel "Oh no, I have failed!"

Those close to me, their eyes red and swollen due to sobbing in sorrow and tears running down their faces, knowing that there is nothing that could help finally lose hope and I see the faces of the messengers of Yama, the lord of death. Tormented by the memory of my evils and hearing the sounds of hell, I will be so afraid that, pooping and peeing on myself, I will clothe my body in excrement and then what virtue could I do in such a crazed state?

Mind, if even in this life I become filled with fear like that of a live fish being rolled in burning hot sand to cook, what need is there to mention the sufferings that will be experienced when I fall into the unbearable hells that will be the future result made by the cause, the evils I have done?

If those of youthful flesh come into contact with boiling water, they will not be able to bear the pain. If I assess that, why then do I remain at ease like this when I have done karmic actions that will result in birth in the Extreme Heating Hell?

Much harm befalls those who want results without being diligent at making the causes and those of little tolerance meaning small fortitude who in the clutches of death will, like the gods when they have all sorts of unwanted things coming down on them[143], cry out, "Oh no, I am overcome with sufferings!"

That being so, rely on this boat of a human body to liberate yourself from the great river of suffering! If you do not, in the future it will be difficult to obtain this sort of boat, so, calling out to yourself, "You stupid fool!" be advised that, "Now that you have obtained one, this is not the time to fall asleep!"

If you are clinging to bad things, why do you abandon the supreme joy of the holy dharma that has limitless causes for joy then become distracted by causes for suffering and find joy in things that make your mind unpeaceful, agitated, and so on?

Hence, I must do the following: be without procrastination, that is, have an uplifted mind;[144] have the supporting forces for perseverance assembled; be industrious at abandoning afflictions and bad conduct; be in control of myself through the antidotes; see myself and others as equal; and practise exchanging self for other!

---

[143] At the time of death, gods experience all sorts of very unpleasant occurrences as portents of their impending death.

[144] The word for procrastination also means despondency, the absence of despondency means there is no procrastination which in turn means that there is a cheerful state of mind.

Moreover, I should never indulge in procrastination by entertaining thoughts such as, "How could I possibly gain enlightenment?" This is how to judge that. The tathāgata, one who speaks the truth, has told this truth in the *Sutra Petitioned by Subāhu*,

> If they develop the strength of their diligence, even those with inferior supports, those who are flies, meat flies[145], insects in general, and likewise worms will gain this difficult to gain, unsurpassed enlightenment.

If that is the case, then for someone like myself who has been born in a fortunate race, one in which the body is a special support[146], the race of humans and can recognize what is beneficial and what is harmful, as long as I do not let go of the conduct of enlightenment, what could stop me from obtaining enlightenment?

"Well yes, in the long run I will obtain it, but it frightens me to think that in order to obtain it I will have to give away my arms, legs, and so on". In limitless samsara there is a heavy burden of suffering that has to be borne and in accomplishing enlightenment there is a light burden of austerities that must be undergone. **Being stupid in regard to what is heavy and light, I have ended up not being afraid of the heavy burden but being afraid of the light one.**

The reasoning connected with the heavy suffering of wandering in cyclic existence and the light suffering of accomplishing enlightenment is as follows.

---

[145] "Meat flies" does not mean mosquitoes. Tibetans regard flies that feed on meat as a separate type of fly, which they call a meat fly, though they are the same as what is referred to as the common house fly in English.

[146] Special support means the support specifically of a precious human body.

During countless tens of millions of aeons I have been cut, stabbed, burned, and split apart many times, but it—those tiring experiences—has not resulted in my gaining enlightenment.

Yet this suffering that comes with my accomplishing enlightenment has a measure of being relatively small or light. It is like the suffering of having an incision made on the body by a doctor in order to remove the greater pain of something such as an arrow lodged inside and damaging it.

All doctors use somewhat unpleasant medical procedures such as bleeding, burning, and so on, to remove major illnesses and in the same way I should tolerate smaller discomforts in order to overcome manifold great sufferings.

The supreme physician, the buddha, does not employ common medical procedures such as these—the relatively coarse ones of bleeding, and so on—but treats fathomless great illnesses with extremely gentle techniques.

When starting familiarization with that with giving, the Guide taught giving cooked food and the like as a beginning preparation. Later, having become familiar with that, he taught that one could gradually reach the point at which one could even give away one's own flesh.

When a mind has been produced that regards one's own body like cooked food, and so on because of having no essence to it, what difficulty would there be in giving one's own flesh, and so on? *The Condensed* says,

> Having understood that phenomena have a nature of lacking
>   a self, of having no truth,
> I can give even my flesh and do it without mind shrinking
>   away from it.
> At that point, what need is there to mention giving external
>   things?

Moreover, such things are done in order to abandon evil, so there will be no suffering involved and they are done in order to develop expertise by abandoning clinging to substantial things, so there will be no unhappiness involved. This is how it is: we have been producing wrong concepts and doing evil actions that have harmed body and mind, whereas if we had been making merit, we would have been making the body happy and if we had been developing expertise, we would have been making the mind happy. Thus, the Compassionate Ones may have to stay in samsara for a long time for the sake of others, but how could they ever become disheartened by it, thinking, "It has been too long"?

I would have been making the body happy and if I had been developing expertise I would have been making the mind happy. Following that reasoning, the Compassionate Ones might stay in samsara for the sake of others, but how would they ever be disheartened?

Thus this one, the bodhisatva, using the strength of his enlightenment mind exhausts his previously-done evil deeds and collects, like taking in a profit, an ocean of merit, therefore he is said to be supreme when compared to the śrāvakas.

Having mounted the horse of enlightenment mind which dispels all despondency and physical weariness, he goes from happiness to happiness, so who on knowing of this mind would procrastinate?

2.2.3.2.3.2 The way to create a force of antidotes

This has three parts: a synopsis made by distinguishing four forces; an extensive explanation of the first three forces; and a short presentation of the last one.

2.2.3.2.3.2.1 A synopsis made by distinguishing four forces

What are the forces to be developed in order to accomplish sentient beings' aims? They are the four forces of intention, steadfastness, joy, and rejection. How are they developed? Intention and the others are developed through being afraid of suffering and through considering their benefits and abandoning what is not conducive to them.

Industriously working at intention which is wanting and aiming towards virtuous dharmas, **pride** or steadfastness which is about creating and applying the antidote type of pride, **joy** which is having delight in virtue, **and rejection** which is to rest up for a while when weary from making efforts at virtue, **will develop the strength of my control over myself—over my body, speech, and mind—and because that can increase perseverance I must exert myself at them.**

2.2.3.2.3.2.2 The first three forces extensively explained

The first three forces are the forces of intention, pride, and joy.

2.2.3.2.3.2.2.1 The force of intention

The wrongs of myself and others are fathomless, but I must eradicate them for that will accomplish the purpose to which I have committed. **It will take an ocean of aeons to eradicate each one of those wrongs, but if I do not see in myself even a fraction of the diligence needed to exhaust all of those wrongs, why doesn't my heart burst on seeing this place of fathomless suffering?** As a consequence it should!

The good qualities needed for myself and others will be many, so I will have to work at familiarization for an ocean of aeons in order to accomplish every one of them.

However, I have never gained familiarization with even a fraction of those good qualities, so what have I gained while I have been here? I am embarrassed to say that I am amazed at how meaningless I have made this excellent birth!

I have not worshipped the Bhagavat who came into this world with offerings and not found happiness in the celebrations honouring

him, meaning that I have not been a steady provider of offerings; I have not done the activities required by the teaching, meaning that having entered the teaching I have not done the activities of taming those with afflictions; I have not fulfilled the wishes of the poor; I have not provided those who have fear with no fear; and I have not given comfort to those sentient beings who are downtrodden by suffering. I who do not have the protection of loving kindness have ended up doing nothing more than making pains of pregnancy for my mother in my mother's womb, and following that, having been born, creating only suffering for her because of her caring for me. That being so, I will not behave that way henceforth, but will diligently perform those activities of making offerings to the buddha, and so on.

In past lives and the present one too, I have kept away from the intention to follow dharma because of which this sort of paucity of good qualities has arisen. Who, knowing of such a mind, would ever relinquish the intention to follow the dharma? It is not all right to do so!

The Capable One said that intention is the root of everything virtuous. And its—intention's—root in turn is constant meditation on full-ripening results—the bad destinies with their disadvantages and the higher levels and emancipation with their advantages.

The disadvantages of samsara that are meditated on—physical suffering, mental unhappiness, the various fears, and separation from what is desired and meeting with what is not desired—come from doing evil. Because of not wanting that sort of full-ripening, I think to myself, "I must abandon its cause, evil".

By doing virtue—outflowed and un-outflowed—with a beneficial intention, I will go here to the higher levels or there to emancipation but here or there wherever it is, the merit involved will offer up manifest good results.

The evil done might come from wanting the happiness of a happy full-ripening, but wherever I go in a future life, whether to a bad migration or, because of the relative strength involved, one of the higher levels, that evil will cause the weapons of suffering to overwhelm me completely in that place.

And, by doing virtue, I will dwell in the spacious, fragrant, and cooling heart of a lotus, my radiance developed by the food of hearing the dharma, the Conqueror's sweet speech, my supreme body bedecked with the marks and insignia arising in miraculous birth from a lotus opened by the Capable One's light, and will stay before the conquerors as a son of the sugatas.

Because of doing many non-virtues in the past, my whole skin will be peeled off by the henchmen of Yama and in that extremely feeble state, boiling molten copper melted by an extremely hot fire will be poured into my body. On top of that, stabbed by flaming swords and daggers, my flesh will be cut apart into hundreds of pieces and I will collapse onto and be dragged about the fiercely blazing iron ground.

That is how it is, so I should have the intention to accomplish virtue and cultivate it with respect.

2.2.3.2.3.2.2.2 The force of pride

Having undertaken the accomplishment of what is meaningful using the rite in *The Vajra Victory Banner Sutra*, I should then cultivate pride[147]. The rite is explained in the dedications of the sixth chapter of *The Victory Banner Sutra* which in turn is found in the

---

[147] Pride here, as earlier explained, has the meaning of steadfastness. Pride in this case has the positive sense of self-confidence, that one can actually start something and, by persevering, see it through to the end. You will see that these themes are explored in this section.

Buddha Avatamsaka Sutra. What does it say there? It gives this example:

> Son of the Gods! When the sun arose, objects that were suitable because whatever bad there was—blindness, smoke, haze, mountains of unequalled height, and so on—had not been turned back were illuminated ...

That example is set out and then it says,

> Likewise, the bodhisatva mahasattva possessing mindfulness and alertness not shrinking at all from the mind of the vast and profound, coursing in good qualities, and coursing in wisdom to the limit is repulsed by the bad behaviour that comes from sentient beings with a temperament of hatred. All such sentient beings who have been born in hell and all such sentient beings who are dwelling in the places of the bad destinies will transfer at death and I will take on their great pile of suffering. I will persevere. I will be delighted. I will not turn back. I will not run away. I will not be afraid. I will not be fearful. I will not regress. I will not procrastinate ...

And so on, it goes on at length.

First of all I should examine a task to find out whether I am capable of accomplishing it or not. If I am capable of it, then **I should undertake it or else if I am not, I should not. Not to start might be best, for once it has been started, there is no turning back.**

If I try to accomplish what I am not capable of accomplishing, that will bring a downfall and **in future births I will have a habit of that and evil and suffering will increase** given that the downfall will bring forth a bad full-ripening. And if I do not work at accomplishing virtue that is suitable to accomplish, that too will bring a downfall **and also in other births at the time of the result** it will be the same as before; for a karmic seed planted during the accomplishment of virtue **there will**

be a low-grade result and as well as that, the task undertaken will not be accomplished.

That being so, pride should be applied to the three of action, affliction, and capability. Saying, "How will it be done? I alone will do it" is pride applied to action.

Made powerless by the afflictions, the migrators of this world are incapable of accomplishing their own aims let alone the aims of others. They are not capable in the way that I am, therefore I will do it for them.

Others may be working at lesser tasks, but how could I just stand by quietly, given that I need to liberate all sentient beings from samsara? I must do that work! Moreover, if I do nothing because of pride that thinks, "Others are doing lesser tasks, but what I am doing is the most excellent kind of work", it would be best for me to have no pride.

When a crow encounters a dead snake, it behaves as though it were a Garuḍa, king of birds and if I have a weak personality like that, even small adversities will trouble me.

How could someone who has shrunk from this task and given up trying with the thought, "How could someone like me do this?", have emancipation through such poverty—of method—mentality? He could not. About not being able to have it, the *Ornament of the Sutras* says,

> They start out carrying the great burden of sentient beings, so
> The supreme satvas[148], find nothing attractive about going slowly.
> The various fetters of self and other are utterly binding, so

---

[148] The supreme satvas or heroes are the bodhisatvas or enlightenment heroes.

> The correct approach is to make one hundred times the effort.

That is saying that someone who is using the antidote type of pride to develop exertion will be very difficult to overcome, even by great adversities.

> Therefore with steadfast mind I shall overcome all adversities, for if I am defeated by an adversity, my desire to conquer the three realms will be worthy of ridicule.

> Therefore, I will conquer everything and no-one will conquer me! I, a son of the lion-like conquerors, will dwell in this sort of pride.

If I think, "Yes, but pride is to be discarded, is it not?", the reply is that the migrator who is overpowered by pride which is an affliction is not the person with pride being shown here. The person with pride shown here is a hero, so does not fall under the enemy's control, whereas the other does fall under the control of the enemy, pride.

The one who is puffed up with the pride of the afflictions will, because of falling under its control, be led to the bad migrations and not only that but will have the festival of being human destroyed, be turned into a servant dependent on another's food, and be stupid, ugly, weak, and despised everywhere. If that sort of person also were included among the ones with pride, tell me, what could be more demeaning than that?[149] [150] It is worse than being someone who has no pride!

Someone who carries the antidote kind of pride in order to conquer the enemy type of pride is called "the one with pride" and also a totally victorious one and a hero. Someone in whom the enemy the affliction kind of pride has taken hold but who then defeats it is someone who completes the fruition of becoming a conqueror, fulfilling what is wanted for migrators.

That being the case, if I find myself amidst a crowd of afflictions, I will withstand them in a thousand ways; like a lion not being bothered by jackals and the like, I will, applying the antidotes, not be bothered by the afflictions.

Just as people will guard their eyes to prevent them from being hit in the midst of a terrible beating, likewise through guarding the antidotes in the midst of terrible upheavals, I will prevent myself from falling under the control of the afflictions.

Regarding the degree of stability of the antidotes: It would be better for me to be picked out and burned to death or have my head cut off, than to bow down to the enemy, the ever-present afflictions.[151]

---

[149] The Derge edition of the text has an extra line which is missing from Padma Karpo's text. The line is present in the major Sanskrit commentary, the *Pañjikā*. With the line added, the text says this: "If tough sorts who are puffed up with pride were also included among the ones with pride, tell me, what could be more demeaning than that?"

[150] Altogether, the meaning here is, "If people with the afflicted type of pride were also to be included among the heroes who have the non-afflicted type of pride, that would be very demeaning to the heroic type, wouldn't it?"

[151] This verse is present in Tibetan editions but the Sanskrit *Pañjikā*
(continued ...)

2.2.3.2.3.2.2.3 The force of joy

Similarly, in all circumstances I will not conduct myself in any way other than what is correct. Like those who want the enjoyment that comes from a game, this sort of person—the bodhisatva—is attracted to whatever tasks are suitable for him to be done and he never has enough of such tasks, which only bring him joy.

Worldly people work for the sake of happiness, but with no certainty of whether there will be a happy outcome or not. On the other hand, it is certain that this work of mine will in both the short and long term have a happy outcome, but if I do not do the work, how could it have a happy outcome in either short or long term? It could not!

If there is no satisfaction in desirable objects that are like licking honey on a razor's edge given their small short-term profit and great long-term disadvantages, why would there be satisfaction with the merit for the peace of enlightenment whose full-ripening is happiness in the long term?

In view of that, in order to finish an activity that was suitable to be done, I shall enter it again and again like an elephant who, tormented by the heat of the late spring's midday sun, on finding a lake plunges into it with joy and delight.

2.2.3.2.3.2.3 A short presentation of the last one

When, due to exerting myself at virtuous actions, my strength of body and mind declines, I should put aside whatever I have been doing for a while so that I will be able to pick it up and continue with it later. In short, finding the work objectionable and becoming disenchanted with it will turn into a cause for it not being accomplished.

---

[151] (... continued)
commentary does not have it as part of the Indian text.

Furthermore, when it—a task of body or speech—has been done well, it can be abandoned while wishing to accomplish what comes next. What Jowo Atisha said is fitting,

> If the mind of equipoise has become stable, that one thing is enough;
> Virtue of body and speech should not be made most important.

2.2.3.2.3.3 Drawing a conclusion

Like old warriors who are expert at dodging an enemy's weapons and at striking the at the enemy meeting the enemy on the battlefront I will dodge the weapon-like afflictions and skilfully use the antidotes as weapons to deal with the enemies that are the afflictions.

If someone skilled in the use of a sword drops his sword during a battle, he quickly picks it up out of fear and likewise, if I lose the weapon of mindfulness, remembering the fears of hell I will quickly retrieve it.

Just as when a poison arrow pierces the body, the poison spreads throughout the body due to the circulation of blood, likewise if mindfulness and alertness degenerate and the afflictions find an opportunity, wrongs will spread throughout the mind. Therefore, mindfulness and alertness must be used to stay attentive.

How is that done? Those who practise the yogic disciplines should be as attentive as a frightened man carrying a vessel full of mustard oil who is being followed by someone holding a sword and threatening to kill him if he spills even a drop of it.

Just as I would swiftly stand if a snake came into my lap, should sleep or idleness—the causes of slipping away from mindfulness and alertness—come, I will quickly repel them.

Each time something wrong occurs, I should berate myself saying, "Oh my! I have done something that is not good, I have debased myself", then contemplate for a long time that, "In future, I will do whatever it takes so that this does not happen to me again".

I will examine myself like this: "How in these circumstances of the afflictions, will I develop familiarization with the antidote, mindfulness?" And then, because of such a thought that wants to know how to rely on mindfulness, I will want to meet with spiritual friends or obtain appropriate tasks they assign me such as hearing, contemplating, and so on from them.

Before having such a task, one needs to be prepared in all ways—in all of body, speech, and mind—and for that I should recall what was talked about in the chapter on the need to rely on **heedfulness**. Then I should rise to any task with a light heart, meaning that I should face whatever will be encountered in a cheerful frame of mind.

Just as the wind blowing back and forth governs the movement to and fro of cotton wool, so shall I be governed by delight in all types of virtue and in all circumstances of things begun and ended.

That was the seventh chapter of *Entering the Conduct of a Bodhisatva*, called "Perseverance".

CHAPTER EIGHT

Meditative Concentration

2.2.3.3 Meditative concentration and prajñā are explained in relation to the last two higher trainings[152]

This has three parts: their connection with the three higher trainings is explained as the meaning in general; the chapter on meditative concentration shows the higher training of mind; and the chapter on prajñā explains the higher training of prajñā.

2.2.3.3.1 Their connection with the three higher trainings is explained as the meaning in general

Carrying out the higher discipline that has six branches completes the heap of discipline whereby all distraction is pacified through which the higher training of mind is gained. Training in that to the end completes the heap of samadhi and by staying in that samadhi prajñā is acquired. Through its acquisition the heroism of having defeated all affliction comes about and when it has, that is called "the heap of prajñā" and the person who has defeated affliction is "completely liberated". That liberation happens in relation to what is to be abandoned and there being many such liberations, it is the heap of complete liberation.

---

[152] "Meditative concentration" is the most general term in Sanskrit for what we in English call "meditation". The word we mostly translate into English as "meditation" means "cultivation". "Samadhi" in Sanskrit corresponds to the English "concentration".

Together with that liberation wisdom is seen which happens in relation to what is to be realized and there being many such seeings of wisdom, it is called "the heap of seeing the wisdom of complete liberation". Therefore, the sequence goes like this: higher discipline is taught first, entrance into higher mind is taught next, and higher prajñā is taught after that.

2.2.3.3.2 The chapter o meditative concentration shows the higher training of mind

This has three parts: the need for mind to be in equipoise; where samadhi is placed; and accomplishing its cause, absence of attachment to the world.

2.2.3.3.2.1 The need for mind to be in equipoise

Having developed perseverance in that way, I should set my mind in the equipoise of samadhi in order to accomplish the higher good qualities. What problem would there be if I do not place it in samadhi? The person whose mind is distracted to frivolous entertainments dwells between the fangs of the afflictions, afflictions that will have no difficulty consuming the person.

What good would there be if I do place it in samadhi? Through solitude of body and mind distraction does not arise. And through not being distracted samadhi is accomplished.

2.2.3.3.2.2 Where samadhi is placed

Therefore I will abandon the world and entirely discard conceptual thinking.

The world is not abandoned because of past attachments or by craving for material gain and the like, therefore I should entirely abandon these things, given that those who are expert see it this way—because of their investigations they know the causes to be attachment and craving and so know the antidotes.[153]

In order to *calm* the afflictions, mind is made to *abide*, so the process is called "calm abiding". Its entity is a samadhi of one-pointed mind. Its characteristic is a meditative concentration in which mind is focussed on a referenced object. Its divisions are that it consists of four meditative states that are the actual four form meditative concentrations and four formless states and the corresponding eight preparatory states[154]. The actual first level of the form meditative concentration s has seventeen sub-strata.

The entity of superior seeing[155] is prajñā which references the just-as-it-isness of phenomena. Its etymology is that it is a *superior* knowing of the nature of phenomena which is precisely *seeing* their just-as-it-is-ness[156]. Its divisions are that it has five aspects: the knowing of things in their extent; knowing them as they are; that arising from labels; that arising from thorough seeking; and that arising from individually discriminating.

Vipashyana arises from its cause, calm abiding, then is unified with calm abiding resulting in vipashyana that fully possesses calm abiding. That sort of vipashyana based on these six—the preparatory step of the first meditative concentrations, the four actual meditative concentrations, and a specific case of the actual first meditative concentration—operates

---

[153] Derge edition has "behave this way" rather than "see it this way".

[154] These are also known as "access" states. They are a level of attainment which is immediately prior to the actual state and which thus prepare for or allow access to the actual state.

[155] Sanskrit "vipaśhyanā", Tibetan "lhag mthong", in English commonly called "insight".

[156] "Superior" translates the Sanskrit "vi" and "seeing" translates the Sanskrit "pashyana".

to completely overcome the seeds of the afflictions which are the discards discarded by the path of seeing and that sort of vipashyana based on these nine—the six levels of meditative concentration just mentioned with the actual first three meditative concentrations of the formless realm added—operates to completely overcome the seeds of the afflictions which are the discards discarded by the path of meditation. **Having understood that those seeds of the afflictions are completely destroyed by superior seeing fully equipped with calm abiding**, it is understood that superior seeing is needed to overcome the afflictions. With that, the need for calm abiding arises, so **to begin with**—meaning first of all—**I will seek out calm abiding** and then I will seek out superior seeing, **which** as well as the calm abiding **will be accomplished through the strong joy of being unattached to worldly life** and living in isolation.

In regard to that, the Middle Way tradition represented here and some other Middle Way traditions differ as to how to carry this into meditation. The others assert that one first does a preliminary of analysing using scripture and reasoning, after which it is essential to accomplish a calm abiding before going further. This appears in the *Lamp of the Path*,

> By scripture and reasoning
> All phenomena are ascertained to be
> Without birth in being without nature and then
> Without discursive thought which is to be meditated upon.

It is why our tradition says that analysis is not done as a preliminary to calm abiding.

2.2.3.3.2.3 Accomplishing its cause, absence of attachment to the world

This has three parts: the way to abandon attachment to desirable things; the way of being joyful at isolation; and the way of meditating on the enlightenment mind that is like climbing stairs.

2.2.3.3.2.3.1 The way to abandon attachment to desirable things

This has three parts: abandoning the cause of attachment, relatives and friends; abandoning clinging to the eight dharmas; and a conclusion to those two.

2.2.3.3.2.3.1.1 Abandoning the cause of attachment, relatives and friends

The true attachment that impermanent—meaning having no essence—beings have for other impermanent beings such as relatives, friends, and so on due to clinging to them as something that is true, means that they will not see the objects of their desires, their beloved ones who will have been born in the bad destinies, again for thousands of lives.

Not seeing them makes me unhappy. Tormented by it my mind will not settle into equipoise and, even if I do see them, I am not satisfied, so like before am tormented by craving.

When I become attached to sentient beings—relatives, friends, and so on—it totally obscures me from seeing the fact of the authentic, the disengagement from hearing, contemplating, and cultivating destroys my disenchantment with cyclic existence, and in the end when I am on the verge of death, tortures me with the anguish of the separation of mutually attached people.

By thinking only of them—relatives, friends, and so on who are the objects of my desires—this life will pass without meaning. These impermanent relatives and friends distracted by listening only to others' opinions, and so on will even destroy the thoroughly good, everlasting dharma through which nirvana can be gained, and so become a hindrance.

If I live at the same level as the childish, associating with ordinary beings and acting out the eight worldly dharmas, it is certain that I will go to the bad migrations—I will go where they go in future lives. If by not living at that level I lead myself upwards to the higher levels, what would be gained from entrusting myself to the childish beings? Our wishes are not in accord.

Even if I did change to being in accord with those childish ordinary beings, they will become close friends in an instant and turn into enemies a short time later. You tell them, "Behave nicely!", but after that even when they meet joyful situations, the situations make them angry. It is difficult to please the ordinary beings.

If something is said for their benefit, such as to turn away from criminal behaviour, it makes them angry and they attempt to turn me away from accomplishing what is beneficial. If I do not listen to what they say, they become angry at me and because of that will one day go to the bad migrations. The *King of Samadhis Sutra* says,

> Words of being in accord with dharma are told, but
> Strong words of anger, hatred, and untrusting mind
> Are given back—this is a thing of the childish
> Whose meaning, though understood, should not be relied
>   upon.

They are envious of superiors, competitive with equals, proud towards inferiors, disregarding them, haughty when praised, and if something unpleasant is said and they hear it, they become angry; therefore nothing of benefit can possibly be gained from the childish.

If I associate with the childish, some kind of non-virtue will definitely arise, such as praising myself and reviling others and discussing the joys of cyclic existence with expressions of how good are desirable things.

The mutual support and association of myself and the childish others will, because of amassing evil, end up in nothing but ruin for both. They the childish associates do nothing for my sake and I do not work for theirs, so I should go far away from these childish people.

When I do meet them, I should please them by telling stories for the purpose of making them happy, but apart from just that without becoming too familiar with them should behave well out of simple courtesy. Likewise, I should not treat them with aversion.

In the same way as a bee takes honey from a flower, I should take from them merely what is needed for the purpose of dharma—alms, and so on—but with remain unfamiliar with all of them, as though not having seen them before.

2.2.3.3.2.3.1.2 Abandoning clinging to the eight dharmas

"Compared to others I have many material gains and am more honoured, so many people like me". If I maintain that kind of self-importance, the distraction involved will prevent me from having the time to do virtue and because of that I will become afraid at the time of death. It makes you feel a little anxious, doesn't it?

Thus, out of total stupidity I become attached to this and that internal and external object, adding to them one after another, with the result that suffering a thousandfold will ensue.

That being so, the learned do not make attachments because fear is born from the attachment, fear of the suffering result. With an unflinching mind fully understand that by nature these things—the objects of attachment—will be discarded at death!

I might have many material gains and be famous, and be well spoken of, but at the time of death, the gain and fame I have amassed will have no power to accompany me to my destination. Leaving the material gains, and so on behind, I will wander on alone to the unknown.

If there are others who deprecate me, what cause for joy would there be in being praised by some? And if there are others who praise me, what cause for sorrow would there be in being deprecated by some?

If even the Conqueror could not please sentient beings of varying inclinations and, concerned about the ways of the Tīrthikas and the barbarians, said unpleasant things about them, if it was like that even for the buddha, what need to mention a bad person such as I? Therefore I should give up all ideas of being in accord with the world.

These sentient beings deprecate others who have no material gain saying, "You have no merit" and express unpleasant things about others who do, saying, "You have bad livelihood". They are by nature hard to be with, so how could any of them be a source of joy?

2.2.3.3.2.3.1.3 A conclusion to those two

The tathāgatas have said, "Do not befriend the childish at all, because they are not happy unless their own purposes are being fulfilled." The *King of Samadhis Sutra* says,

> No matter how long one has banded together with the childish,
> The day will come when they will turn and stop being close, becoming an enemy;
> When experts have first-hand knowledge of that nature of the childish,
> They will not rely on the childish.

2.2.3.3.2.3.2 The way of being joyful at isolation

This has three parts: aspiring to isolation; while there, considering the disadvantages of desired things; and commending isolation.

2.2.3.3.2.3.2.1 Aspiring to isolation

In forests, the gentle creatures, birds, and trees do not express unpleasant sounds, so being with them is a happy event, and one day I shall stay together with them.

May I while dwelling in a cave, empty shrine room, or at the foot of a tree not look back one day at the things of the householder or of worldly life, but be without attachment to them.

May I dwell in places that, not being held to as "mine" by anyone, are naturally spacious for the mind, where without needing to concern myself with what others might think, I can behave as I wish and do so without attachment.

One day I will dwell there with just a begging bowl and a few other articles and with the three dharma robes that no-one wants for their use,[157] not having to hide myself, yet not at all afraid.

2.2.3.3.2.3.2.2 While there, contemplating the disadvantages of desired things

Having gone to the charnel ground, one day I shall understand that both the skeletons of others who have already died and my body are the same in having the feature of being subject to decay.

This body of mine that I have treasured so much will be a decaying and rotting corpse that will smell so bad that even the foxes will not come close to it; such is what will become of it.

If I think, "In isolation I will not be able to stand the separation from relatives", then although this body first arose as one whole thing, it and the flesh and bones with which it was created will break down and separate into pieces. If so, what will I say about each of the others whom I hold dear?

At birth I was born alone and at death I shall die alone. If others cannot take on a share of this suffering, what use are close ones who create obstructions when I am doing virtue?

---

[157] ... the robes of a monastic ...

Like travellers of the roads find a place such as a guest house and stay in it, travellers of the paths of rebirth find a place to be born and stay in it and all of them have the suffering of birth.

I shall retire to the forest until, as a corpse on a bier **supported by four pall-bearers**[158] **and with the world standing there with tears on their faces and stricken with grief, I have to go on.**

Having gone to the forest, I might think, "Won't death strike?" But even if death strikes, because of **befriending no one I have no attachments and because of having no enemies I am begrudging no one, this body will dwell alone in solitude. Having already been counted as a dead man, there will be no mourners when I die.**

There will be no one around to trouble me with their mourning, so in this isolated place there will be no one to distract me from my recollections of the Buddha and the others.[159]

That being so, I shall dwell by myself alone in the forest of exceptional beauty and joy where having only minor difficulties leaves me at ease and with all distractions quelled.

Dwelling in that place having completely let go of all other ideas and with single-minded purpose, I shall persevere in order to set the mind in equipoise and tame the afflictions in it.[160]

---

[158] In ancient India, a funeral bier was carried to the charnel ground by four pall bearers.

[159] There are three recollections of the Three Jewels, one each for Buddha, dharma, and sangha, and there are other sets of recollections too. See *Unending Auspiciousness, the Sutra of the Recollection of the Noble Three Jewels* published by Padma Karpo Translation Committee, 2010, authored by Tony Duff, ISBN: 978-9937-8386-1-0.

[160] This is persevering in order to achieve calm abiding and then vipa-

If I think, "Yes, but staying there alone I will not be working for others' sakes, which contradicts the training to be done", this explanation has been given,

> Even though no energy is being expended on actions that
>   benefit others,
> The intention to do that is always being made.
> Someone who has that intention
> Is meaningfully engaged in working for others' sakes.

Samadhi is developed for a while and if through that the extra-sensory perceptions and miracles are accomplished, a tremendous wave of energy for others' sakes results. In that way, working for others' sakes happens, so meditation in isolation does not adversely affect working for others' sakes.

In this world and the next one too, desires bring down ruin; in this one they produce being killed, bound, and flayed and in the next, they produce the hells, and so on.

For the sake of a woman many requests are first made through messengers for her to join the family and evils and notoriety are not avoided for her sake; I engage in fearsome deeds—in terms of this and future lives—and even exhaust my wealth for her. However, if I examine the woman who I think is "the source of supreme joy at the time of total sexual embrace", she is a skeleton obscured by the machinery of skin and flesh, and nothing else. If so, then instead of utterly wanting and thoroughly clinging to this thing which is not autonomous and not mine, why do I not go to nirvana, the state beyond sorrow?

The first time, when she was a new bride, I made an effort to lift her veil and, when it had been raised, she bashfully looked down.

---

[160] (... continued)
shyana.

Previously, whether anyone could see her or not, her face was covered with a cloth.

Now afflicted one, this woman to whom you were so attached has been thrown away into the charnel ground where, with its skin torn off by the vultures' beaks, you see her face clearly as it actually is, as though you were seeing it directly without the covering of a cloth. Now that you see it for what it is, why do you run away?

Previously, although other men fixed their eyes upon my wife's body, staring at it out of jealousy, I thoroughly guarded it using many methods, so why jealous one[161], do you not guard it now, while it is being eat by vultures?

If vultures and others—jackals, and so on—having seen this flesh are eating it, there is no offering of flower garlands and sandalwood ointments to be made now that it has become the food of others.

And, having seen her bleached skeleton, if I am frightened by it even though it does not move, why am I not frightened by zombie corpses which are propelled by a few impulses?[162]

Although I was attached to it, her body, when it was covered with clothes and the like, why do I not desire it when as a corpse it is not covered? If I have no need for that, why do I embrace it when it is covered?

---

[161] The Sanskrit says "jealous" whereas the Tibetan says "stingy". Out of jealousy the husband is keeping his wife for himself and not sharing her with others, which is the meaning here of being stingy.

[162] Zombies or corpses which have risen from being dead and move around were an accepted phenomenon in Tibetan culture. They are considered to be propelled by impulses of attachment in the mind that belonged to the corpse and which is still connected to it or by impulses coming from the mind of spirits who have taken over the corpse.

At the time of sexual activity, I will swallow the woman's saliva. If excrement from below and saliva from above come solely from food, why do you not like excrement yet like saliva? This is about being nauseated.

About craving for contact: a pillow, whose cotton is soft to the touch and its interior clean, does not give me sexual enjoyment whereas I mistakenly believe that the pores of a woman's body do not emit a bad odour. Thus you, desirous one, are deluded as to what is unclean believing it to be clean!

Some stupid fools saying that they cannot sleep on cotton although it is soft to the touch, become angry towards and do not like it. That is about being angry at what is clean and attached to what is unclean.

If you think, "I am not attached to what is unclean", why do you copulate with your woman whose body is a cage of bones linked together with muscle and plastered over with the mud of flesh and therefore unclean in nature?[163]

Yours—your body—too has many unclean parts that you have to live with, yet that not being bad enough, your obsession with what is unclean makes you want another bag of uncleanliness, a woman's body.

If you have attachment to a woman, is that attachment to a woman's body or attachment to her mind? "I enjoy the flesh of the body", so I want to touch it—a woman's body—and gaze upon it with my eyes. In that case, it would be right for you to enjoy a woman's corpse too, but you do not want the flesh—the flesh of that corpse—that by nature is without mind!

---

[163] Mud was used in India as plaster for walls.

If it is attachment to her mind, the mind of a woman desired cannot be touched or viewed and anything that could be touched would not be a consciousness. Thus, sexual embrace of the body is meaningless, so what use is it?

It is not so strange not to realize that the bodies of others are unclean in nature, but it is very strange not to realize that one's own body with its ever-present impermanence of death is something unclean! It is like this: even if you do not intellectually understand that the far-off heap of poop and pee is unclean, there is no cause for not being directly aware that the close-by heap of poop and pee is unclean.

If I think, "I am attached to its colour and shape", then having abandoned what has a fine shape and bright colours like a fresh lotus flower opened by rays of the sun in a cloudless sky, how is it that, with a mind that has until now clung to this uncleanliness, I am still finding joy in a cage of the unclean?[164]

Similarly, if you do not want to touch places such as the ground that are smeared with excrement which are also referred to as nauseating, how is it that you want to touch the body from which it—the excrement—came?

If you have no desire for the excrement that so nauseates you, why do you embrace another's genitals? And again, you do not want to touch an unclean little maggot that came to life in a pile of unclean excrement and whose seed was nourished by the excrement, but you want to touch a big worm that was born from impurity—it is contradictory.

---

[164] You like your consort because you like her fine colour and shape. Well, a freshly-opened lotus flower has fine colour and shape and is free of the muck in which it grew up, but you have abandoned that in favour of something that does have fine colour and shape but which is a bag of muck.

Not only do you not condemn your own uncleanliness, but your obsession with what is unclean makes you want another bag of uncleanliness as well!

Attractive things such as camphor, and so on, and savoury foods or cooked rice having been put into the mouth then spat out make the ground unclean. Although such a mass of uncleanliness is obvious to the senses, if I still have doubts, I should go to charnel grounds and look at the bodies and other uncleanliness thrown away there! It is no different from that.

Knowing that if the skin of the body is opened up and red is displaying everywhere, it will give rise to great fear, how will that body give rise to joy again?

The scents rubbed on a woman's body are sandalwood and the like, not the scents of that woman's body, why then do I become attached to others' bodies because of scents like sandalwood that are other than their own? It makes no sense.

If I am not attached to this body because of its naturally bad odour, that is good is it not? How is it that those who crave the meaningless things of the world apply pleasant scents to the unclean body then speak about it being clean?

Well, if it is the pleasant scent sandalwood, how could it come from this body? It could not. Why then do I become attached to others' bodies because of scents that are other than theirs?

The long hair and nails, yellowish teeth, smell, and taint of dirt of that woman's body shown naked in its natural state is frightening. Why do I make such an effort to pretty it when that is like sharpening a weapon that will cause me harm? Oh my! The back to front efforts of my stupidity are the bases for the world's being totally disturbed by a crazed mind.

When, having seen some skeletons, renunciation is produced in the charnel ground, will there be any joy in charnel grounds of cities that are filled with moving skeletons?

Women, who are in that way unclean, are not obtained without paying a price. In this life I exhaust myself gathering wealth for that purpose and in future lives will be harmed in the hells, and so on.

As a child I am not able to increase my wealth and for that time must stay at home. As a young man I need to run after wealth and how could that be an easy situation? At the end of a long life of amassing wealth when I have become aged, what use will sex with my wife be then?

One type of bad, desirous person wears himself out by working all day and then, having arrived home in the evening, leaves his exhausted body lying there like a corpse.

One type has the suffering of becoming afflicted by having to travel and go far away from home. That person longs in his heart for his spouse, but does not see her for years at a time.

Some who want to benefit themselves through stupidity sell themselves for their own purposes, but not getting what they want are aimlessly driven by the winds of others'—women and so on—actions.

Some sell their bodies into the service of others and powerless are employed by others. And if their wives give birth, the children end up at the foot of a tree in an isolated place because they are, powerless, born in the bed of enjoyment that goes where the work takes the parents.[165]

---

[165] This is not as strange as it might sound. In India, poor people would make a simple shelter for a home at the foot of a large tree. This situation is still found, at the time of writing, in India and Nepal.

Some fools who are deceived by desire, thinking, "I want sustenance to stay alive", go to war for the sake of a small wage all the while apprehensive that they might lose their lives. Some go into the service of others for the sake of a small recompense.

Some desire-filled people have their bodies cut up into pieces on account of women or wealth. Some because of being sentenced to it by the law, get impaled on the impaling stick. Some others are stabbed with a—another's—dagger. Others still are burned. Such things as these are readily seen.[166]

Therefore, due to the pains involved in first amassing, then guarding, and finally losing it, I should realise that wealth is the root of infinite problems. Those who become distracted by their attachment to wealth have no opportunity to be liberated from the suffering of rebirths in becoming.

In that case, there are many disadvantages to having desire, such as the ones listed above, and little profit. People like that are for example like the livestock used to draw carriages who get to eat just a few mouthfuls of grass; they get to experience all kinds of hardship.

For the sake of a little recompense—which is not so rare given that even animals manage to get some—this perfect leisure and endowment so difficult to find is destroyed by the deep suffering created by previous actions.

The things of desire will certainly perish for they are impermanent, without essence, and cause me to fall into the hells, and so on.

---

[166] This paragraph could be understood to mean that the various types of people mentioned inflicted injury on themselves. However, the grammar and also Padma Karpo's commentary indicate that these are things done by others to the people. An impaling stick is a shaft of wood with a very sharp end that is forced up through a person's anus all the way through to the head. It was a capital punishment in India and also in Tibet.

Because this is not very meaningful, it comes with the constant difficulty of total weariness, whereas the attainment of buddhahood comes with difficulty that is a ten-millionth fraction of that. Thus, compared to those following the conduct of enlightenment, those having desire experience another, greater suffering yet have no enlightenment. Do not choose the latter!

If I have contemplated the sufferings of the hells, and so on, I will understand that the ruin brought on by weapons, deadly poison, precipices with their falls, burning fire, and enemies cannot compare with the harm caused by desire, and in that way having become disenchanted with desire, I shall arouse joy for isolated places where such things do not arise.

2.2.3.3.2.3.2.3 Commending isolation

Inside forests that are peaceful without disputes and without the sights and sounds of others, fortunate ones—bodhisatvas, mindful of their purpose to benefit others, tread in pleasing places such as those of excellent houses of broad flat stones that are cooled by the sandal-scented moonlight, in the forest peaceful without enemies,[167] a place fanned by gentle breezes.

They dwell for as long as they wish in empty houses, at the foot of trees and in caves, having abandoned the suffering of guarding and caring about possessions.

Not relying on anyone, they live carefree, independent and detached, having no ties to anyone, relatives or friends. Even the leader of the gods[168] has difficulty finding a life that is as contented and happy as this. What need to consider others?

---

[167] Derge edition has "sounds".

[168] "Leader of the gods" refers to the god Indra who lords over all the other gods below him in the upper reaches of the desire realm.

Having in those ways and others contemplated the good qualities of isolation, I should take joy in that. Following on from that, I shall completely pacify discursive thought and meditate on the enlightenment mind as follows.

2.2.3.3.2.3.3 The way of meditating on the enlightenment mind that is like climbing stairs

This has three parts, which are three ways of meditating on enlightenment mind: meditation on the enlightenment mind of self and other being equal; meditation on the enlightenment mind of exchanging self and other; and meditation on enlightenment mind that does not reference self and other.

2.2.3.3.2.3.3.1 Meditation on the enlightenment mind of self and other being equal

There, in that isolated place, I will completely pacify discursive thought and meditate on enlightenment mind. Of the meditations on enlightenment mind, first I will make an effort to meditate on the enlightenment mind of self and other being equal.

How are they equal? All sentient beings, myself and others, are equal in wanting happiness and not wanting suffering. Like me, all of them equally guard against suffering. Like me, all of them work at producing happiness.

Moreover, if you think, "It is not possible is it for all of them to be like me in guarding against suffering and producing happiness?" To answer with an example: my body has many parts such as the hands, but as a body to be guarded all of them are one. Likewise, migrators in their happinesses and sufferings might not be the same, but myself and all of them are one in being something that guards against suffering and produces happiness.

Although my suffering does not harm another's body, that suffering of mine is, because of clinging to a self, unbearable. Similarly, when I am cherishing another with compassion, although the other's sufferings do not come down on me, I suffer because, due to the compassion, I am clinging to a self in the other's person whereby the other's suffering becomes something difficult to bear, like when a mother sees the suffering of her only child.

Hence I should dispel the suffering of others because it is suffering, like my own suffering, and I should benefit others because they are other sentient beings, just like me.

When both myself and others are matched in wanting to be happy, what is so special about me? Why with such a small mind do I work for my happiness alone? It is not right.

When both myself and others are matched in not wanting to suffer, what is so special about me? Why do I not guard others from suffering but guard myself alone?

If I think, "Because their suffering does not harm me, I am not guarding them against it", then it is the same also for future sufferings, why guard myself against them if they are not harming me now?

If I think, "I will experience the suffering of my next life", it is a wrong-minded concept, given that it is one person who dies in a past life and another who is born in a later one. The two are different.

If I think, "When another has some sort of suffering, that other person will have to guard himself against it; I do not need to guard against it." The suffering of the foot is not also that of the hand, why then does the hand guard against the suffering of the foot?

If I say, "It might not be correct, but because of this world's style of grasping a self there is the idea of foot and hand being mutually one", then grasping at dual self and other also is not right and whatever is not right should be thoroughly rejected.

The reason for self and other not being right is as follows. What are referred to as "a single continuum" and "a collection" are in fact many instants and many things that have been exaggerated by referring to them as one thing; they are false in the same way as a rosary being called a single continuum, an army being called a collection, and so on. All sentient beings are empty of a nature, which means that there is no sufferer, no self who has the suffering, in which case who governs it? No-one does.

There being no owner who has the suffering, there is no special case among us—myself and all others—hence to dispel my suffering but not others' would not be right. It is suffering, therefore it must be removed. Then why am I so sure about dispelling my suffering and not that of others?

"Why should everyone's suffering be turned away?"[169] There is no argument over this. If it is to be turned away, then it is right that all of it should be turned away. If it should not be turned away, then I too am to suffer just like other sentient beings are to suffer.

Then, regarding the cultivation of compassion, you might ask, "Compassion brings much suffering, so why should I persistently develop it—compassion—for others?" When the suffering of migrators is considered, it is true that the person with compassion suffers much more.

However, if a compassionate person by the single suffering that would come from giving away the body for the sake of others was to eliminate many sufferings of himself and others, out of love he would accept that one suffering for himself and others. It would be

---

[169] ... given the reasoning just explained, that sufferer and suffering are empty of nature ...

suffering for that person but it would be beneficial and would produce much benefit and ease.[170]

In regard to the acceptance of one suffering in order to eliminate many sufferings, there is this. Previously, **the bodhisatva Supuṣhpachandra, although aware that a vicious king would harm him** by having him murdered, **did not try to prevent his suffering in order to prevent the suffering of the many** people belonging to the palace. Because of that greater purpose he sent the palace staff to a forest where dharma teachings were being given while he stayed behind at the palace.

When through seeing self and other to be equal **the bodhisatva's mindstream has become familiarized like that, he takes joy in pacifying the suffering of others, so will, like a swan entering a lake of lotuses, like and be delighted to enter even the hell of Unremitting Torment.**

Will the ocean of joy gained by such a bodhisatva **when he has accomplished his wishes and sentient beings have been liberated** from the bonds of karma and the afflictions, **not be most excellent?**[171] It will. When it is others that must have emancipation, what am I doing wanting it for myself? Many oceans of beings have actually set themselves on doing this, it is not an allegory or an idol. **What does wanting emancipation** for myself **achieve** for others? Note that the use here of "ocean" is not merely an example or a poetic picture.

Although the bodhisatva works for others' sakes like that, he has no conceit and does not consider himself to be wonderful. Due to having joy only in working only for others' sake, he has no hope for a full-ripening result.[172]

---

[170] Benefits means goodness that comes within the context of samsara and ease means the relative ease and happiness of enlightenment.

[171] The Derge edition has "sufficient" rather than "excellent".

[172] "Full-ripened result" meaning that he has no hopes for getting some
(continued ...)

Proceeding like that, just as I guard myself against unpleasant words however small, so I should cultivate a mind to guard others from any unpleasantness however great and I should cultivate a mind of compassion that wants them to be free of suffering.

Familiarization like that has for example led me to regard the drops of semen and blood of others[173] as "me" even though they are not things of mine. In the same way, why do I not also apprehend the bodies of others as "me". I should do so!

2.2.3.3.2.3.3.2 Meditation on the enlightenment mind of exchanging self and other

This has three parts: the way of being able to exchange self and other; the way to defeat the non-conducive side, grasping a self; the way of foremost instructions that straighten out bends in that.

2.2.3.3.2.3.3.2.1 Meditation on the enlightenment mind of exchanging self and other

It is not difficult following on from that to see my body as also that of others—the ones who I currently do not cherish.

Moreover, having made myself aware of the faults of cherishing myself and the ocean of good in cherishing others, I will completely reject all cherishing of my self and will take up the cherishing of others. That is to be cultivated in meditation.

In the same way as the hands and so forth are maintained to be limbs of the body, why are bodied beings not claimed to be limbs of migrators?

---

[172] (... continued)
good karma out of working for sentient beings sake that will ripen as a good result for him in the future.

[173] Where semen and blood coming initially from the parents combine to make my own body.

It is difficult to give rise to the exchange of self and other in the mindstream, so, even though I have not accomplished it yet, it is not necessary to let that mind die, instead, familiarization with it will result in its being accomplished in the greatest degree. In the same way as familiarization with this body that does not have a self gives rise to a mind thinking, "It is myself", why would familiarization with other sentient beings not give rise to a mind that thinks, "They are myself?"

When doing that sort of familiarization, even though I am working for the sake of others, I should not be thinking that I am wonderful nor having conceit arise. It is similar to feeding myself then not having hope for something in return.

Therefore, just as I guard myself from unpleasant words however small, so I will familiarize myself with a mind that guards migrators and a mind that has compassion for them.

Therefore, guardian Avalokiteshvara, lord of great compassion, has even blessed his name in order to dispel fears of being amongst migrators[174]. He spoke like this, "May anyone who hears my name be freed of the fear which is the anxiety of being in that group of people" and so on.

I might think, "Exchanging self and other is a greater good quality, but the exchange is extremely difficult to do". However, I should not turn away from it because it is difficult. This is so given that, because of the power of familiarity, I could become unhappy later upon hearing that someone whose name was previously frightening to hear was not around. It does happen and because of that self and other can be exchanged.

---

[174] "Amongst migrators means being in cyclic existence.

Therefore, someone who wants quickly to protect himself and others should carry out this holy secret, the exchange of self and other.

2.2.3.3.2.3.3.2.2 The way to defeat the non-conducive side, grasping a self

The non-conducive side to carrying that out is attachment to my body, so that has to be turned away. How is that done? Because of attachment to my body there is fear of smaller things such as the pain of being pricked by a thorn, so who would not be hostile towards, as one's enemy, **this body that** is the basis for or **gives rise to great fear**? It is right that anyone would!

Wanting a means to cure the body's distress of hunger and thirst, and so on, I might kill birds, fish, and gentle creatures, and so on and lie in wait at the sides of roads in order to ambush travellers.

If for the sake of profit and respect I were to kill even my father and mother or steal the property of the Three Jewels, I would burn in the hell of Unremitting Torment. In that case, what wise person would worship this body by desiring and guarding it? It would not be right to do so. Who would not regard it as an enemy and who would not denigrate it too? It would be right to do.

"If I give it away to others, what will be left for my use?" A mind that thinks of my own sake like that is going the way of the malicious spirits. "If I use it for my own purposes, what will be left for me to give?" A mind that thinks of the other's sake is taking the approach of the gods.

If I harm others for myself, for my own happiness, I will end up tormented by suffering in the hells, and so on, but if I harm myself for others, I shall gain everything that is excellent.

Wanting for the higher levels I will not get them but will end me up in the bad migrations, ugly and deeply stupid. If I shift that attitude to others, and want the higher levels for them, in future I shall obtain an honoured place in the happy migrations.

If I use others and have them work for my own purposes, later on I will experience being a servant to them, will carry loads for them, and so on. If use myself for others' purposes, later on I will experience being a lord over others.

The reason for this is that, however much happiness there is in the world all of it comes from wanting others to be happy and however much suffering there is in the world all of it comes from wanting myself to be happy.

What need is there to explain it further? The childish, ordinary beings, act for their own sake and the lords among capable ones[175] work exclusively for others' sakes. Look at the difference between the two and understand it!

That being the case, if I do not genuinely exchange, like trading one for the other, my happiness for others' suffering, ultimately I will not accomplish buddhahood and temporarily even in samsara will have no happiness.

As far as working for my own sake goes, put aside the absence of happiness of the next world that comes from it—between my servants not working and my masters not paying me a wage for my service, the aims of this life will not be accomplished in this life either.

Similarly, confused ordinary beings completely cast aside the happy situations they could have gained as the result of having made a perfect set of causes for the production of happiness seen in this life and happiness not seen until a future one, and, through the cause of having made suffering for others, take on unending suffering.

---

[175] See the glossary.

That being so, if all of however much injury, and fear and suffering exists in the worlds arises from its root, grasping a self, then what use is that great malicious spirit of grasping a self to me?

If I do not completely let go of my own such self, I will not have let go of grasping a self and if I have not, I will not be able to abandon suffering, in the same way as I will not be able to avoid being burnt if I do not let go of a fire that I am holding.

Having seen that, then in order to alleviate my own harms and pacify the sufferings of others, I shall give myself over to others and hold them as I do my self.[176]

Having in that way already given myself over to sentient beings in general, henceforth I must be certain of the mind that thinks, "I am governed by others"! Now, except for the sake of all sentient beings, you mind must not think of anything else.

And, it is not correct to do anything for my own sake using these eyes, and so on that are now governed by the other. Hence, it is not correct to do anything with these faculties of the eyes, and so on that have been given over to sentient beings that would be contrary to their sakes. Looking at another with angry eyes, and so on must be stopped.

Thus, sentient beings, not me, should be my principal concern. Anything I see on my body that would be useful I will take from my body then use for the benefit of others!

2.2.3.3.2.3.3.2.3 The way of foremost instructions that straighten out bends in that

This has three parts: straightening out bends; one's own fault of distraction; and hiding my good qualities.

---

[176] Meaning "see them as myself and cherish them accordingly".

2.2.3.3.2.3.3.2.3.1 Straightening out bends[177]

Ancillary to setting those lesser than myself and the others—those equal to myself and those better than myself—as myself and myself as the other,[178] and using a mind that is without the conceptual thought of a self in myself, I should cultivate envy towards those better, competitiveness with those equal, and pride in view of those who are lesser.

How is that done for envy? You point your index finger at your own physical form, then have the following conversation.[179]

This one is honoured by the world but from the perspective of sentient beings I am not. I have not acquired material things like this one has and this one is praised by everyone, whereas I am deprecated. This one is happy, whereas I suffer.

I do all the work while this one sits about at ease. This one is renowned as greater in the world because of his good qualities, whereas I am reputed to be inferior, with no good qualities at all.

What is gained from this talk of no good qualities? We all possess good qualities! Compared to some this one is inferior, that is how it is, so I should not become timid and compared to some I am superior, that also is how it is, so we should not be haughty.

---

[177] Straightening out bends is explained at the very end of this section.

[178] In other words, you put yourself in the other's shoes and the others in your shoes.

[179] In this section, self has been changed to other. Therefore, when referring to what would be I before the change, the words "this one" are used. And, to refer to what is now oneself, the wording "I" followed by "sentient being" is used. In this case, it means we or us because it is now the side of what was other.

The degeneration of my discipline, views, and so on happens because of the force of the suddenly-occurring afflictions, it is not something I have control over, so it is not right to berate me when they happen. You assert that you have enlightenment mind, thus you are someone with compassion and if so, **you must cure me** and sentient beings from that **degeneration to the best of your abilities and if it causes harm, I must be willing to accept that as well.**

However, if I and these sentient beings **cannot be cured by him** and he provides no help, "Why does he berate me and sentient beings?"

What use then are his good qualities—which are transient ordinary good qualities—to me and sentient beings? **This one has the** nature type **of good quality, the buddha essence, that I and sentient beings have yet has**[180] **no compassion for migrators who are caught in the cruel mouth of the bad migrations. This one who outwardly displays conceit over his good qualities wants to join ranks with the experts** who are expert in all the particulars of myself and sentient beings, but his mind is not up to it.

---

[180] This sentence in the Derge edition reads like this: "This one has the so-called 'good quality', of having a self". The idea is that the person who has been shown in the preceding verses to have good qualities has proved himself to have only transient, worldly good qualities that have so far been useless. At this point I and sentient beings can either say, "His good qualities are of no use to me and sentient beings, being no more than the negative quality of having a self" or "We are just as good as him, because all of us have the good quality of the buddha essence, the tathāgatagarbha". From there it goes on to say that, even though this one is proud of what are no more than worldly qualities, he wants to be included with those who really are expert spiritually speaking and who have the good qualities of enlightenment. The text leaves the reader with the feeling of "Wow! The arrogance!" which is mentioned as his "conceit". Pride is what this and the last several paragraphs have been about and that has been brought to a head here.

Now, cultivating competitiveness in view of those who are equal.

In order to make myself and sentient beings better than this one who, from the perspective of material acquisitions and honour, and so on, is regarded as equal with me, I certainly will amass material gains and honour for myself, even if it means taking them away from this one by verbal dispute.

I shall by all means make my and sentient beings' good qualities evident to the whole world and furthermore shall not let anyone hear of this one's good qualities, whatever they are.

And for my and sentient beings' faults too, I will hide them and be worshipped but this one will not be worshipped for that is appropriate. In the coming days I and sentient beings will abundantly obtain material gains and will be honoured, but this one will not.

I and sentient beings shall make this one appear horrid then watch for a long time with pleasure as he is made into a laughing stock of all migrators, someone whom they revile back and forth.

Now, cultivating pride in relation to those who are lesser.

It is indeed well known that, "This afflicted one is attempting to compete with me and sentient beings", but how could this one be equal to me and sentient beings in hearing, contemplating, and meditating prajñā or in bodily appearance, family line,[181] or wealth? He could not!

Upon hearing of my and sentient beings' good qualities that have become in that way well-known to all as superior, I shall be thrilled with joy, my body hairs standing on end.

---

[181] In Śhāntideva's time in India caste was all-important. It is equivalent in our context to family line.

Even if this one has some possessions, if he is working for me, I shall give him just enough to live on and take any extra by force.

I and sentient beings will spoil his happiness and perpetually bring him harm, for in samsara for all of hundreds of lives he has harmed me and sentient beings.

Those verses are not only about changing self and other intellectually. Their meaning has to take effect which is done by cultivating it with by meditation. The branches of a willow tree are exceptionally flexible and when one is straightened out, it immediately goes back to its former, bent-over state. Similarly, when both self and other are strongly bent in the direction of self, the antidote to that is to meditate on other and self and on self and other.

2.2.3.3.2.3.3.2.3.2 One's own fault of distraction

In the section below, the conventions of one's own terms and others' terms are explained.

You mind, while wanting to act for your own sake have seen countless aeons pass by, but the great weariness involved has meant that you have accomplished nothing but suffering.

Thus, no longer proceeding like that, from this point on I certainly shall cast aside my own sake then fully engage in working for the sake of others! The command of the Capable One that when others' sakes are worked for great good qualities will be gained is not deceptive, so by following it I shall directly see its good qualities in the future.

If in the past you had done this sort of act that is concerned with the other's sake, then just by that this situation of yours of not having gained the perfect happiness that comes with the rank of a buddha could not possibly have come about.

Therefore, just as you, mind, have come to grasp an "I" in these drops of semen and blood of others, likewise you shall also familiarize yourself with others!

Having made a grand concept about others that is an inner deception, I will steal away any good quality that appears on my body and then you must live benefiting others!

"I am happy, others are sad. I am high, others are low. I benefit myself, not others", why am I not envious of myself?

In terms of intending and connecting: I will separate myself from my own happiness and connect myself with taking on the sufferings of others. Asking, "At this point now, what exactly am I doing?", I must examine myself for faults. That is needed in order to produce a mind that identifies faults then abandons them. Moreover, the *Compendium of the Vehicles* says,

> If someone knows his wrongs as wrongs,
> He will at some point part ways with them.
> A proud person who holds his wrongs as
> Good qualities will not part ways with them.

And the *Mirror of Charm* presents a similar view.

Although others do wrong, I will transform the wrongs saying, "I will take them on", into faults of my own! Although I do even a small wrong, standing before many people I will totally lay it aside!

2.2.3.3.2.3.3.2.3.3 Hiding my good qualities

By describing another's renown in the best of terms—regarding his excellent discipline, amount of teachings heard, and so on—I will make it outshine my own renown! Like the lowest of servants, I will employ myself for the sake of all sentient beings!

Like the tailor who saved a leper-woman from a river, I should not praise this naturally fault-ridden self for some little transient good quality it may have for that would not be right. No matter which good qualities this self has, not letting even a few people know, I shall hide them!

In short, may the harm that I have done to others for my own sake from now on descend upon me for sentient beings' sakes!

I should not become aggressive and overbearing but should have the manners of a new bride—bashful and timid, and restrained in both body and speech.

You mind are to remain in that sort of conduct and not behave as you did before. If you stay within that mode of conduct, you will be governed by the antidotes, but if you go outside it, that will be your destruction.

However, even though you mind have been advised like that, if you do not act to train yourself in that way, since all wrongs will depend on you, the effect will be that they will end up in your destruction in particular.

Mind, that previous time when you could ruin me is another time; now that I see you and where you go—actually mind goes nowhere—I shall completely destroy your haughtiness.

I reject you, mind that thinks, "Still, I have my own sake to take care of"! I have traded you to others—who are the antidote—so do not be downhearted but offer them all your strength.

If having lost heedfulness I do not give you over to sentient beings, it is certain that you will give me over to the guards of the hells.

Up till now you have given me over like that many times and I have suffered long. Now, recalling all my grudges that have come from your doing that, I will defeat you, the mind that thinks of its own sake.

If you want joy for me, it will not happen by making me joyful in relation to my own sake. If I want to be guarded, it will happen through constantly guarding others.

The more I take enormous care of this body, the more I fall into a state of extreme fragility, unable to tolerate anything.

For falls like that, if nothing on earth can satisfy the desires, who could fulfil them? No-one could!

Those desires give rise to afflictions that come with the desires not being accomplished and also to a dissatisfied mind. However, by not being attached to any desired thing I end up not depending on anything at all and because of that will never know the exhaustion of an excellent accumulation of desired things. I will be like an undemanding pauper.

Therefore, I shall never allow an opportunity for the desires of the body to increase and not grasping at attractive things will be the finest of all things. The *Letter to a Friend* says,

> Amongst all of the things of wealth, a satisfied mind is
> The most supreme, the teacher of gods and men has said.

In the end, my body will turn to dust and, unable to move itself, will be moved by others with a mind[182]. This unclean form of thirty-six constituents is unbearable. Why do I grasp a self in it?

Whether it lives or whether it dies, what use is this machine of a body to me? What difference is there between this body and clods of earth, stones, and so on? Is it better or worse than them? Oh my! Why do I not dispel the pride that comes with thinking, "There is an I in this!"

---

[182] Others with a mind means pall-bearers ...

Concerns for the body have led me to an accumulation of meaningless suffering, then produced attachment and anger towards it, but what use is this thing that is equivalent to a lump of wood?

"How is the body equivalent to being wood?" Whether I am taking care of my body as I am now that it is alive or whether it is being eaten by vultures, and so on, it has no attachment to the past and no hatred coming—that is how. Why then do I become attached to it?

When someone belittles it there could be anger, when someone praises it there could be pleasure, but if they—the belittling and praise—are not recognized by the body, all the continual cherishing that I do for it does nothing but wear me out.

You say, "I want this body to be happy for it and I are friends who like each other", but you have to wonder, since all beings want their own body to be happy, why do I not find joy in theirs?

Therefore, I shall without attachment give up this body in order to benefit migrators. In that case, though it may have many wrongs connected with it, I will look after it for others' sakes while experiencing the results of my previous actions.

The childish behaviour that has gone before has been enough! Now I shall follow along after the experts—the buddhas, and so on—and having recalled the talk about heedfulness, shall turn back sleep and mental dullness.

Like the compassionate Sons of the Conquerors, I shall bear what is right to do, for if I do not exert myself single-mindedly day and night, when will my suffering come to an end? This is saying, "How will I *arrive* at the *end*, the other shore, the doing of which is the meaning of paramita?

2.2.3.3.2.3.3.3 Meditation on the enlightenment mind that does not reference self and other

Therefore, in order to dispel the obscurations I shall withdraw my mind from mistaken ways and constantly place it in equipoise upon the perfect object.

Therefore, in order to dispel the obscurations, the self is negated and therefore not referenced. Thereby and after that, "other" is sent away and therefore not referenced. Through that the mistaken referencing of a self that was going on before is abandoned by a path on which there is no abandonment to be done and no use of an antidote.

That way I shall withdraw the mind from its mistaken ways and, the resulting not referencing of any grasped-grasping at all will be the true or authentic referencing. By not wavering from it, the authentic is viewed and by that there is continuous placement in equipoise on the authentic. This is because of what Guardian Maitreya said,

> In this there is nothing at all to remove and
> There is not the slightest to be added.
> The authentic views the authentic itself.
> When the authentic is seen, that is complete liberation.

That was the eighth chapter of *Entering the Conduct of a Bodhisatva*, called "meditative concentration".

CHAPTER NINE

Prajna

2.2.3.3.3 The chapter on prajñā explains the higher training of prajñā

This has three parts: the style of teaching, that all of the preceding branches were taught for the sake of prajñā; the prajñā to be generated is shown using the two truths; and the differences between the rational minds that determine the two truths are explained.

2.2.3.3.3.1 The style of teaching, that all of the preceding branches were taught for the sake of prajñā

Because all of those branches—generosity, discipline, patience, perseverance, and meditative concentration—were taught by the Capable One for the sake of prajñā ... In regard to that, *The Commentary Ascertaining the Intent of the Sutras* says,

> When a bodhisatva has no concern for body and possessions, he will take on genuine discipline. When he is keeping the disciplines, he will start to possess patience. When he has gained patience, he will undertake perseverance. When he has undertaken perseverance, he will arrive at the accomplishment of meditative concentration. When he has accomplished meditative concentration, he will go on to gain beyond-worldly prajñā.

And *The Inconceivable Secret* indicates the way in which they become branches when it says,

Shāntimati! Furthermore, the bodhisatva being expert in method, no matter which meditative concentrations he cultivates every one of them will be cultivated in order to entirely complete, accomplish, and increase the Prajñāparamita ...

And *The Condensed* says,

> For generosity, the preliminary to generosity is prajñā ...

And the *Middle-Length Mother* says,

> Kaushika, in that way these five paramitas are like blind people. If there is no Prajñāparamita, they are without a guide, so are not able to make a path to enlightenment either, and if that is the case, how could they see their way to go to the city of the knowledge of all superficies?

That is what makes all of generosity and the others into paramita, so it also has to be defined as the preliminary for all paramitas.

Continuing on ... those wanting to quell the sufferings will develop prajñā. *The Condensed* says,

> By prajñā the nature of phenomena is entirely known and then
> One truly departs from the three realms in their entirety.

And the *Treasury of Abhidharma* says,

> Without utterly distinguishing phenomena there is
> No way to thoroughly quell the afflictions ...

2.2.3.3.3.2 The prajñā to be generated is shown using the two truths

Truth is twofold—Fiction and Superior Fact. It is said that Superior Fact is not the domain of rational mind and rational mind is the

Fictional[183]. Fiction is that which obscures the fact of the authentic and Superior Fact is the fact[184] sought after as the superior or holy fact. The first of the two is to have entered a state marred by delusion, but from the perspective of mere convention that state of delusion is not confused, so the fiction is defined as being true. *Entering the Middle Way* says,

> The nature of delusion is that it obscures, therefore it is fictional, and
> What is contrived by it appears to be true,
> Thus the Capable One called it "fictional truth".

The Sutra that Shows Fiction and Superior Fact says,

> Son of the Gods, if for superior fact, the superior fact truth became the domain of ordinary body, speech, and mind, it would no longer be counted as superior fact, but would be the fictional truth itself.
>
> Son of the Gods, the superior fact truth is beyond all conventions, is truly not born and not ceasing, and is free of that to be expressed and expressor of it and of known and knower. For as long as it is, in the all-knowing wisdom that has the excellence of all superficies, beyond an object, it is the superior fact truth.

It is not possible to show it, though if it is not shown, it will not be possible to comprehend it. Hence the buddhas, being expert in method, make it understood through reliance on the fictional; saying, "Superior fact is like this", they show it using over-statement.

Going further, *The King of Samadhis Sutra* says,

> For phenomena that are without letters

---

[183] The Buddha gave at least one teaching in which he declared the two truths and how they are to be understood.

[184] Fact in "superior fact" means a fact for the mind.

What listener would have what shown?
The fact heard and shown is how
Overstatement gets at that which is without letters.

And Jetsun Milarepa said,

> The full realization of the authentic fact
> Does not belong to someone stupid like me.
> As with a mute or young woman's bliss,
> A true complete buddha can only
> Illustrate it and except for that
> Is not able to show it.

That being so, Nāgārjuna said,

> Without relying on conventions
> The superior of facts will not be understood.

And having seen the relationship between method and what comes from method as expressed in those quotes, this is the assertion of two truths.

Going further, that superior fact is defined through overstatement, but the *Root Prajñā* shows it using negation like this,

> Peace not known from someone else,
> Not elaborated using elaborations,
> Without conceptual thought, not a differenced fact,[185]
> That is the character of just-that-ness.

Chandrakirti says,

> The falling hairs caused by vitreous floaters[186] and similar
>   things
> Are mistaken entities come from conceptual designation and

---

[185] A differenced fact is something that is thought to be other, that is different from the observer. The term implies duality. Conceptual thought only operates with differenced facts.

[186] For floaters, see the glossary.

Then there is what is seen when the eyes have been corrected.
That is how the situation here should be understood!

Chandrakirti shows it using words of negation, but not non-affirming negation[187]. How does he do that? He first points out that "a person who has vitreous floaters in his eyes has falling hairs appearing in the space before him". He goes on to say that by correcting his eyes then looking again, he will not see the falling hairs anywhere. Then, meaning that his concepts of existence have been abandoned, not the slightest amount of falling hairs will exist for him.

Going further with that, in regard to the concepts of existence, negation is a word that conveys working industriously, whereas in superior fact no negating and no establishing is done. In line with that, the childish conceive of the skandhas, dhatus, and ayatanas as existing, so they are given the task of "freeing themselves from existence and non-existence using negation to do it". It is expressed like that, but the superior fact is not the domain of rational mind, so how could it be related to negation or establishment?

One lot asserts that the view of the Madhyamaka is that everything exists in the fictional and nothing at all exists in superior fact, but for us that is not acceptable. "Not existing in superior fact, existing in fiction" means that the fictional is these things themselves, hence "they appear yet are not established, so are like illusions" is how it is posited. For that reason when there is one rational mind that is positer and posited, that rational mind is said to be the fictional. When a seen object is seen by that rational mind, both aspects—seen and seer—are a fiction. A seen object of the noble ones dwelling on the levels is not seen by a seer, and just that is defined as seeing superior fact for a moment. It happens because the obscuring veil of fiction is removed.

That sort of thing also appears in the *Condensed* which says,

---

[187] Nāgārjuna shows it using a non-affirming negation and Chandrakirti through an affirming negation.

> The childish describe it with the words "seeing space".
> The meaning of "how could space be seen?" has to be examined!
> The seeing of dharmas like that was also taught by the tathāgata.
> The seeing of it cannot be illustrated with another example.

If in regard to that quote you think,[188] "That to be seen that cannot be illustrated by another example is the emptiness of having let go of grasped-grasping", then that is even worse than grasping it as a thing; *The Sutra Petitioned by Kaśhyāpa* says,

> The view of a person is a mountain of a view, but a very
> proud person's view of emptiness exceeds even that; that view
> is not how it is.

And the *Root Prajñā* explains,

> If they go wrong and view emptiness,
> Those of little prajñā will be ruined.

If this is distilled down, the definition that we consider to be acceptable is this: "Superior fact is not the domain of rational mind. Rational mind conceives of things saying, 'It is this, it is not this', yet wanting to assess it as space is as ridiculous as trying to measure space. For us, there is no position to proclaim.[189]"

2.2.3.3.3.3 The differences between the rational minds that determine the two truths are explained

This has three parts: the way that the understanding of the two truths progresses in a sequence of lower and higher; in general, objections of

---

[188] "Think" here carries the implication of being sure that one's conceptual understanding of emptiness is correct.

[189] The idea of having no position to proclaim is the final understanding of the Madhyamaka or Middle Way.

the Sautrantikas regarding the explanation of phenomena being illusion-like and replies; and in particular, objections of the Chittamatrins regarding the explanation of mind being without truth and replies.

2.2.3.3.3.3.1 The way that the understandings of the two truths progress in a sequence of lower and higher

Regarding that, the world is seen to consist of two types: the yogins who are involved with the tenets of the buddhas and the commoners of the world who are not.[190]

Others say that this refers to those who do not develop their rational mind's view using those tenets and those who do, which is a division into the outsider Tīrthikas and the Buddhists. However, Chandrakirti said,

> The Tīrthikas, propelled by the sleep of not knowing,
> Have their way of designating an atman and
> Designating illusions, mirages, and so on,
> But the world does not have those approaches.

He is saying that compared to the Tīrthikas' view, the correct view of worldly beings is superior and that the worldly beings are of two types, the worldly ones possessing that superior view and the yogins who have gone higher than them. His approach in which only Buddhists are posited is a good way to do it.[191]

---

[190] "Commoners" here translates a Sanskrit word that, in this context, has the sense of "all the others besides the yogins, the ordinary people of the world".

[191] This section is meant to clarify the two types of person who have the fictional and superior factual views. There are both Buddhist and non-Buddhist yogins. In the end, the non-Buddhists, who Padma Karpo exemplifies using the Tīrthikas, do not meet superior factual truth because of their various mistaken understandings, which means that "yogins" can be understood to mean Buddhist yogins alone.

The world of commoners is harmed by the yogins' world and amongst the yogins also, those of less refined view are harmed by those who are successively higher with their more refined rational minds. The commoners are the ones who proclaim a correct view amongst the worldly and it is their view that is harmed by the sight of the yogins who see that phenomena are like illusions. The word order of "the world of commoners is harmed by the yogins' world" differs in various editions of the text, but it makes no difference; the meaning of "the world of commoners is harmed by the yogins' world" is that the fictional aspect of the yogins' world harms the world of the commoners. And similarly for the yogins, the successively more refined rational minds of those who are successively higher harm those who are lower than them; the Sautrantikas harm the Vaibhāshikas, the Chittamatrins harm the Sautrantikas, and the Madhyamikas harm the Chittamatrins.[192]

Note that the word "harm" used in logical argument does not mean harm in the usual sense. "Harm" in this context means that someone whose view is higher because it is a more refined understanding is advocating a position that is not flawed compared to the position of someone whose view is lower.

How is it that the yogins harm the worldly ones? **When both worldly ones and yogins are using the examples**—of an illusion, mirage, gandharvas' city, and so on—**that go with their assertion in common that phenomena lack a nature but are not analysing for the purpose of determining the superior fact, fruition**, then the basis of each one's analysis is the fictional. In regard to that, **the worldly ones are seeing**

---

[192] These are the names of the followers of the four main philosophical schools of the Buddhists. The Vaibhāshika are the followers of the Vaibhāsha school, meaning the Particularists. The Sautrantika are the followers of the Sautranta or Sutra school. The Chittamatrins are the followers of the Chittamatra or Mind Only school. The Madhyamikas are the followers of the Madhyamaka or Middle Way school. The Sanskrit names of the schools will be used throughout. Śhāntideva is a Madhyamika or follower of the Madhyamaka, the Middle Way.

visual forms and the other sense objects as **substantial things and moreover conceiving of them as real**. The yogins on the other hand see that those things are without essence, which they see is illustrated using the example of being illusion-like. Because of that **the worldly ones are not seeing them in the way that the yogins do, as illusion-like. Thus the worldly ones and yogins are not in accord, so have a dispute over this**. The dispute comes down to this: the worldly ones declare "Visual forms and so on are true", whereas the yogins declare, "No, they are not true".

The disputes that happen internally amongst yogins of successively higher realization has already been explained elsewhere.[193]

2.2.3.3.3.3.2 In general, objections of the Sautrantikas regarding the explanation of phenomena being illusion-like and replies

How do the worldly ones and the followers of the Lesser Vehicle, such as the Sautrantikas, object?[194] They say, "If all phenomena are not, as with the horses and oxen of illusion, established in fact, it contradicts that **visual forms and so on are established**[195] **by direct perception.**" We reply, "The position you have just now declared will next be overcome using valid cognition, then we will successively overcome your claims of contradiction of scripture and your consequences of

---

[193] This is referring to the presentations of the four main Buddhist schools of philosophy in which the views of the higher ones invalidate the views of the lower ones—the Sautranta school invalidates the arguments of the Vaibhāṣha school, and so on.

[194] This section contains a refutation of objections concerning fictional truths. Following the sense of Shantideva's text, this is the worldly ones who are objecting to the yogins. However, the two lowest of the four Buddhist philosophical schools, the Vaibhāṣha and Sautranta, have been included with the worldly ones because they assert, like the worldly ones, that phenomena are truly established, not illusory.

[195] ... as being true or are proved to be true ...

worship of the conqueror being meaningless, not being conceived, no virtue and evil, and enlightenment conduct being meaningless."

They say, "Well yes, but both Śhrāvaka sections[196] say that,

> Compound phenomena are viewed as being like
> Stars, vitreous floaters, votive lamps,
> Illusions, dew drops, water bubbles,
> Dreams, lightning, and clouds."

If they are thinking that since we both accept that compounds are illusion-like it makes no sense to argue over it, they must consider this. Those examples are about visual forms and the other sense objects that, after existing in superior fact for an instant, become non-existent outside of that. Thus, the *Complete Commentary*[197] says,

> Substantial things arisen before, that have then become non-existent,
> Are said to be "impermanent".

In other words, the examples given in what they cited just above were set out due to having the common attribute of existing only for a short while. But we are not talking about impermanence here, we are talking about something that exists for its own period—call it an instant—of time and which, in terms of its style of existence, is explained to be "illusion-like". Thus their talk of impermanence does not agree with what is being presented here, so has to be disputed.

They said at the start of this section that "visual forms, and so on are established by direct perception" and the teaching which is relevant to that is that visual forms and other sensory appearances come into appearance in a sequence of moments and are established by direct

---

[196] Of the four main Buddhist philosophical schools, the first two are the schools called the Vaibhaśha and the Sautranta that are followed by śhrāvakas.

[197] Skt. Pramāṇavarttika.

perception in their first moment." We reply, "Yes, but that is establishment through renown[198]—it is the confused worldly beings establishing them through renown—not through valid cognition[199] that evaluates a sense object as being true or false. It—that validation of them using mere renown—is false the same as what is actually unclean—such as a woman's body, and so on is renowned in the world as being clean, and so on."

Again they object, "Your advocating that 'visual forms, and so on are, like illusions, not established,' contradicts the scripture in which the Buddha said, "All Brahmans! 'All' refers to the five skandhas, twelve ayatanas, and eighteen dhatus." Our reply to that objection is that for the sake of bringing worldly ones who would be scared by emptiness in to his teaching, the Guardian taught substantial things which in suchness are not momentary. At that time, he used the words "things which in suchness ...", not the words "the entityness[200] of things", thus there is no contradiction between the words we use when advocating our position and the words used in scripture. In line with that, *The Sixty Verses on Reasoning* says,

> Like the conquerors out of their understanding
> Speak of "I" and "mine"
> They likewise out of their understanding

---

[198] "Establishment by renown" means that someone in the world speaks of something being a certain way and in the end most if not all people accept it as such. It can also be called "establishment by hearsay". The problem with renown is that it is not necessarily true, even if it is true some of the time. In logic, renown is regarded as the worst of several ways to assess something as being valid or not.

[199] Skt. pramāṇa, Tib. tshad ma is rendered throughout as valid cognition.

[200] The teaching of substantial things using the terms "skandha", and so on, is a Lesser Vehicle approach to reality taught to bring people into the fold of the Buddha's teaching. The term "entityness" is only used in the Great Vehicle approach to reality, where the "entity" of any given phenomenon is emptiness and its "-ness" is its appearing superfice.

Speak of the skandhas, dhatus, and ayatanas.

If they say, "If things are not existent in superior fact, visual forms, and so on would not be established as momentary and that being so, it would contradict scripture which says, 'All compounds not remaining for a moment, how could they function?'", then we say, "In just-that-ness, those compounds are not momentary because they are without nature." They say, "Yes, but if you consider what that scripture was concerned with, it was concerned with the fictional, so it is teaching that they are momentary."

If they say, "For the fictional too, it would be contradictory for it would contradict scripture that says, 'Not seeing moments is seeing the truth'", we reply that the yogins have no fault in regard to the fictional for, in contrast to the world, their seeing of moments is that they see the fictional in actuality, so they are posited as seeing truth. Otherwise, if they did not, their perception that women are unclean would be harmed by the world. In the world's twisted apprehension, women's nature which is in fact unclean, is taken to be clean. Compared to that, when the yogin thinks, "I am seeing it just as it is", he is seeing it as unclean.

In regard to the consequence that worship of the conqueror would be meaningless, if they say, "Because the object of worship, the buddha, is like an illusion, a result of the worship would not arise and because the worship is not true, it could not be a cause for a result", then we say that merit from having made illusion-like worship to an illusory sort of conqueror is gained in the same way as with your worshipping a truly existent one.

In regard to the consequence of not being conceived, if they say, "If these sentient beings are an illusory sort of thing, how could they, after having died within the process of craving and appropriation, be reborn? The consequence is that they would not be born", we say, "It is because for as long as the conditions for it—substances and mantras[201]—are assembled, illusion will arise."[202] If they then say, "Illusions are false because they last for a short while, whereas sentient beings remain in samsara without beginning, so it is not the same", we say, "**How could sentient beings exist in truth merely because of having a longer duration?**" If they did, it would be all right to distinguish the horses and oxen of illusion that stay for one day and the horses and oxen of illusion that stay for a whole year as false and true respectively and that being so, it would not be all right to advocate that 'illusion is false'."

In regard to the consequence of virtue and evil being non-existent, if they say, " Because of the illusory not being true, it is not correct that benefit and harm done to sentient beings would result in the occurrence of virtue and evil", then we say, "**There is no mind involved in the killing, and so on of a being of illusion, hence there is no evil.**" If they say, "If a sentient being is killed, evil does occur, so this is not the same", then we say, "**For someone possessing an illusion-like mind who has done something beneficial or harmful, illusion-like merit and illusion-like evil will occur.**"

"Well then", they say, "Is it due to the difference of there being or not being mind in the two?" We reply, "**Minds of illusion never happen in those cases because the mantras, and so on**—where and so on refers to the substances used by an illusionist—**do not have the ability to create mind. The illusions that arise from a variety of conditions arise in a whole variety of ways that additionally have mind, therefore there is a difference in the amount of the conditions needed to provide the causes for the two. There is no single condition existing anywhere that has the ability to produce all such effects.**"

---

[201] Illusion happens by the use of certain substances and mantras.

[202] These are the two of the twelve links of interdependent origination that are crucial in terms of propelling the next rebirth. For appropriation, see the glossary.

In regard to the consequence of enlightenment conduct being meaningless, they object, "If this is how it is—that in superior fact all sentient beings are the nature of nirvana and that wandering in cyclic existence they occur as mere illusions in the fictional—then the buddhas also would be in cyclic existence, so what use would enlightenment conduct be given that although enlightenment has been gained, there will once again be birth in cyclic existence?" We reply, "When the continuity of the conditions for the illusion of cyclic existence—fundamental ignorance, and the rest—has not been cut, the illusion will not have been brought to an end and there will be cycling around again and again, whereas when the continuity of the conditions has been cut, birth in the fictional will not occur again." That is saying that conduct done for enlightenment will not be meaningless.

2.2.3.3.3.3.3 In particular, objections of the Chittamatrins regarding the explanation of mind being without truth and replies

This has three parts: objections of the True Aspectarians and replies; objections of the False Aspectarians and replies; and ancillary to those, the Chittamatrins refute the Madhyamika's assertion of phenomena being illusion-like.[203]

2.2.3.3.3.3.3.1 Objections of the True Aspectarians and replies

The True Aspectarians do not assert facts that are grasped such as sand and stone. They make mind into two parts—the aspect of the grasped fact and the aspect of the grasper. Then they assert the two to be truly established in superior fact and argue the point.

The Chittamatrin says, "For you, when the referencers, the confused consciousnesses do not exist, what will reference the illusions?" The

---

[203] There are a number of sub-schools of the Chittamatra or Mind Only school. Two of them are dealt with here, the ones called True Aspectarian and False Aspectarian respectively. True and False refer to the superficies of facts (objects of the senses) being regarded as true or false respectively.

Madhyamika fires back, "As a consequence, there is no referencing!" then says, "**When for you Chittamatrins elephants or other illusions do not exist, what can be referenced at that time?** As a consequence, there is no referencing, because the object to be referenced, the illusion, does not exist". The Chittamatrin states, "**If in suchness they—mind and the sensory appearances of visual form, and so on—exist as other, the aspect grasped as the seeming appearance does not exist externally, it is internal to mind itself.**" The Madhyamika replies, "**When it is illusion manifested by mind itself**, object and mind being the same substance[204], **then at that time what** object to be known **will be seen by what** rational mind that is the knower? As a consequence there will not be such seeing. If there is such seeing, it will be in relation to an object seen. If that is asserted, every migrator without exception would be blind! **The Guardian of the World himself said in** *The Descent into Lanka Sutra* that 'mind does not see mind'. It says,

> The way that a sword's own blade and
> The way that a finger's own tip
> Do not cut and do not touch themselves,
> Likewise mind does not see mind.

Hence, just as a sword's blade does not cut itself, so it is for the mind; it is not acceptable that a single, partless consciousness could have a threefold personality of object known, knower, and knowing of it."

The Chittamatrin states, "**It is like the way that** a source of illumination, such as **an oil lamp** placed in the dark **truly illuminates itself** without relying on something else. For consciousness also, because it has been produced with the personality of knowing, we claim that it is 'self-knowing' that does not rely on some other knower." The Madhyamika refutes that example saying that **the oil lamp will not illuminate itself by itself for the reason that beforehand it was not obscured by darkness.**

---

[204] Tib. rdzas gcig. "Same substance" is a term from Indian logic meaning that two or more items have the same entity.

In regard to that the Chittamatrin states, "There is no fault in what we say! **There is the blue colour like that of a crystal which exists in relation to something else and the blueness of an Utpala lotus which does not exist in relation to something else**[205], likewise some things in a dark room **are illuminated in reliance upon something else and some other things** such as an oil lamp being illuminated **are seen even without reliance on something else.**" The Madhyamika replies, "**If it—the Utpala—is not a blueness** of its own causes and conditions, **then it has not made itself blue by itself,** so its being blue also happens in reliance on causes and conditions."

Saying that "**the lamp is illuminating** without reliance on something else" **is about** your idea of **consciousness being known by consciousness. If we now talk about that, it is saying that** "**rational mind is what illuminates** itself by itself", **but this begs the question** "**known by what** knower?" There is no knower!

If it is known by other-knowing, your proclaimed position fails and if by self-knowing then the basis of the dispute ends. You have made a decisive proof that the consciousness is both a self-knower and an other knower!

In that way rational mind, the comprehender, does not exist and because of it *The Sutra Petitioned by Kaśhyāpa* says,

> Kaśhyāpa! The buddha has not seen, does not see, and will not see mind.

If mind is never seen by anyone, any description of it as being self-illuminating or not would, like a description of the beauty of a barren woman's daughter, be meaningless given that any description of it could never lead to certainty about it.

---

[205] This is referring firstly to a transparent crystal, such as a quartz crystal, that is dependent on something else because of assuming the colour of the light being passed through it. Then it refers to the blueness of an Utpala or blue lotus which is not dependent on something else.

CHAPTER NINE

The Chittamatrin says, "If the self-knowing that is knowing itself by itself does not exist, how will a consciousness be recalled, thinking, 'I had a consciousness like that arise in me'?" There would be the consequence that it would not be possible to recall a consciousness. The Madhyamika says, "A connection exists because remembering is the result of experience".

Self-knowing has not been established for us Madhyamikas, so memory will not be established as its result. You ask us, "Well then, how do you assert this matter?" For us, there is no self-knowing, but when something other is experienced in consciousness, there is a connection in which that consciousness is the experiencer due to which it—the experiencing consciousness—will be remembered, as with a rat's poison. A bear hibernating in the wintertime does not experience being poisoned when bitten by a rat, but, on being woken by thunder in the springtime, experiences illness and knows that it has been affected by poison.

If you, the Chittamatrin, say, "Because a mind possessing other conditions—knowledge of the future and the like and the extra-sensory perception of knowing another's mind—sees another's mind from the furthest possible distance, it is established that one's own mind which is at the closest possible distance is self-illuminating", then we say that that is not right. We say that due to the application of a consecrated eye-lotion a vase of treasure can be seen from afar, but the applied eye-lotion itself, which is close-by, will not be seen.[206]

Here, it is not how the grasped objects of the consciousnesses are known—the eyes seeing visual forms, the ears hearing sounds, the nose smelling smells, and so on—that is being negated because the arising of knowables is not something that is to be analysed. "Well" you ask, "What is being negated?" Here, it is the cause of all suffering, the

---

[206] The argument here relies on the assumption that if mind can see or perceive the future and the minds of others, and so on, then it must be possible for mind to perceive itself, that is, to be self-knowing.

great negative force of strongly clinging to substantial things, the mind conceiving substantial things as true, that is to be repelled because by doing so, all sufferings will be repelled.

2.2.3.3.3.3.3.2 Objections of the False Aspectarians and replies

You Chittamatrins say, "The other-dependent illusion-like phenomena are neither thought of as other than—different from—nor not other than—one and the same as—this wholly-established mind, so there is the consequence that no distinction can be made between mind's entity and any of its elaborations." We reply, "If they are substantial things—meaning other-dependent substantial things—how could they not be other than the mind given that they are not wholly established? In which way are they not? As a consequence they are! And if you say, "They are not other than, not different from it", then the assertion that mind is wholly-established has the consequence that they, similar to illusions, do not exist as substantial things.

The Madhyamika says, "We accept that, like an illusion is not true but its un-examined fact can be viewed, so it is for the viewer, the mind." The Chittamatrin says, "If not examined and not analysed, samsara has a nebulous basis in mind's substantial things and will perform the functions of cyclic existence, otherwise, if it is examined and analysed, mind having been cleared off, mind itself would become pure the same as space, so would not perform the functions of cyclic existence and that is referred to as 'having gone to nirvana'."

The Madhyamika replies, "How could those non-existent things of samsara because of being dependent on a substantial thing—mind—come to have the ability to perform the functions of samsara?" It would be like a rabbit dependent on a goat's head not having the ability to perform the function of goring.

And, for you, mind is an unaccompanied—meaning without grasped and grasper—singularity of superior fact, self-knowing alone. If not, there is the consequence that, when mind has been freed from the grasping—meaning both grasped and grasper—and has gone to a singularity of non-dual wisdom alone, at that time all sentient beings would have effortlessly become tathāgatas. Even if so—even if there is such a fault—in the end, what good will come from considering everything to be false aspect mind only? None will, so give up clinging to it!

2.2.3.3.3.3.3.3 Ancillary to those, the Chittamatrins refute the Madhyamika's assertion of phenomena being illusion-like

Chittamatrin: It may be that all phenomena are illusion-like and that there is transcendence of them in nirvana or in something even better. However, even if all phenomena are understood to be illusion-like and one thinks, "They are like a dream", how will afflictions be repelled given that grasping at illusion is itself a subtle form of grasping a self of phenomena? This is proved using the following example. The illusionist who has manifested a beautiful woman does not have a mind to embrace her, and so on, arise, but thinking, "She is very fine!" could have a mind of desire for her arise.

Madhyamika: The creator of the illusion sees everything about her as illusion-like, but the illusion can make him desirous like that because he still has not eliminated the latencies for becoming afflicted towards knowables nor the latencies for the obscuration of the knowable. Therefore, when he sees her as illusion-like, he grasps at the illusion because his latencies of emptiness meditation are weak.

The content of the preceding two paragraphs is spoken of in the *Sutra Petitioned by Shrīmāla* in connection with cycling through the births and transferences at death of inconceivable, un-compounded cyclic existence.

2.3 The conduct that goes with accomplishing buddhahood

This has three parts: the path of the Madhyamaka on which one goes to buddhahood; the function of the Great Vehicle in which one travels to buddhahood; and discarding arguments concerning its cause, meditation on emptiness.

2.3.1 The path of the Madhyamaka on which one goes to buddhahood

Someone who claims that phenomena are illusion-like says, "For you as well, if you grasp all phenomena as emptiness, then that too, as with viewing them as an illusion, will turn into samsara" and that is indeed true! Nevertheless, we determine them to be empty as follows. A beginner is at the level of provisional meaning and your assertion of being illusion-like applies to a buddha too, so the doubt "This does not match" is brought up for him and then, because of this weak latency of emptiness meditation he is not propelled into samsara[207]. **By starting to familiarize himself with the latencies** of absence of truth, that is, emptiness, **his latencies of** strongly clinging to **substantial things**, that is, of grasping a self in them, **will start to be eliminated and**, having examined substantial things with calm abiding and individually discriminating prajñā, he will determine that "they are nothing whatsoever". Then, by familiarization with their being "nothing whatsoever" the actual prajñā that utterly dissects phenomena is produced. Thereby, **that grasping at their being empty also will later be eliminated.** That sort of thing is also found in the sutra *Petitioned by Kaśhyāpa*, which says,

> Fire arises through rubbing two sticks,
> But by its arising, the two are burned up.
> Likewise, the faculty of prajñā is born,
> But by its birth the two are burned up.[208]

Then, when the point has been reached that "there is nothing still existing of that to be negated", the substantial things to be examined—visual forms, and so on—are not being referenced. At that time how could non-existent things free of basis that have come from

---

[207] The meaning here is that he has a latency of emptiness because of the doubt that has occurred. It is weak, but it is strong enough to start turning him away from further involvement with samsara.

[208] "The two" in the second couplet refers to the mind and all phenomena.

substantial things having been halted, given that they are not able to be referenced, be present before rational mind? They could not.

When things and non-existent things are not present before a stain-free rational mind, at that point there is no superfice that is not one of those two, so the three spheres having been thoroughly purified, **there is the utter peace of being without references.** It is like when the firewood for a fire has been consumed the fire goes out of itself.

In regard to that, moreover, at the time of the equipoise of bodhisatvas who have attained the levels, the rational mind that does the referencing does not become manifest, so the objects that would be referenced end in not appearing. However, it is not that they have ended forever, because when these bodhisatvas arise from their equipoise, the objects, appearing as mere illusion, arise again.

Then, when someone has become a buddha, the rational mind and all of the references it has put in place have been thoroughly pacified into the dhatu,[209] so there is no cause for them to continue to arise. Nāgārjuna was heard to say,

> I prostrate to the holy ones,
> The advocate complete buddhas who show
> That something that arises in interdependence is
> Without cessation, without production,
> Without nihilism, without permanence,
> Without coming, without going,
> Not different facts, not a single fact,
> The thorough pacification of elaborations, peace.

With that he was explaining interdependent arising, the trail of the Madhyamaka. And Chandrakirti said,

---

[209] "Dhatu" here is short for "dharmadhatu". It literally means "the zone in which all phenomena can come about". In the sutras, it is equivalent to the zone of emptiness which is the womb of all dharmas.

> By having incinerated all the dry firewood of knowables
> There is the peace of the conquerors' dharmakāya.
> At that point, there is no birth and no cessation;
> The mind having ceased, the kāyas are directly visible.

That being so, the object, in reference to "buddha", and the subject, knowing wisdom, are non-dual. Thus, buddha in its own appearance does not have wisdom and buddha itself having been posited as wisdom, the two or three or four and so on kāyas are its divisions. That is the actual Prajñāparamita, which is called "fruition Prajñāparamita".

If, when someone has become a buddha, there were the fictional, it would indeed be necessary for the buddha to see it, but buddhas do not see it at all, so it is not present for them. The fictional obscures what is prior to it, the authentic; it has already been defined as something that just suddenly and adventitiously happens, so it is like dreaming a dream whilst having fallen into a sleep of delusion. The circumstance here is one of waking up from the sleep of delusion, so how could those dream-like appearances possibly appear? When one has become a buddha, anything other than that is not at all possible.

2.3.2 The function of the Great Vehicle in which one travels to buddhahood

Question: "If buddhahood is like that, then nothing else but that would appear to a buddha, because of which a buddha would not enact other's sakes, would he? If he did, it would be necessary to appear to others, which contradicts what was explained before."

Answer: If you think that, then consider this. **Like wish-fulfilling gems and wish-fulfilling trees**, do not appear for others, but **completely fulfil others' wishes**, bodhisatvas, prior to becoming a buddha, act to ripen those to be tamed and when they complete the results of prayers of aspiration for them, purify a buddha-field. **Their** accomplishment of a buddha-field in that way through their **prayers of aspiration** for those to be tamed causes a conqueror's form to appear to those to be tamed.

For example, a person named "Brahmin Śhagu" once made a Garuḍa-bird pillar for worship then passed away and, even for a long time after he had passed away, if prostrations and offerings were made to it, it could alleviate poisons of nagas, and so on. Similarly, in accord with a bodhisatva's enlightenment conduct done in the past a conqueror's pillar for worship is accomplished in the present and even though the bodhisatva who created it has passed into nirvana, he is still enacting the sakes of all sentient beings.[210]

Lesser Vehicle follower: "Yes, but how would worshipping buddha who has no samsaric mind bring about a result of the worship? It would be like offering food to a cairn of stones." Madhyamika: Because it has been explained in *The Stacked Flowers of Authoritative Statement Sutra* that the merits derived from worshipping a buddha both while he is present and from worshipping his relics after he has passed into nirvana are the same. The sutra says,

> Someone who on seeing the tathāgata arhat true complete buddha develops an admiring mind and because of that admiring mind honours the buddha with material goods, clothing, food, bedding, medicines, and useful articles, and all things that bring happiness and makes offerings and praises, and someone who offers a mere seed of mustard to a stupa containing the relics of a tathāgata who has passed into nirvana are to be known as having full-ripenings that are equal—there are no special points or differences in regard to offerings made to tathāgatas.

---

[210] "Pillar for worship" in this verse in its first use means a pillar of wood that was consecrated by its creator, an ancient Indian adept, to give it certain beneficial powers. In its second use, it refers to the body of a conqueror, which is like a pillar and which has enormous beneficial powers.

Madhyamika: It is established **through scripture** that **there** is equally a result of offering to a buddha whether in fiction or suchness. For example, as with how a result accompanies a truly-existing buddha as asserted by you, by an illusion-like offering made in an illusion-like object, an illusion-like result arises.

2.3.3 Discarding arguments concerning its cause, meditation on emptiness

This has three parts: setting out the arguments; explaining the objections and replies; showing emptiness interdependent arising as the path of the Madhyamaka.

2.3.3.1 Setting out the arguments

Vaibhāshika: We Vaibhāshikas and the others like us do not tolerate the explanations of familiarization with the latencies for emptiness, and so on, that bring about purification of the three spheres. For us, the path of **seeing** on which one sees the sixteen aspects—impermanence, and so on—of **the four truths** of the noble ones and the path of meditation on which one familiarizes oneself with a steady stream of that is what will **liberate us** from the bonds of the discards of the paths of seeing and meditation through which nirvana will be gained. **What use then is there in seeing an emptiness** that is not referencing anything at all? We say, "Nothing meaningful would be accomplished by it".

2.3.3.2 Explaining the objections and replies

This has three parts: establishment by scripture; establishing the Great Vehicle as the buddha-word by scriptural citations; and showing it extensively using logic.

2.3.3.2.1 Establishment by scripture

Madhyamika: **Because a** Prajñāparamita scripture says, "Without this path of realizing emptiness, there can be no enlightenment." It says,

> Because of thinking to change the Shrāvakas and

> Because of wanting to change the Pratyekabuddhas and
> likewise the dharma kings,
> He said that unless they were tolerant of this, they would not
> be able to attain sugata-hood ...

2.3.3.2.2 Establishing the Great Vehicle as the buddha-word by scriptural citations

Vaibhāshika: "You can explain it that way, but for us the citation is not credible because **the Great Vehicle is not established** to be the Buddha-word. Rather, it was made up after the teacher had passed away by some people, for example Nāgārjuna, according to their own ideas." The Madhyamika replies: "**How can it be that your Shrāvaka scriptures are established** as the Buddha-word?" The Vaibhāshika responds, "**Because** our scriptures are established as the Buddha-word for us shrāvakas, obviously, and because that is not disputed by you Great Vehicle followers, **they are established** as the buddha-word **for both of us.**"

The Madhyamika says, "It is the case, is it not, that they were not established for you at first but, later on, due to certain circumstances, you developed trust in them?" The Vaibhāshika responds, "The teacher gave them to Kashyapa, who gave them to Ananda, who gave them to Shanavastri, who gave them to Upagupta, who gave them to Dhidhika, who gave them to Sudarshana. The Madhyamika says, "Then if you consider this carefully, it means they can be trusted to be the Buddha-word due the characteristic of lineage. **It is the same for the Great Vehicle as well**; the Bhagavat gave them to Maitreya, who gave them to Mañjugosha, who gave them to Vajrapani, and then they went to Nāgārjuna, Asanga, and so on, so there is lineage there too."

If something is true simply because two parties other than ourselves **assert** agreement about **it, there would be the consequence that the Vedas, and so on,** the scriptures of Kanāda and the others, **also would be true.**

If he says: "Our scriptures are not disputed at all, but those of the Great Vehicle are disputed by one party even as they are claimed by another party to be the Buddha-word, therefore the Great Vehicle is to be rejected", we reply, "It is like that with your scriptures too. Because your scriptures are disputed by the Tīrthikas and because some scriptures of the eighteen Buddhist sects are disputed by you and others, your scriptures should be rejected also."

2.3.3.2.3 Showing it extensively using logic

If the root of the teaching is the full monks, the full monks of superior fact taught as the four truths are in a difficult position, the difficult position of not realizing emptiness. And, if they do not realize emptiness, their minds will have referencing, so nirvana also will be a difficult position for them, that is, it will not be possible to attain.[211]

If he says, "Emptiness is not necessary for liberation happens when the afflictions have been abandoned", then we say that as a consequence, immediately an arhat has abandoned the afflictions he must be liberated from suffering.

If he says, "That is what we assert", we say the arhats have no afflictions, but they have been seen to have the suffering of the potentials of karmic actions done previously when they were ordinary beings—Maudgalyayana was beaten to death by some parivrājakas of a Hindu sect, Angulimala was burned to death, Udāyin had his throat cut, and so on."

---

[211] The "difficult position" appearing twice in this verse is a literal translation of a construction that refers to a situation that presents a great or even insurmountable difficulty. The first couplet means that the śhrāvaka monks, who do not accept emptiness, have for themselves the difficult situation of not realizing emptiness. The second couplet adds to that, saying that, because of not realizing emptiness, they also have the unsurmountable situation of not being able to attain nirvana.

He responds, "By seeing the truth fundamental ignorance is has been abandoned, so the links of dependent origination from formatives up through craving have been abandoned. Thus it is ascertained that in a subsequent birth, craving, the cause of appropriation, 'does not exist'. Therefore, later lives are not taken on, so when the aggregates of this life have ended, arhats pass into nirvana without remainder and then all of the karmic potentials will have been ended."

The Madhyamika replies: "You just now said, 'This craving does not exist' for them, but that is not acceptable. Why could they not have craving that is not an afflicted type of craving, but a total stupidity type of craving in which case there would be craving, just not an afflicted type of craving?"[212]

Generally speaking, this is because the condition of feeling brings about craving and they do have feeling. While all phenomena are being realized in non-referencing, the mind having referencing will be supported by and dwell on and so become attached to some objects[213] and because of that nirvana without remainder will not be attained.

For that reason, in a mind that is separated from the realization of emptiness, causes of movement can stop functioning for a while and then start up again, as happens with the meditative equilibrium "non-perception". Therefore, one should cultivate emptiness as the cause of enlightenment.

---

[212] Vasubhandu's *Treasury of Abhidharma* states that there can be two types of craving—one with afflictions and one without afflictions that still has total stupidity regarding objects. Śhāntideva is suggesting that śhrāvaka arhats have the latter, even if they do not have the former.

[213] *The Pañjikā* gives: "some objects" refers either to the four truths of the noble ones that are the domains of attachment or to the results of meditation on the four truths.

❋ ❋ ❋

At this point, some editions of the text have three verses included, beginning with "If you acknowledge the verbal utterances that correspond to the sutras ..." The *Pañjikā* great commentary and Vibhuti say that the three verses were added later. The Indian Acharya Vairochana says in his commentary that they were not seen in his time, therefore the Tibetan Translator Ngog did not include them in his Tibetan commentary. However, later Tibetans such as Tsang Nagpa and others did find them to be acceptable, so did include them in their Tibetan editions of the text. In this commentary they have been excluded from the text in accordance with what Translator Ngog said.[214]

❋ ❋ ❋

2.3.3.3 Showing emptiness interdependent arising as the path of the Madhyamaka

This has three parts: the way of gaining the fruition using emptiness; it is not right to fear that; and turning back the cause of fear, the self.

2.3.3.3.1 The way of gaining the fruition using emptiness

---

[214] The three verses are as follows:

If you acknowledge the verbal statements comprising the sutras as the words of the Buddha, how is it that you have no respect for the Great Vehicle which for the most part is similar to your own sutras?

If the whole is faulty because one part is not acceptable, why not consider the whole as taught by the Conqueror given that one part is similar to your sutras?

What person would not accept the teachings that leaders such as the Mahā Kashyāpa could not fathom simply because that person did not understand them?

In general, the task of staying in samsara for the sake of all those sentient beings who are suffering as a result of their stupidity of believing in a self, is accomplished by becoming liberated from the extremes of remaining in attachment, the cause of clinging, and fright the cause of fear, which are the extremes of permanence and nihilism. However, the Madhyamikas specifically define it this way: "'existence' is the extreme of permanence and 'non-existence' is the extreme of nihilism" and then say that by not conceiving of the three spheres, one will be liberated from those extremes. By remaining in that liberation from extremes the bodhisatva is not contaminated with the flaws of samsara and by arousing compassion the bodhisatva stays in samsara for the sake of others rather than entering the dhatu of peace. By those two factors, the bodhisatva passes into non-abiding nirvana. All of this is a result of emptiness.

Therefore it is not acceptable to reject such emptiness and hence, without doubting whether emptiness is the path to enlightenment or not, one must meditate on it. In regard to this the *Four Hundred* also says,

> For those of small merit
> Doubting this dharma does not arise.
> By just a little doubting
> Becoming will fall into tatters.[215]

Emptiness also is the antidote to the darkness of the obscurations of the afflictions and of the knowable, so, wanting to abandon those two obscurations and have all-knowing quickly, how could one not meditate on it, emptiness?

---

[215] The meaning here is that those of small merit—such as the Lesser Vehicle advocates with whom he has just been arguing—will not even have a doubt in regard to things being empty because they do not believe in the Great Vehicle teachings. However, someone with some merit will have faith in the teaching that phenomena are empty and that in itself will begin to reduce the mind of samsara and eventually eliminate it.

2.3.3.3.2 It is not right to fear that

The advice is given: "Grasping substantial things brings suffering as a result, so why, given that emptiness destroys the cause of suffering—grasping a self—with the result that it is what quells suffering, would one be afraid of it?"

2.3.3.3.3 Turning back the cause of fear, the self

This has three parts: an overall presentation of refuting a self in the five aggregates; specific refutations of the self done through examinations using tenets; and determining the non-self of phenomena.

2.3.3.3.3.1 An overall presentation of refuting a self in the five aggregates

If being afraid of emptiness has a cause, it is this grasping a self. If there were a self somewhere that came from grasping a self in something, then one could become afraid due to anything at all, any condition whatever it might be, but there is not a self anywhere, so who is there to be afraid?

Teeth, hair, and nails are not the self. The self is not bones and not blood. It is not nasal mucous nor phlegm, nor is it lymph or pus. The self is not fat nor sweat and the lungs and liver are not the self. The other internal organs are not the self nor is the self excrement or urine. Flesh and skin are not the self nor are warmth and the energy-winds the self. The nine orifices are not the self. Never are the six types of consciousness the self.

2.3.3.3.3.2 Specific refutations of the self done through examinations using tenets

This has three parts: refuting the Sāṃkhya's self; refuting the Naiyāya's self; and the reply to saying that if there is no self, as a consequence it would not be all right for results to be experienced nor for compassion to arise.[216]

2.3.3.3.3.2.1 Refuting the Sāṃkhya's self

Followers of Rishi Kapila state, "Consciousness of sound and so on, the personality of mind, is the self of conscious knowing. Moreover, it is permanent, all-pervasive, has qualities, attachment, and has functioning mind,[217] though when related to rational mind, it is not something having functioning mind because rational mind is material. It is not the maker of results nor the utilizer of them. Being free of something to be done, the prime substance whose nature is three equal factors of sattva, rajas, and tamas, is the doer of everything, so the self is what has the force of fruition[218]. When the self wants to course in objects, because it possesses mind and because it is pervasively free of good qualities, it is without something to be done."

The Madhyamika refutes the Sāṃkhya's self: Regarding the self, **if the consciousness that grasps sound was permanent**,[219] there would be

---

[216] A refutation of the self of both the Sāṃkhya and Naiyāya schools has already been presented in one section of chapter six. A summary of the Sāṃkhya school's views is also presented there in a footnote. The reader is advised to look at that section and the several sections in this chapter that deal with the Sāṃkhya view in order to better understand it.

[217] Tib. sems pa. This term is not the same as "sems" which is the general term for samsaric mind. "Sems pa" refers to a specific aspect of mind which is one of the mental events and which has sometimes been translated as "volition" or "mental drive", though I have translated it as "functioning mind". The term is used frequently over the next few pages.

[218] These are the Sanskrit names for the three factors of the primal substance. "Sattva" corresponds to pleasant, "rajas" to unpleasant, and "tamah" to darkness, not-knowing.

[219] ... as in the case of the Sāṃkhya's permanent self ...

the consequence of the apprehension of sound at all times[220]. If you say, "We assert that", then at that time when there is no sound knowable, what sound would be known given that there is no sound object? And if you assert that, then what characteristic would it have that would result in its being called "consciousness that is the apprehender of the object, sound"? Because of not being conscious of an object, the convention "consciousness" would not be applicable.

If you say, "Although there is no object consciousness there can be consciousness of an object", then we say that there would be the consequence that wood also could be conscious of an object, because even though it does not have consciousness of knowables, it would be conscious of objects. Thus it is certain that, "There will not be a consciousness apprehending its object unless its knowable object is within range." Thus it is proved that the apprehender of sound is impermanent.

If you say, "That sound consciousness later becomes conscious of and apprehends visual form and because the two are of one nature, when there is no sound, its consciousness will not become non-existent", then we ask, "At that time when visual form is seen, why is sound not also heard?" You say, "Because there is no sound within range." We say, "Therefore, the consciousness of it also would not exist, so sound is proved to be impermanent."

Madhyamika: How could that whose nature is to apprehend sound apprehend visual form? The consequence is that it could not apprehend it. The pervasion is that it is not all right for one part-less moment of consciousness to have two natures. If you say, "This is like one person being a son in relation to his father and a father in relation to his son, so positing one consciousness in dependence on two objects has no fault", then we say, "One person being father and son is a conceptual designation, not the actual—meaning true—situation for in superior

---

[220] ... even when sound was absent ...

fact one thing does not have two natures. Given that what you have referred to exists as a conceptual designation, you have not proved your case. The reasoning is given: **This is how it is: the individual qualities of rajas** meaning duḥkha, suffering, **tamas** or darkness meaning delusion, **and sattva** meaning happiness having combined, the primal substance is present in its own entity. All migrators have that personality, so in superior fact **are not son and not father either.**

Moreover, **if you say, "That** apprehender of visual form **is not seen by rational mind to have the nature of possessing an apprehender of sounds, but like an actor, the apprehender of sounds assumes another guise and sees", then** as a consequence, **that** grasper or apprehender of visual form **is not permanent** given that it is produced in another guise and ceases from it. **That situation of two having the nature of being oneness is an unprecedented oneness;** if I tell you "that is a new style of expression" it is to ridicule you!

If you say, "If another guise and the changing into another guise **is not the true one,** then, because that is not how it actually is, there is no fault, it is like crystal", well then, tell us the actual nature of that conscious knowing self! If you say, "**It is consciousness that operates at all times continuously", then we say, "In that case, there is the consequence that all beings would become identical** because they would be the same in having mere consciousness in common."

And, not only that, but if they become of one nature due to being the same in one respect, as a consequence **that which has a functioning mind**—meaning conscious and knowing beings—**and that without mind**—meaning the primal substance that has a nature of being without mind—**also would become of one nature because of being the same in being existent.** If that is asserted, **when all the specifics**—meaning the particulars that become differences between the two—**are up-ended in that way, what basis would there be for positing similarity? As a consequence there would be no such bases, because difference would not be possible. The pervasion: because for two things to be the same without difference there can be no similar thing.[221]

2.3.3.3.3.2.2 Refuting the Naiyāya's self[222]

Followers of the Naiyāya school assert that, "The self is: permanent; all-pervading; different for each living creature; without mind; connected with functioning mind, so having functioning mind; the support that is the cause for the qualities of happiness and so on; the doer of virtuous and un-virtuous minds; the utilizer of the resources that are the results of that; and the one that goes on to the next world."

The Madhyamika refutes the Naiyāya's self: **That without mind is moreover not a self because of its quality of being without mind, as with a piece of cloth, a vase, and so on.** The Naiyāya follower says, "Yes, but due to including the rational mind of mind **it does possess mind and because of that it is conscious** meaning that it does function as an object consciousness." The Madhyamika says, "**If so, there is the consequence that when it**—the self—due to possessing the mind of rational mind **becomes somewhat unconscious** in the circumstances of being intoxicated, in a faint, and so on, **it could perish** in the circumstances when the rational mind is included. This is because beforehand, that partial non-consciousness is produced as a consciousness knowing its fact at the time of inclusion of rational mind.

If you say, "**If the self is not subject to change** at either of the two times, **what effect would the mind** that includes the rational mind **have on that self?**", we say that the consequence is that it would have

---

[221] If two things are identical, there is no basis by which they can be said to be similar because for two things to be similar they have to be different.

[222] The Naiyāya is one of the six main Hindu schools. The name means the school of logicians. The Naiyāyikas or followers of the Naiyāya accept a self as a permanent, partless, material phenomenon within the being of an individual. This self is claimed to be able to experience objects because it is has a mind, one which is separate from it.

none because the self is changeless. In accord with that assertion of a self which has a consciousness like that which has not the slightest effect on it and which is free of activities because of its permanence, space also could be made out as a self.

2.3.3.3.3.2.3 The reply to saying that if there were no self, as a consequence it would not be all right for results to be experienced nor for compassion to arise

Rishi Kapila and others like him say, "If the self that having made karmas in this world goes on to the next world does not exist, a relationship between virtuous and non-virtuous karmas done and their results that would come from them would be not be tenable; if having done a karma the doer were to perish, then whose karma would it be? The experiencer of the result being someone else, the action done would go to waste and the result of it would not happen."

We reply that we both concur that the bases of an action and its result are different in this and a future life respectively and that the self has no bearing on this matter, hence it is meaningless to argue about this, is it not?

"The one possessing the cause—the karma—is the one who has the result of that karma and will experience it" is something that could not possibly be seen. If you say, "Well yes, but eating food that is not healthy brings on sickness, giving increases resources, and so on can be seen", those are cases where the one involved is being clung to as the same throughout, but this is not a case of being the same throughout because the one involved perishes by the moment.

Nevertheless, in dependence on the world's clinging to the belief that it is one continuum of mind that is involved with the things of both cause and effect, the Buddha taught that "the doer is the experiencer of the result" out of consideration for those to be tamed. A sutra says,

> Monks, the karmas you have done and accumulated will not ripen on such things as the external earth element and not on

water, fire, and air, but will ripen on these skandhas, dhatus, and ayatanas that you have taken up.

Thus there is no self, but it is acceptable that one continuum experiences the result; it is like a red flower comes about when stained by Gyakeg, the seed of Madu-lung-ga.[223]

If you say, "That continuum is the self, is it not?", then we say "That continuum is the continuum of mind". If you think, "Mind is the self", past mind and future mind are not the self because having ceased and not been produced respectively, they are not existent. You say, "Yes, but the mind produced now in the present is the self." We say, "If so, given that it perishes in the second moment, there is no permanent self."

For example, if the trunk of a Plantain tree, which is held to have an essence, is pulled apart layer by layer, in the end nothing, no essence at all, will be found. Similarly, if you search using attribute analysis, a truly-established self also will not be found in the mind or the aggregates.

You say, "If, when self and sentient beings have been evaluated, sentient beings do not exist, and because there is then no object of compassion, for whom will compassion be produced?" We say that it is for whoever has been imagined in the fictional by the stupid ones who have promised to work for the sake of their gaining the result, buddhahood.

You say, "If in superior fact there are no sentient beings, then who gets the result of the compassion, given that in superior fact there would be not be anyone having a fruition?" That is true. Nevertheless, there are the needs of the world of those stupid ones. Because of the world's needs, the stupid ones who see a need for the beings of

---

[223] Gyakeg is an intense red stain that is derived from the Madu-lung-ga tree.

the world to achieve **the fruition for the sake of thoroughly pacifying their sufferings are not rejected.** That agrees with what *Entering the Middle Way* says,

> The way that you assert other-powered things
> Is not how I proclaim the fictional.
> In view of the world, I have said, "because of the fruition,
>   these are said to exist although they do not exist",
> But I do not advocate that.

You say, "The promise to take sentient beings to the fruition might be a case of being stupid in regard to a self, but it would not be correct to reject it." We say that **the pride** of grasping an **I that is the cause of** samsaric **suffering** is to be rejected because it **will increase the stupidity of a self.** If you say, "There might be a need, but there is no method for getting rid of it", we say that **there is a method; meditation on the non-existence of self is the supreme one,** the supreme antidote to that.

2.3.3.3.3.3 Determining the non-self of phenomena

This has three parts: showing the first three thorough applications of mindfulness; the last one together with objections and replies; and carrying them onto traversing the path of interdependent origination, the trail left by the Madhyamaka.

2.3.3.3.3.3.1 Showing the first three thorough applications of mindfulness

This has three parts: thorough application of mindfulness of body, thorough application of mindfulness of feelings, and thorough application of mindfulness of mind.

2.3.3.3.3.3.1.1 Thorough application of mindfulness of body

This has three parts: showing that the individual parts are not the body; showing that there is not a singular body that pervades the individual parts; and stopping the confusion of taking a collection of parts to be a body, and so on.

2.3.3.3.3.3.1.1.1 Showing that the individual parts are not the body

If attribute analysed, the body is not the legs above the ankle bones and not the shanks. The thighs and waist also are not the body, nor are the abdomen or back the body. The chest and the shoulders also are not the body. The body is not the ribs, and so on nor the arms. The armpits and shoulders also are not the body. The inner organs also are not it. The head and the throat also are not the body. If not, what here in these individual parts is the body? A body is not found in them.

2.3.3.3.3.3.1.1.2 Showing that there is not a singular body that pervades the individual parts

The Sāṃkhyas and others say, "The individual parts are not the body, rather, there exists something having parts that pervades all the parts, a singular thing that enters all the parts." We say, "If you assert that this body having parts enters and resides in all of the parts, it either enters by sections or at one time. For the first, if that body having parts becomes resident in all parts in a partial way, if you were to examine to find in which particular place it is resident, you would find that it does not reside anywhere. For the second, you might think, "The pieces of the body do indeed become resident in a—an individual—piece at one time", but even then, where would that body asserted to be a singular body itself be residing? Where it was residing would not be found.[224]

---

[224] This paragraph accurately translates Padma Karpo's commentary with original verses. However, when the original verse is read without the commentary, there is only a sense of one possibility, not two possibilities, being presented. The verse without commentary reads: "If this body (the one having parts that has been asserted by the Sāṃkhya and others) is

(continued ...)

If that body having parts was in its entirety and not just partially resident in the hands and other parts—all of them as many as they are—then there would have to be as many bodies as those hands, and so on, which undermines the assertion of a singular body.

If there is no body outside or inside even after the skin outside and the flesh and blood inside have been examined, how could the hands, and so on have a body? They could not. If it—the body—does not exist when observing just the hands, and so on and does not exist somewhere other than the hands, and so on, given that it has not been observed in the places where it could be observed, how could it exist? If examined that way, it does not exist.

2.3.3.3.3.3.1.1.3 Stopping the confusion of taking a collection of parts to be a body, and so on

You say, "Therefore, this body is not the way that it appears", and we say that the body does not exist. However, stupidity in regard to the hands, and so on results in the impression of a body conceived of as a singular blob in the rational mind. It is like the shape of a cairn of stones results in a rational mind apprehending the cairn as a human.

As long as one does not come too close and for as long as the conditions for it are assembled, the body appears as a person. Similarly, for as long it exists in the hands, and so on and individually discriminating prajñā has not apprehended it, a body continues to appear in them.

If you think, "The body does not exist, but the individual parts exist", then in the same way, because the hand is a collection of fingers, and so on assembled together, what will be the hand? It is the same for the fingers because each one being a collection of segments will not

---

[224] (... continued)
resident in all the parts in a partial way, the pieces must have become resident in a piece, but even then where would that body itself be residing?"

be found, and the segments too having been separated into their own pieces will not found, and the pieces too having been separated into their own atoms are broken down, and the atoms too by separation into their directional parts of east, and so on, are not established as singular. Because the separated directions also are free of pieces, they are like space, with nothing about them established at all, so for the Madhyamaka, even the most subtle atoms do not exist.

Therefore, who of analytical mind would become attached to this dream-like form of ours that appears to confusion? When in that way there is no body, what man attached to a woman is there and what woman attached to a man is there? Likewise, with whom does one become angry? And who is stupid? None of these beings are established!

2.3.3.3.3.3.1.2 Thorough application of mindfulness of feelings

This has three parts: refutation of feelings being true; refutation of the cause of feelings, contact; and feeling and feeler not existing, they are established as being without nature.

2.3.3.3.3.3.1.2.1 Refutation of feelings being true

Like form, feeling does not withstand examination either. If **suffering feeling** actually existed, why wouldn't it obstruct the production of minds of **great enjoyment**? If it did exist in actuality, minds of enjoyment would always turn into suffering. If **happy feeling actually existed**, it would not be possible to be overcome with grief, and the like, and even if it were, **why would** the conditions for happy feelings such as **tasty foods**, and so on not bring pleasure to someone afflicted with grief, and so on?

You say, "They do exist in actuality, but **are not experienced because of being overridden by something** which is their opposite, either a happy or suffering feeling, and **which is stronger**". If so, when there is a suffering or happy feeling that does not have the property of experiencing, how could it be feeling given that it does not possess the characteristic of feeling?

You say, "At the time of a happy feeling, suffering feeling exists in a subtle form even though its gross form has been removed by the happy one, isn't that so? It is a mere feeling of enjoyment other than that gross happy one, so the gross suffering having been quelled, the subtle one has been removed."

We say that that subtle one moreover does not depart from its own class. Thus, if a condition that opposes suffering or happy feeling arises and therefore suffering or happy feeling does not arise, it means that feeling, being harmed by opposing conditions and strengthened by conducive ones, ends up being a contrivance. Thus it is established, isn't it, that feeling conceived of as true is what is called "manifest clinging"?

On account of that manifest clinging that has come from conceiving of feeling, there is its antidote, the cultivation of this attribute analysis which is the thorough placement of mindfulness of feeling. The meditative concentration and vipashyana that comes from that field of thorough examination is the food of yogins that they use to develop themselves. By eating that food, the yogin turns away all strong clinging.

2.3.3.3.3.3.1.2.2 Refutation of the cause of feelings, contact

Madhyamika: Moreover, that feeling happens when its cause, contact, occurs. It comes from the meeting of the three things of sense faculty, object, and consciousness. If that meeting is examined with logic, it does not exist, hence there is no arising of feeling due to that condition.

This is how it is: the sense faculty and the object either have an interval between them or do not. If sense faculty and object have an interval between them, where would they meet? The consequence is that meeting would not be possible; because of the intervening interval, they would be like one mountain in the east and another in the west. And if you say that **there is no interval** between them, **they**—sense faculty and object—**would be oneness** because there would not be the slightest bit of non-inclusion of the two. **In that case**, if you make that assertion, **what sense faculty would meet with what** object? The consequence is that there would be no meeting because of being one without difference. The pervasion is that meeting with one partless thing is contradictory.

You say, "There is no fault. This is partless atoms meeting with things. In that, by examining the meeting done by parts and part possessors, no rejection is entered because it is entrance at the coarse level". We say that **there is no entering of one atom into another atom because atoms do not have space that would provide the opportunity and are equal in size**; not larger or smaller, they are like two peas. If you say, "It is because there is no contradiction in their meeting **when there is no entry**," we say that one not having entered the other, as a consequence **there is no merging** with the other, and if you assert **there is no merging** with another, as a consequence **there is no meeting** of the two because of your assertion. The pervasion is that meeting is a coming together. And, if there is a partial coming together, there are parts and if there is a whole coming together, merging would be necessary.

For the partless case moreover, **how could what is called "meeting" or "assembling" be acceptable** when there are no parts? It is ascertained that, for meeting, one part is necessary. **If you have seen a mutual meeting and one which is partless** yet without contradiction, **then show it to us!**

It is not possible for consciousness, which is without body, to have a meeting because a mutual connection is what "meeting" refers to and that exists with the possession of a body and as a consequence **it also is not possible for an assembly of sense faculty, object, and consciousness because it is a non-existent thing**, because in fact there are no existent things, **as with a horse's horn**. This is similar to the way that attribute analyses of the segments of a finger, and so on were done earlier.

If in that way contact does not exist, from what would feeling arise? If it does not arise, what meaning is there to this tiring effort to accomplish pleasurable feelings and abandon suffering ones? It is meaningless.

2.3.3.3.3.3.1.2.3 Feeling and feeler not existing, they are established as being without nature

If you think, "The furthering of pleasant feelings makes no sense, but, due to not tolerating suffering, we want to abandon it", then what feeling of duḥkha would harm who—what feeler of it—given that feeler and feeling are without nature?[225]

Because of that, when there is no feeler at all and the feeling also does not exist, then, having seen this situation of all phenomena being primally pacified, why craving are you not expelled?[226]

If you say, "For Rishi Kapila, the substances of clay pots and so on exist as visible and touchable", then we say that something can be seen by the eye faculty or touched by the body faculty, but mind with its dream-like and illusion-like personality is produced simultaneously with feeling, because of which it does not see the feeling.

Feeling produced earlier is remembered by mind produced later, but when they are produced simultaneously, mind does not experience the feeling. Mind does not itself experience its own personality, feeling, which can be understood by the earlier negation of self-knowing, nor is it experienced by something else because it has already been shown that when mind's experiencing is examined in the three times, such a thing is not possible.

---

[225] This paragraph belongs at the end of the immediately preceding paragraph, but Padma Karpo puts it here to fit with the current heading.

[226] Feeling is a precursor of craving, one of the root causes of rebirth in samsara. Feeling having collapsed, craving also should collapse.

There is no existence of a feeler at all, hence feeling is not real, not established in actuality. How could this assembly which like that has no self, no owner, this phenomenon of interdependent arising, be harmed by this feeling?

2.3.3.3.3.3.1.3 Thorough application of mindfulness of mind

The mental mind and the faculty consciousnesses are shown to be without nature, which is done in two parts.

1. Mental mind is shown to be without nature. **Mental mind does not reside in the five sense faculties. It is not in the objects—visual form, and so on. It is not somewhere in between the two, either. Mind is not inside nor outside the body and even if searched for is not found anywhere else either.**

And, **the mind is not the body nor something other than the body. It is not mingled with body and its flesh; nor is it somewhere apart from the body. The mind is not established in the slightest because of which sentient beings are primally nirvana by nature.**

2. The sense-faculty consciousnesses are shown to be without nature. **If the sense consciousnesses such as the eye consciousness exist prior to their knowables**—the objects of visual form, and so on, **how could a consciousness be produced after having referenced something which is its object?** As a consequence it would not be produced, because at the time of its production, there would be no object knowable. **If consciousness and knowable arise simultaneously**, because they happen at the same time **how could the consciousness be produced after having referenced something?**

Moreover, **if the consciousnesses exist after the object knowable**, the object having ceased would be non-existent then at that point **from what referenced object would the consciousness be produced?**

2.3.3.3.3.3.2 The last one together with objections and replies

This has three parts: setting out what the last one is in a statement; stating the objection; and giving the reply.

2.3.3.3.3.3.2.1 Setting out what the last one is in a statement

What is the thorough application of mindfulness of phenomena? It is about the fact that production prior to, at the same time as, or afterwards is not accepted **in that way** just described, **because of which production for any phenomenon is not something that could be known**. It was in view of that that the conventions of the three, four, and so on doors of complete emancipation with their absence of production and absence of cessation were made.

2.3.3.3.3.3.2.2 Stating the objection

Objection: "**If it is like that**, that all phenomena are a sameness of being without production and cessation, **there would be no fictional truths that are produced and perish in which case how would there be two truths? Moreover, if fictional truths existed due to others** making phenomena into objects of their rational minds, **how could sentient beings pass into nirvana** given that it has been made into an object of rational mind?"[227]

2.3.3.3.3.3.2.3 Giving the reply

Reply: **This** talk of "passed into nirvana" is about the conceptualizing of another's mind, hence that nirvana is one that has been made into an object, it is not about one's own fictional posited by one's own rational mind. The fictional that arises due to being posited by rational

---

[227] The second sentence means the following. If the fictional did exist, it could exist due to other sentient beings making phenomena into objects of their rational minds, thereby imputing arising and perishing onto phenomena that are in fact a sameness. In that case, sentient beings in general would not be able to go to nirvana and even those who had already gone there would not be able to stay there because nirvana would have become a fictional truth due to the one or more of the others having made it into an object of their rational minds.

mind is one of that of this existing that arises, as with due to long existing there is short. Later,[228] if that exists as an ascertained phenomenon, then at that point that fictional exists; if it does not exist, it is a non-existent fictional, like a sky flower.

That being so, **both the conceptualizer** that is the exaggerating rational mind **and the** exaggeration that is the **object conceptualized** by it **are mutually dependent**—because the conceptualizer does the examination and by that examination there is placement of a concept—**just as all of** these **attribute analyses which are expressed in dependence on what is**—the **conventions that are**—**well-known** in the world, but not on superior fact because that is beyond conventions.[229]

Objection: **When an analysis is done using attribute analysis on an attribute analysis already done, at that point the** second **attribute analysis also will have to be analysed** by a third attribute analysis **because of which there would be no end to it.**[230]

Reply: It would not be without end, for **when that thing to be thoroughly examined and analysed has been attribute analysed and** determined, all references having been thoroughly quelled **no basis for the attribute analysis will exist and because** there now is **no basis for it, it will no longer be produced. That non-production** moreover **will be described as "having gone to nirvana"** and having done that, one will have gone beyond all conventions.

---

[228] ... when one has attained nirvana for oneself ...

[229] "Analysis is regarded as a more subtle form of conceptualizing, which itself can also be translated as "examination". In other words, coarser examination is shown to be mutually dependent and then the subtler form, of attribute analysis, which is being done here, is likewise mutually dependent.

[230] In other words, there would be an infinite regression.

According to them—the advocates of substantial things being true—the two of knowable and knower[231] are true, but that position is extremely difficult to maintain because there are no proofs for it and many refutations of it. If they say, "An object to be evaluated is established through the power or force of a consciousness which is a valid cognizer", then we ask what basis or proof is there for positing the existence of consciousness which is a valid cognizer? There is none.

If they say, "Yes, but consciousness is established as true through the knowable being established as true", we ask what basis and proof for the knowable existing is there? Here, nothing has become valid cognition. If they say, "We posit that both consciousness and knowable exist by way of being mutually dependent", in which case we say that both would become non-existent.

Objection: For example, if without a son there is no father because the convention of father would not apply, then from where would a son come? Just as in the absence of a son a father does not exist, likewise consciousness and knowable being mutually dependent, both of them are non-existent.

Moreover, the two are not seen to be established by way of their mutuality. They say, "For example, just as a sprout is produced from a seed coming to life and what the seed is is understood through that sprout, similarly, why for a consciousness—a result—that has been produced from a knowable—a cause—would the knowable not be understood as existing through the consciousness?" We say that the example and what it points to do not match. Understanding what a seed is through the spout is not a case of being understood by the seed itself. If a consciousness which is other than the sprout were to understand through the sign of the sprout that "this seed exists"

---

[231] Knowable and knower here refer respectively to the thing to be analysed and the analyser just discussed.

through what would the consciousness that understands that that knowable exists be understood to be existent? Self-knowing has already been negated. In the case of that being understood by another rational mind, there would be an infinite regression.

2.3.3.3.3.3.3 Carrying them onto traversing the path of interdependent origination, the trail left by the Madhyamaka

This has three parts: showing Madhyamaka by the view; entering it by meditation; and explaining how to traverse it by conduct using method and prajñā.[232]

2.3.3.3.3.3.3.1 Showing Madhyamaka by the view

This has three parts: refuting the assertion that there is production without cause; refuting the assertions of it arising from wrong causes; and explaining emptiness and interdependent arising by pointing them out.

2.3.3.3.3.3.3.1.1 Refuting the assertion that there is production without cause

The Charvakas[233] state, "All substantial things are produced in the mode of there being no reliance on a cause; if it were anything else, what would be the causes of a lotus flower, the eye of a peacock's feather, and so on?"

---

[232] Note that the presentation is being done using view, meditation, and conduct.

[233] The Charvakas are followers of an Indian school of philosophy. Amongst other things, they assert that phenomena do not arise from causes. For a complete explanation of the Charvakas, their views, and their relationship to other schools of thought, see *The Lion's Roar of the Ultimate Non-Dual Buddha Nature* by Tony Duff, ISBN 978-9937-572-79-8.

The Madhyamikas refute it: "Everyone in the world directly sees all causes. The variations in the stalks of lotus flowers, and so on, are created by variations in their causes, their seeds."

If you the Charvakas ask, "What makes the variations of cause?", we say that it is the variations in earlier causes, in other words, by the power of having planted causes earlier the corresponding results are produced and become manifest. You ask, "Why do causes have the ability to create a result?" We say that it is due to the power of earlier causes.

2.3.3.3.3.3.3.1.2 Refuting the assertions of it arising from wrong causes

This has three parts: refuting the assertions that it arises from permanent Īshvara; from permanent atoms; and from a permanent primal substance.

2.3.3.3.3.3.3.1.2.1 Refuting the assertion that it arises from permanent Īshvara

The Tīrthika Īshvara[234] is said to be like this: "The bhagavat, expert at making a variety of manifestations for migrators, sole captain of migrators, pre-eminent among the entirety of migrators, possessor of the ability to be permanently without degeneration, and knower of all. This great Īshvara does not belong to the domain of all that can be seen on this side. Having thought ahead, he makes all of the animate and inanimate. He does all production, dwelling, and perishing for the reason that if it were any other way then he, not having a mind, would not know production."

---

[234] The non-Buddhist Naiyāya and Vaisheshika schools believe the cause of everything to be the almighty god Īshvara. He is regarded as having five principal qualities: divinity, purity and being worthy of veneration, permanence, oneness, and being the creator of everything.

The Naiyāyikas and Vaisheshikas state that Īshvara is the cause of all migrators. We say, "If so, then tell us what, exactly, is this Īshvara?!" If you say, "He is the elements of earth, and the rest", then we say that it is indeed true that the elements create a result, but why tire both of us out arguing over a mere name—that is, over just giving the elements the name "Īshvara"? Nevertheless, if you think that they are of comparable meaning, they are not; earth and the others—the other elements—are manifold[235] and impermanent, are without movement[236] and mind, are not divine and are trodden upon by the feet and are unclean, thus they cannot be Īshvara himself because their characteristics do not match his.

If you say "space is Īshvara," we say that Īshvara is not space because it, being free of performing activities, is without movement. If you say, "Īshvara is the self", we say that he is not the self because that called the "self" has previously been refuted. If you are thinking, "Īshvara seen from his own side is the Inconceivable One", then we say that the Inconceivable One whose function as creator of migrators also is something that cannot be conceived of, so what use is there in describing him as such, as the creator?

Moreover, we question, "What result does he desire to create?" If you say, "a self", then we say that the three things of that self, the four elements of earth and the others, and the entity of Īshvara are permanent, aren't they? If you claim that they are, there is the contradiction that what is permanent is to be created.

If you say, "Īshvara's result is consciousness and with that is happiness and suffering[237]", we say that consciousness is produced from—in dependence on—knowables and the happiness and suffering experi-

---

[235] ... as opposed to being one.

[236] "Movement" here refers to the mobility of thoughts and so forth within mind.

[237] ... and neutral feelings ...

enced without beginning is produced from virtuous and evil **karmas**. Tell us then, what has he—the Īshvara you assert as a cause—created?! If what he has created is not observed[238] at all, then it is not correct to refer to him as "the cause of migrators". **If the cause, Īshvara, does not have a beginning, how could the result** produced by him, the formation of the world, **have a beginning?**

Moreover, why wouldn't he, a permanent cause, not be perpetually making the result, the formation of the world? As a consequence, he would be. You say, "**He, Īshvara the cause, is not reliant on anything else.** He the cause is permanent, but the creation of results is reliant on other conditions, so he is not perpetually creating results." We say that if there is nothing else—no other assembly of causes—not made by him, on what would this assembly made by him rely? As a consequence, a reliance would not be necessary.

If he is reliant, because the cause would be an assemblage of conditions, Īshvara would not be the cause. If all the causes for the creation of a result have assembled, he will be powerless to prevent a result being produced and in the absence of such an assembly will be powerless to produce.

If Īshvara himself makes a result while not desiring to do so due to the power of causes and conditions having assembled, as a consequence it—the result—would be under the control of other because Īshvara would have no control over it. And if you say that he desired to do so, to create a result, even then he would be dependent on newly-created desires. However, if he acts that way, given that such desire is something other than Īshvara, where is the activity of Īshvara?[239]

---

[238] ... as an object of consciousness ...

[239] The implication here is that such activity would not be the activity of the almighty, supreme Īshvara.

2.3.3.3.3.3.3.1.2.2 Refuting the assertion that it arises from permanent atoms

Those who advocate permanent atoms—Kapila, Charya, and others—had their assertions refuted earlier, in the section on the thorough application of mindfulness. They advocate that, "When two or more permanent atoms come together, ground, mountains, and so on arise, so those permanent atoms are the cause of the various migrators."

2.3.3.3.3.3.3.1.2.3 Refuting the assertion that it arises from a permanent primal substance

The Sāṃkhya assert what they call "the primal substance", which they also name "the nature". Moreover, they assert that it does not disintegrate so is permanent and that it is, due to a mode of transformation, the cause of migrators—meaning the cause of the animate and inanimate worlds. Then what is this primal substance? When the qualities called "sattva or happiness, rajas or suffering, and tamas or delusion" are equally present, they refer to it as "the primal substance" and when not equally present, they refer to it as "migrators."

Then they say the following: "From the nature the rational mind or the great one is produced. From that comes pride. From that comes the sixteen assemblages as follows: mouth, legs, hands, urethra, and anal passage are the five faculties of activity; ears, body, eyes, tongue, and nose are the five faculties of rational mind; for both faculties there is mental mind, making eleven; and sound, touch, visual form, taste, and smell simply as themselves makes another five.

"From those five come the five great elements. In regard to those five, their nature is exclusively that of cause. Rational mind, pride, and just the five making seven are both and the eleven faculties and the five elements are exclusively result. Beings are not both cause and result. The root nature is without change. The seven of the great one, and the rest are causes and the set of eleven is what changes. A being is not the nature, is not change."

For the refutation of that, there are five refutations concerned with: the root nature; transformations produced from it; happiness, and so on being material; happiness, and so on being permanent; and cause and effect being of the same substance. And given the consequence of matching it to itself also, there are six positions to be rejected.

For the first of the six, there is the consequence that **it would not be all right for one thing**, the primal substance they assert, **to have a personality of three natures** of sattva, rajas, and tamas. There is no equal presence of the qualities, **thus there is no primal substance, so it**—and everything that results from it—**does not exist. Likewise the qualities do not exist and, moreover, because each one of the three qualities would have three aspects the qualities do not exist in which case the existence of sounds, and so on**—the twenty-three transformations produced from them—**is very far-fetched** and should be thoroughly rejected.

The refutation of happiness, and so on being material. If you say, "Migrators are the personage of the three qualities, so clothing, and so on are of the nature of happiness", then we say that **clothes, and so on being matter without mind, they could not possibly have happiness, and so on**—meaning happiness, suffering, and neutral states.

If you say, "Clothes, and so on are not of the nature of happiness, but the **substantial things** of clothes, and so on **have the nature of being happiness, and so on's cause**", then we say, "**We have already done the attribute analysis of substantial things** such as clothes, and so on—which in this case is that they do not have parts, are not subtle atoms, and are not the personage of the three qualities either—**haven't we?**"

Furthermore, if everything illuminated is the nature of happiness, and so on, it follows that clothing, and so on are not your cause, happiness and so on, because the clothing, and so on are evident[240]. If we make that assertion, then saying, "Moreover, from your cause which is happiness, and so on there is no arising of cloth, and so on and from the cloth, and so on there is the production of happiness, and so on" shows that the result comes after the cause. And if those things—the cloth, and so on—are absent, there will be no happiness, and so on which shows the reverse that when there is no cause, a result does not arise.

The refutation of the assertion that the happiness, and so on are permanent follows. If you say, "That happiness, and so on being the personage of the three qualities are permanent, so clothing, and so on are not produced", then we say that the happiness, and so on are never observed as permanent because the qualities, and so on do not exist. The pervasion: If the illuminations of happiness, and so on perpetually exist, why are they not apprehended as the experience of happiness? There is the consequence that it would be correct for them to be so apprehended.

If you say, "If that happiness, and so on which is a co-present illumination that later on not being referenced has become subtle, like stars in the daytime sky", then how can it be coarse present as illuminated and subtle that has changed to the nature of not being illuminated too given that it is single and permanent? The pervasion is that if it is permanent, that contradicts its changing and if it is single, that contradicts it being of the natures coarse and subtle.

If you say, "There is no fault; it is not that there is the sudden existence as two, coarse and subtle, rather, having left its coarse state, it has become the subtle state", then we say in which case the coarse and subtle states would be impermanent because the coarse having left it

---

[240] The Sāṃkhya claim that sattva or happiness is one of three qualities of the primal substance and that when the three are equally present, the primal substance is a cause. Śhāntideva does not accept that.

is present as the subtle because it has come under the influence of production and destruction. Coarse and subtle being impermanent like that, **why do you likewise not assert all of the twenty-five substantial things to be impermanent?** That has to be asserted for the same reasons.

If the coarse state is not other than happiness, the coarse state which is happiness will be illuminated and thereby will be impermanent.

Refutation of the assertion that cause and effect are of the same substance contains two refutations: firstly of the non-existent not being produced and secondly of being existent but not seen. Here, three arguments made by opponents are dealt with and removed in connection with the consequence of the two being equivalent.

For the first of the three, **if you assert that "something not existent is definitely not produced at all because of being non-existent, like a sky-flower"**, which entails all substantial things existing in the nature of being able to be a cause, **then you will not assert production** later of an illumination **when the illumination** that happens in the circumstance of not illuminating **is not existent, but not doing so you are caught** at being an advocate of existence. This is because of the consequence that something else being referenced later is also being referenced earlier.

If the entity of the result is present in the cause,[241] **then someone eating food would be an eater of excrement** because by eating the cause of excrement, the excrement also would be present. If you want to wear cotton clothing, **you should use the money for the cotton clothing to purchase seeds of cotton then wear them** because the seeds would have cotton cloth present in them.

---

[241] ... which is cause and effect being of the same substance or entity ...

Refuting the assertion of existing but not being seen is as follows. If you argue that in superior fact the result exists in the cause, but the stupid people of the world do not see it, then we say it does not end with the stupid people of the world for that is the case even for others who know about suchness, such as your own Sāṃkhya leader who was conceited about his knowledge of suchness, which has the consequence that you are stupid in regard to this too.

That knowledge of the result existing in the cause exists even for the world, so tell us the reason why is it not seen by the world! If you argue, "It is because the rational minds of worldly people do not have valid cognition", then we say that they see the illuminations—sounds, and so on—but as a consequence that is not true because their rational minds are not a valid cognizers.

The argument of the consequence of matching it to itself is as follows:[242] If a conventional type of valid cognizer is not a valid cognizer, would not an evaluation done by it and even if it were an overall analysis[243] become false? The consequence is that it would.

Madhyamika: You assert that then say, "Meditation can be done in suchness on the emptiness of all phenomena having no nature, but if it has to be evaluated by valid cognition, because of that situation[244] in which everything will be evaluated as false there will be the consequence of it not being accepted." We then say that, not having detected with rational mind the substantial thing under investigation—the substantial thing to be investigated not being referenced within rational mind—its non-existence will not be apprehended, which does not match with meditation. Therefore, for any substantial thing that is false that is to be refuted, its non-existent thing is clearly false

---

[242] One source says that this is an argument put forward by the Sāṃkhyas.

[243] ... as opposed to an attribute analysis ...

[244] ... referred to in the previous paragraph ...

is what is asserted. That false thing to be refuted is therefore a preventative false valid cognizer; on the death of a dream child, the conceptualizing thought that thinks, "That child does not exist" functions to prevent the previous conceptualizing thought, "That child exists". It too is false. It is like that.

2.3.3.3.3.3.3.1.3 Explaining emptiness and interdependent arising by pointing them out

Performing attribute analysis like that—as was just explained—reveals that there is no production at all of a result without a cause, nor is there such a result present in either its individual or combined conditions, the conditions that produce the result.

It has not come from somewhere else, does not dwell as such, and in ceasing, does not go off to another place. What difference is there between this that stupid fools make out through clinging to be true and the illusions manifested by an illusionist?

Examine where the illusions of horses and elephants manifested by illusionists and the things manifested by causes come from—they are not produced—and also to where they go—they have no cessation.

Thus, any given thing will be seen due to the causes and conditions for it being nearby. If they—the causes and conditions—are not there, it will not be seen. Because its coming about depends on something else, it is a contrivance analogous to the appearance of a reflected image in a mirror, so how could there be any truth to it? There is none.

Similarly, the *Sutra Petitioned by Matisāgara* says,

> Those that arise in interdependent relationship
> Do not have the slightest nature.

If at the time of the cause, the result is already existing as a substantial thing, what need would there be for a cause? This is because the result having already been accomplished, it has no requirement for dependence on something else. Nevertheless, if you think, "Although that result does not exist now at the time of the cause, later it will become a result that is a substantial thing", then what need would there be for a cause?" This is so because even with a thousand million causes there is no turning a non-existent thing into a substantial thing.

In that situation, how would that result be a thing or not? What else could change later into a thing?

If at the time of being non-existent, the result could not possibly exist as a substantial thing, the nature of a non-existent thing having been rejected, when would it become an existent substantial thing? This is so because it definitely would not change. A thing for as long as it has not been produced is a non-existent thing and will not be separated from being so, which is what defines it.

If not separated from being a non-existent thing, the time of being an existent thing is not possible because that is the time of a thing being halted. A thing also does not change to being a non-existent thing because if it did, there would be the consequence of it having two natures.

When analysed in that way there is no cessation and there is no thing that has been produced because of which all of these knowables in the migrations have not been produced and do not cease in a permanent way, which would be like the birth and death of a barren woman's son.

If you say, "Well yes, but what would it be like, this appearance of production and cessation?", we say that the appearances in confusion of the migrations are like a dream; when attribute analysed, they are similar to the Plantain tree with its layers of covering. Similarly, *The Mother* says,

> Emptiness of form is not being empty of form, it is being empty of form-ness. Emptiness is form.

And the others were connected there as well. The *Sutra Taught by Vimalakīrti* says,

> The bodhisatva Joy on Seeing said, "Empty of form-ness is not being empty due to form having collapsed, it is being empty of nature.

Likewise, feeling and the rest are connected there. And, *Stacked Jewels* says,

> Something that has been produced from conditions, has not
>   been produced.
> It does not have a born nature.
> Anything that comes about requiring conditions is emptiness.

Nāgārjuna said,

> Why externals arise interdependently
> Is that they arise from assemblages.
> They are asserted to be like the sound of a drum and a sprout
> And analogous to a dream and an illusion.
> Phenomena are produced from causes and
> Have not the slightest cessation.
> As for cause, they are empty of cause,
> So are understood to be without production.
> It is explained that all phenomena in being totally without
>   production
> Are emptiness.

2.3.3.3.3.3.3.2 Entering it by meditation

If attribute analysed, **there is no difference between those who have and have not passed into nirvana**, given that they are equally without nature.

What is there to gain and what is there to lose in regard to appearances of things which are empty like that? Similarly, what is there in being honoured or totally abused by someone?

Where do happiness and suffering of body and mind come from? What is there to be liked and what is there to be disliked? When I use my intellect to look into the nature of it, who is craving and what is craved?

If analysed, who—what person—in this world of the living dies? Who will come into life and who has come into it? And who are relatives and who are friends?

You must thoroughly grasp as I Śhāntideva have done, that everything when not being referenced is like space then cultivate that in meditation! As Nāgārjuna said in his *Enlightenment Mind Commentary*,

> The mind that is freed of referencing
> Is present with the characteristic of space;
> Doing this space meditation is what is
> Maintained to be emptiness meditation.[245]

2.3.3.3.3.3.3.3 Explaining how to traverse it by conduct using method and prajñā

Nāgārjuna said,

> If you have meditated on this emptiness,
> The rational mind that takes joy in others' sakes
> Will arise, there is no doubt.

That is to say that those wanting happiness here in this life who rely on the causes of fighting with enemies and delighting in relatives and friends, gradually create utter conflict and overwhelming joy.

---

[245] "Maintained" here means what is asserted by those who have full knowledge of their system.

CHAPTER NINE

Their desires failing, they are miserable and strive to accomplish them; and on account of their desires they argue with others, beat[246] and stab one another, and intimidate each other all of which causes them to live very difficult lives.

Due to relying on virtues with outflows they come again and again into happy migrations where many types of happiness are available for their use, but then when the virtuous potentials have been exhausted, they die and fall into the long and unbearable sufferings of the bad destinies.

Thus they wander in becoming, a place of many pitfalls where there is no mention, no understanding, of suchness. And there, these two sides of samsara and emptiness meditation are mutually incompatible, therefore in becoming there is no mention, no understanding, of this sort of suchness.

And there in that becoming too, because it is a limitless ocean of suffering whose difficulty to bear is beyond analogy, there is little fortitude for that sort of thing—abandoning suffering and accomplishing virtue—and because of it life is very short as well.

And there too, they work at meaningless activities such as various methods for the purpose of living long and without illness, attending to hunger and weariness, sleeping for about half their lives, being injured by enemies, keeping company with childish associates, and so on. In that way their lives pass quickly without meaning and as a result, it is extremely difficult for them to find the prajñā that does this sort of attribute analysis.

And there too, how could there be the samadhi that is the method for turning away from familiarization with complete distraction?

---

[246] The Derge edition of the Tibetan text has "cut" rather than "beat".

And there too, the maras together with evil persons, wives, and the four types of government ministers are striving to ensure that they fall into the great bad destinies, the hells.

There are many wrong paths in there and, not having the supreme prajñā, it is difficult to get past doubt; due to non-virtue being greater in amount, it will be difficult to gain leisure again and extremely difficult to have the occurrence of a buddha—why?—because the river of afflictions is difficult to stop. E MA Compassion! Suffering arises in a non-stop succession, like a wheel turning around.

For those in samsara like that there is extreme suffering, but not seeing their own suffering and not giving rise to disenchantment with samsara they stay in the river of suffering. For them, whose sufferings are unbearable, it is right that I should be pained and exclaim "Oh my!" because I cannot bear their suffering.

For example, there are some ascetics who pour water over themselves again and again then enter fire again and again. They stay like that, suffering in the extreme but priding themselves on being happy.

Like them, there are others who carelessly continue to perform such activities, going ahead as though there were no aging and no oncoming death. First they will be killed by the lord of death, then they will fall into the three bad destinies where they will have unbearable suffering.

Observing the pain produced by the fires of their individual sufferings like that, I consider these beings with compassion. In order to take away their pain, I look on them as strongly as I can like a mother whose child is distraught with suffering. The *Enlightenment Mind Commentary* says,

> One who has developed stability through meditation will,
> Because of not being able to bear the suffering of others,

> Reject the bliss of stable meditation—meditative
>   concentration—and then
> Will enter even the hell of Unremitting Torment.

For that, the two accumulations are to be completed using the appropriate means. The first of the two is the accumulation of merit, which is gathered using the methods shown—generosity and the others.[247]

For those who like that are pained by the fires of their sufferings I will one day become a rain of all that is needed for sentient beings' happiness, a rain that falls nicely from the clouds of my merit accumulation and quells their sufferings.

The second of the two is the accumulation of wisdom, as follows. **I will one day, in the mode of not referencing the three spheres, out of respect have gathered the accumulation of merit within an illusion-like state and will teach emptiness to those ruined by referencing until they become buddhas.**[248]

That was the ninth chapter of *Entering the Conduct of a Bodhisatva*, **called "Prajñāparamita".**

---

[247] The heading for this section, several pages back, mentions method and prajñā. The next paragraph is the accumulation of merit which is done with the use of method and the paragraph after that is the accumulation of wisdom which is done with the use of prajñā.

[248] Ruined by referencing means that beings have spent countless lifetimes operating in the framework of dualistic mind and been caught in samsara because of it, including the ones who have entered the path to enlightenment.

CHAPTER TEN

Dedication

3 The Goodness of the End, the Concluding Matter

This has three parts: the virtue of the composition given to sentient beings in general; prayers of aspiration made for individual cases; dedication for accomplishing what is meaningful for oneself.

3.1 The virtue of the composition given to sentient beings in general

The complete dedication of all conduct is a feature of the Great Vehicle, therefore, Shantideva says, **By the virtue I have obtained through composing** *Entering the Conduct of a Bodhisatva* **may all migrators enter the bodhisatva's conduct.**

May all beings everywhere as many as there are, the beings in samsara who are sick with the illness of fundamental ignorance and its **sufferings of body and mind obtain an ocean of happiness of body and joy of mind by my merits.**

While they, those sentient beings, **are arousing the enlightenment mind in order to gain the happiness of buddhahood, may their happiness never decline and moving along quickly may they obtain an uninterrupted flow of the unsurpassed happiness.** This was about giving virtue to others; it is saying, "By this virtue may they be freed from fundamental ignorance and have all-knowing wisdom instead".

3.2 Prayers of aspiration made for individual cases

This has three parts: prayers for the lesser beings in the bad destinies; prayers for the lesser beings in the higher levels; and prayers for those who have entered emancipation.

3.2.1 Prayers for the lesser beings in the bad destinies

May the bodied beings in all of the hells as many as there are in the world realms enjoy happiness of the sort enjoyed by the sentient beings in Sukhāvati.

May those feeble with the cold found in the cold hells "Blistering" and the others find warmth. May those feeble with heat be cooled by limitless rivers of water pouring down from the great clouds of the bodhisatvas' miracles.

May the forest of trees with sword-like leaves become a beautiful pleasure grove. May the forest of Śhalmari tree trunks turn into wish-fulfilling trees.

May the regions of hell become places of joy beautified by exquisite calls of wild ducks, geese, and swans and have lakes with fragrant lotuses.

May the heaps of burning coals turn into heaps of jewels and the burning ground become a polished crystal floor. May the iron mountains of Crushing Hell turn into celestial palaces of worship then be filled with sugatas.

May the rains of lava, blazing stones, and weapons from now on become a rain of flowers. May all the exchanges of the blows of weapons from now on be a playful exchange of flowers.

May those sinking into fiery pits at the Fordless River, their flesh falling away and their lily-white bones revealed, by the force of my virtues obtain the body of a god and stay together with goddesses in gently flowing rivers.

"Why are these hell beings who were not afraid before, the unbearable henchmen of Yama, the crows, and the vultures now full of dread and afraid? Through whose excellent strength is darkness everywhere dispelled and joy brought upon us?" On thinking that, they look up and see, in the centre of the firmament above, the blazing form of Vajrapani! May they, by the force of the utter joy and faith born within them be free from evil then go together with him to his buddha field called "Adakavatī".

When they, the beings in the hells, see hell's heaps of fire extinguished by a rain of falling flowers mixed with incense-scented water, immediately satisfied they wonder whose work this was and in this way may these beings in the hells see Padmapani, that is, may they see Avalokiteshvara come there.

Those beings in hell say to one another, "Friends, come here, come here quickly, we will be rescued! Do not be afraid! The fearless youthful one with long tresses[249] has arrived, the one whose power removes all of our suffering and relieves us with the force of joy, the one who has produced for us the enlightenment mind that protects all migrators and love like that of a mother for an only son."

Upon seeing Mañjughoṣha in this way, may the beings in hell cry out, "Friends! See him in a delightful palace resounding with praises and songs sung by a thousand goddesses, with the tiaras of a hundred gods being offered to his lotus feet, with eyes moist with compassion and a rain of many flowers falling upon his crown."

Like that, having seen by my roots of virtue a pleasant fall of cooling, sweet-smelling rain coming from clouds created by the

---

[249] This is Mañjughoṣha.

bodhisatvas Samantabhadra and the others, bodhisatvas with no obscurations, may all beings in hell be truly happy.

May all animals be free from the fear of being eaten by one another—like that of a fish being swallowed by an alligator. May the hungry ghosts be happy like the men of Unpleasant to Hear[250] in having, unhindered, possessions for their use.

Furthermore, may they be satisfied by a stream of milk pouring from the hand of the noble Lord Avalokiteshvara and, for the hungry ghosts who are stricken by heat, by bathing in it may they always be cool.

3.2.2 Prayers for the lesser beings in the higher levels

May the blind see with their eyes, may the deaf always hear the sounds of dharma, and just as it was for Mayadevi, may pregnant women give birth without harm.[251]

May the ones who wander naked find clothing, the hungry find food; may the thirsty find water and non-intoxicating delicious drinks.

May the poor find the wealth of possessions. May those weak with sorrow find joy. May the forlorn find a cheerful mind. May they find steadiness of mind and an excellent situation.

May those who are sick with any of the types of disease there are quickly be freed from their sickness. Henceforth may every one of the sicknesses of migrators permanently not happen.

---

[250] This is the name of the northern continent of our Mt. Meru style world system.

[251] Mayadevi was the mother of Śhākyamuni Buddha. Her birth of the Buddha was painless.

May the frightened cease to be afraid. May the imprisoned be freed. May the powerless to accomplish something of great meaning come to have the power needed for it, and may people have a mind of acting for mutual benefit, a mind that is gentle and flexible.

May all travellers to various places find happiness and no fear everywhere they go. May they accomplish their purpose in going without need of effort.

May those who sail in boats and ships accomplish their wishes and having safely returned to the shore may they joyfully reunite with their relatives.

May wanderers who have lost their way in dangerous places meet with other travellers, and without fears of thieves, tigers, and so on, may their going be easy and without fatigue.

May those who find themselves in isolated and other such places, intimidating places without a path—the children and the aged without a protector, those stupefied and the insane—be guarded by divinities.

May beings be free from all states of no leisure—meaning the places where there is no time, no freedom to do what is meaningful—and have faith, prajñā, and love and with excellent food meaning properly obtained and excellent conduct, may they be always be mindful throughout their lives.

May all sentient beings have unending resources like those in the storehouse of space. May those resources being free of dispute over their ownership and injury because of them be theirs to use as they please.

May those who have little splendour come to great splendour. May those whose form has become degraded through facing difficulties come to have a most excellent form.

May the females however many there are in the world come to be males. May the bad types, the ones of inferior class, gain a higher position in a future life and the proud ones at that time also be overcome.

By the power of the merits I have accumulated, may all beings, none left out, abandon all forms of evil and perpetually engage in virtue.

3.2.3 Prayers for those who have entered emancipation

May those who are arousing the mind for enlightenment not be parted from the enlightenment mind and diligently perform the conducts of a bodhisatva and may they be cared for by the complete buddhas and abandon—or overcome—the works of the maras.

May all of those sentient beings who are arousing the enlightenment mind have lives that are unfathomably long. May they always live happily and not even hear the word "death".

May all directions be filled with gardens covered in wish-fulfilling trees, gardens in which the sweet sounds of dharma are being proclaimed by the buddhas and the buddha sons.

May the lands everywhere be places devoid of stones and the like and level like the palm of the hand, of the nature of lapis lazuli—on which latticework patterns have been drawn in gold and which if depressed comes back to being smooth again—and smooth.

There are several circles of disciples, but may the majority, the bodhisatvas, be present in every land adorning them with their excellences, their good qualities.

May bodied beings uninterruptedly hear in all their places the beneficial sounds of dharma issuing from birds and trees, rays of light and even space itself.

May they always meet with complete buddhas and buddha sons. May those gurus—teaching buddhas—to migrators be worshipped with infinite clouds of offerings.

May celestials bring timely rains to this world so that harvests are bountiful. May kings act to protect their kingdoms in accordance with dharma. May the people of the world be perfectly happy.

May all medicines for removing sickness be effective and those who recite mantras be successful, accomplishing the abilities they desire. May dakinis, rakshasas, yakshas, and so on—malevolent beings, some flesh-eating, and as well as those, the ghosts—be endowed with compassionate minds.

May no living creature ever be sad, commit evil, or ever fall ill. May none ever be afraid or berated, or develop an unhappy frame of mind.

May reading the words of the teacher, the buddha, and recitation flourish and stay nicely present in all viharas[252]. May the sangha always be in harmony and the sanghas's aims be fulfilled.

May members of the sangha who want to do the trainings find isolated places that are not the cause of downfalls. May they, in having abandoned all distraction cultivate the mind of samadhi so that it becomes workable.

May the fully-ordained nuns be materially sufficient and abandon quarrelling with each other and harming each other. Similarly may all ordained ones never let their discipline become corrupt.

---

[252] A vihara is the Sanskrit name for a place where Buddhist monks dwell and carry out Buddhist practices.

May I, on seeing that my discipline has become lax resulting in a fault, give rise to renunciation then repair it, starting with even the smallest downfall and thereby always put an end to evil acts. May I in future lives moreover obtain a happy migration then in that place guard my yogic conduct so that it does not become corrupted.

May the experts be honoured by all and receive excellent alms. May their, those experts', minds be completely pure without pride or jealousy, and because of that may they be renowned in all directions.

May beings in all their places of birth not experience the suffering of the bad destinies and without hardship obtain a body better than that of the gods, one of leisure and endowment, and thereby quickly accomplish buddhahood.

May sentient beings make offerings many times to all the buddhas and as a result always have the happiness of the inconceivable happiness of the buddhas.

May the bodhisatvas accomplish the welfare of migrators just as they have intended. May sentient beings receive the happiness that the guardians intended for them when the guardians were training.

Similarly may the pratyeka buddhas and the śrāvakas also find happiness.

3.2.4 Dedication for accomplishing what is meaningful for oneself

Until by the kindness of Mañjughoṣha I have gained the first level Utter Joy,[253] may I always remember my lives and immediately upon birth obtain ordination.

---

[253] Utter Joy is the first of the ten bodhisatva levels.

CHAPTER TEN

May I be sustained by basic foods that will nourish me. May I in all my lives have a place with all of the qualities needed for staying in isolation.

May I, whenever I want to see guardian Mañjughoṣha or want to ask him a small question, see him without hindrance.

May I, in order to accomplish the sakes of all the sentient beings who reach as far as the ends of space in the ten directions, have a conduct like the conduct done by the bodhisatva Mañjughoṣha.

For as long as space remains and for as long as migrators—sentient beings—remain, for that long may I too remain in order to dispel the suffering of migrators.

May all the sufferings of migrators big or small whatever they might be ripen on myself. May the sangha of bodhisatvas set all migrators in happiness.

The sole medicine for dispelling the suffering of migrators, the source of every happiness is the Buddha's teaching; may it together with material support and honour remain for a long time.

He then adds, "I prostrate to Mañjughoṣha through whose kindness virtuous minds arise". Furthermore, he adds, "I prostrate to my virtuous spiritual friends through whose kindness I have developed my body of analytical thinking through hearing, contemplating, and meditating."

That was the tenth chapter of *Entering the Conduct of a Bodhisatva*, called "Dedication". *Entering the Conduct of a Bodhisatva* by Śhāntideva is complete.

GLOSSARY OF TERMS

Affliction, Skt. kleśha, Tib. nyon mongs: This term is usually translated as emotion or disturbing emotion, etcetera but the Buddha was very specific about the meaning of this word. When the Buddha referred to the emotions, meaning a movement of mind, he did not refer to them as such but called them "kleśha" in Sanskrit, meaning exactly "affliction". It is a basic part of the Buddhist teaching that emotions afflict beings, giving them problems at the time and causing more problems in the future.

Alertness, Tib. shes bzhin: Alertness is a specific mental event that occurs in dualistic mind. It and another mental event, mindfulness, are the two functions of mind that must be developed in order to develop shamatha or one-pointedness of mind. In that context, mindfulness is what remembers the object of the concentration and holds the mind to it while alertness is the mind watching the situation to ensure that the mindfulness is not lost. If distraction does occur, alertness will know it and will inform the mind to re-establish mindfulness again.

Appropriation, Skt. upādāna, Tib. nye bar len pa: This is the name of the ninth of the twelve links of interdependent origination. Tsongkhapa gives a good treatment of all twelve links in his interdependent origination section of the *Great Stages of the Path to Enlightenment*, a translation of which is available for free download from the PKTC web-site. It is the crucial point in the process at which a karma that has been previously planted is selected and activated as the karma that will propel the being into its next existence. In other words, it is the key point in a being's existence when the next type of existence is selected. There is the further point that, at the time of death, the particular place that the wind-mind settles in the subtle body, a place related to the seed syllables mentioned in the tantras, also determines the next birth. The two points are not different. The selection of the karma that will propel the next life then affects how the wind-mind will operate at the time of death.

Arousing the mind, Tib. sems bskyed: This is a technical term nearly always used to mean "arousing the enlightenment mind", though it is occasionally used to refer to the deliberate production of other types of mind, for example renunciation. There are two types of arousing the mind—fictional and superior factual; see under fictional enlightenment mind and superior factual enlightenment mind.

Attribute analysis, Tib. rnam dpyad: "Attribute analysis" and "overall analysis" are a pair of terms used to highlight a crucial difference between conceptual and non-conceptual approaches towards understanding something, for example, the view of emptiness.

Attribute analysis is an assessment done using rational mind; it examines (Tib. dpyad) the individual, surface attributes (Tib. rnam pa) of something to come to a rational understanding of what the thing is. It conceptually eliminates the attribute which something is not in order to establish the concept of what something is. Therefore, it could also be called an "eliminative analysis". It entails what is called "distinction-removal" which is the conceptual process of distinguishing something as being this rather than that and in doing so eliminating what "that" is from the understanding of the thing.

Overall analysis is an examination (Tib. dpyod) done using wisdom to discover the actual thing itself; it works by taking in the whole thing (yongs) at once in a single moment of non-dual comprehension. Rather than dealing with the attributes of the thing one at a time in a conceptual way using a process of distinguishing and eliminating, it is a non-conceptual, non-eliminative process of direct comprehension.

Becoming, Skt. bhāvana, Tib. srid pa: Becoming refers to the style of existence that sentient beings have within samsara. Beings in samsara have a samsaric existence but, more than that, they are constantly in a state of becoming. They are constantly becoming this type of being or that type of being in this abode or that, as they are driven along without choice by the karmic process that drives samsaric existence.

Bliss, Skt. sukha, Tib. bde: The Sanskrit term and its Tibetan translation are usually translated as "bliss" but in fact refer to the whole range of possibilities of everything on the side of good as opposed to bad. Thus, the term will mean pleasant, happy, good, nice, easy, comfortable, blissful, and so on, depending on context.

Bodhichitta, Tib. byang chub sems: See under enlightenment mind.

Bodhisatva, Tib. byang chub sems dpa': A bodhisatva is a person who has engendered the bodhichitta, enlightenment mind, and, with that as a basis, has undertaken the path to the enlightenment of a true complete buddha specifically for the welfare of other beings. Note that, despite the common appearance of "bodhisattva" in Western books on Buddhism, the Tibetan tradition has steadfastly maintained since the time of the earliest translations that the correct spelling is bodhisatva; see under satva and sattva.

Capable One, Skt. muni, Tib. thub pa: The term "muni" as for example in "Shakyamuni" has long been thought to mean "sage" because of an entry in Monier-Williams excellent Sanskrit-English dictionary. In fact, it has been used by many Indian religions since the times of ancient India to mean someone "who could withstand the rigours of gaining spiritual attainment".

Clinging, Tib. zhen pa: In Buddhism, this term refers specifically to the twofold process of dualistic mind mis-taking things that are not true, not pure, as true, pure, etcetera and then, because of seeing them highly desirable even though they are not, attaching oneself or clinging to those things. This clinging acts as a kind of glue that keeps a person involved with the unsatisfactory things of samsara.

Compassionate activity, Tib. thugs rje: This does not mean compassionate activity in general. Rather, it is a specific term that refers to that aspect of wisdom which spontaneously does whatever needs to be done, throughout all reaches of time and space, for all beings. Although it includes the word "compassion" in its name, it is more primordial than that. It is the dynamic quality of enlightenment which choicelessly, ceaselessly, spontaneously, and pervasively acts to benefit others.

Confusion, Tib. 'khrul pa: In Buddhism, this term mostly refers to the fundamental confusion of taking things the wrong way that happens because of fundamental ignorance, although it can also have the more general meaning of having lots of thoughts and being confused about it. In the first case, it is defined like this: "Confusion is the appearance to rational mind of something being present when it is not" and refers, for example, to seeing an object, such as a table, as being truly present, when in fact it is present only as mere, interdependent appearance.

Cyclic existence: See under samsara.

Dharmakaya, Skt. dharmakāya, Tib. chos sku: In general, this refers to the mind of a buddha, with dharma meaning reality and kāya meaning body.

Dharmata, Skt. dharmatā, Tib. chos nyid: This is a general term meaning the way that something is, and can be applied to anything at all; it is similar in meaning to "actuality" *q.v.* For example, the dharmatā of water is wetness and the dharmatā of the becoming bardo is a place where beings are in a samsaric, or becoming mode, prior to entering a nature bardo. It is used frequently in Buddhism to mean "the dharmatā of reality" but that is a specific case of the much larger meaning of the term. To read texts which use this term successfully, one has to understand that the term has a general meaning and then see how that applies in context.

Elaboration, Tib. spro ba: This is a general name for what is given off by dualistic mind as it goes about its conceptual business. The term is pejorative in that it implies that a story has been made up, un-necessarily, about something which is actually nothing, which is empty. Elaborations, because of what they are, prevent a person from seeing emptiness directly. Being elaboration-free implies direct sight of emptiness.

Enlightenment mind, Skt. bodhichitta, Tib. byang chub sems: This is a key term of the Great Vehicle. It is the type of mind that is connected not with the lesser enlightenment of an arhat but the enlightenment of a true complete buddha. As such, it is a mind which is connected with the aim of bringing all sentient beings to that same level of buddhahood. A person who has this mind has entered the Great Vehicle and is either a bodhisatva or a buddha.

It is important to understand that "enlightenment mind" is used to refer equally to the minds of all levels of bodhisatva on the path to buddhahood and to the mind of a buddha who has completed the path.

Therefore, it is not "mind striving for enlightenment" as is so often translated, but "enlightenment mind", meaning that kind of mind which is connected with the full enlightenment of a true complete buddha and which is present in all those who belong to the Great Vehicle.

Entity, Tib. ngo bo: The entity of something is just exactly what that thing is. In English we would often simply say "thing" rather than entity. However, in Buddhism, "thing" has a very specific meaning rather than the general meaning that it has in English. It has become common to translate this term as "essence" *q.v.* However, in most cases "entity", meaning what a thing is rather than an essence of that thing, is the correct translation for this term.

Evil, evil deed, Skt. papaṃ, Tib. sdig pa: The original Sanskrit means something which someone has done which is truly bad, rotten. Anyone who has done such a thing is looked down upon. The Tibetan for it relates to the idea of a scorpion, a nasty creature that will sting you and injure you. In Buddhism, the term does not have the Christian sense of evil but simply means action done that, being done under the influence of an affliction, degrades you now in others' eyes, degrades you now because of the bad karmic seeds that you have planted by doing it, and degrades you in the future because of the ripening of the bad karmas into unpleasant results.

Exaggeration, Tib. sgro 'dogs: In Buddhism, this term is used in two ways. Firstly, it is used in general to mean misunderstanding from the perspective that one has added more to one's understanding of something than needs to be there. Secondly, it is used specifically to indicate that dualistic mind always overstates or exaggerates whatever object it is examining. Dualistic mind always adds the ideas of solidity, permanence, singularity, and so on to everything it references via the concepts that it uses. Severing of exaggeration either means removal of these un-necessary understandings when trying to properly comprehend something or removal of the dualistic process altogether when trying to get to the non-dualistic reality of a phenomenon.

Fact, Skt. artha, Tib. don: "Fact" is that knowledge of an object that occurs to the surface of mind or wisdom. It is not the object but what the mind or wisdom understands as the object. Thus there are two usages of "fact": fact known to dualistic and non-dualistic minds.

Fictional, Skt. saṃvṛtti, Tib. kun rdzob: This term is paired with the term "superior factual" *q.v.* In the past, these terms have been translated as "relative" and "absolute" respectively, but those translations are nothing like the original terms. These two terms are extremely important in the Buddhist teaching so it is very important that they be corrected, but more than that, if the actual meaning of these terms is not presented, then the teaching connected with them cannot be understood.

The Sanskrit term saṃvṛtti means a deliberate invention, a fiction, a cover-up. It refers to the mind of ignorance which, because of being obscured and so not seeing how things are ultimately, is not true but a fiction. The things that appear to that ignorance are therefore fictional. Nonetheless, the beings who live in this ignorance believe that the things that appear to them through the filter of ignorance are true, are real. Therefore, these beings live in fictional truth.

Fictional and superior factual: Fictional and superior factual are our greatly improved translations for "relative" and "absolute" respectively. Briefly, the original Sanskrit word for fiction means a deliberately produced *fiction* and refers to the world projected by a mind controlled by ignorance. The original word for superior fact means "that *superior fact* that appears on the surface of the mind of a noble one who has transcended samsara" and refers to reality seen as it actually is. Relative and absolute do not convey this meaning at all and, when they are used, the meaning being presented is simply lost.

Fictional truth, Skt. saṃvṛtisatya, Tib. kun rdzob bden pa: See under fictional.

Fictional truth enlightenment mind, Tib. kun rdzob bden pa'i byang chub sems: One of a pair of terms explained in the Great Vehicle; the other is Superior Factual Truth Enlightenment Mind. See under fictional truth and superior factual truth for information about those terms. Enlightenment mind is defined as two types. The fictional type is the conventional type: it is explained as consisting of love and great compassion within the framework of an intention to obtain true complete enlightenment for the sake of all sentient beings. The superior factual truth type is the ultimate type: it is explained as the enlightenment mind that is directly perceiving emptiness.

Field, Field realm, Tib. zhing, zhing khams: This term is often translated "buddha field" though there is no "buddha" in the term. There are many different types of "fields" in both saṃsāra and nirvana. Thus there are fields that belong to enlightenment and ones that belong to ignorance. Moreover, just as there are "realms" of saṃsāra—desire, form, and formless—so there are realms of nirvana—the fields of the dharmakāya, saṃbhogakāya, and nirmāṇakāya and these are therefore called "field realms".

Floaters, Tib. rab rib: This term has usually been mistakenly translated as "cataracts". It is the medical term for eyes with a disease known as *Muscaria volante* in Western ophthalmology. The disease is common to a large portion of the world's population and has the common term "floaters" given to it by the medical profession. Almost anyone who looks out at a clear source of light will see grey threads, sometimes twisted, sometimes straight, floating in the field of vision. When an eye is moved, because the gel of the eye shifts, the floaters can seem to be like hairs falling through the field of vision and so are sometimes called "falling hairs". They seem to be "out there" when in fact they are shadows being cast on the retina by fissures in the gel inside the eye. The point is that they seem real when in fact they are an aberration produced by an illness of the eye.

Formative, Skt. saṃskāra, Tib. 'du byed. This term is usually translated as "formations", but a formation is the product of that which caused its formation, whereas this term refers to the agent which will cause a formation. The formatives, which are the contents of the fourth of the five aggregates, cause the production of a future set of aggregates for the mindstream involved. There are two types of formatives, ones which are a type of mind and ones which are not. The former includes all of the afflictions both those which are virtuous and those which are non-virtuous.

Four close placements of mindfulness, Tib. dran pa nyer gzhags pa bzhi: This is a set of four practices taught by the Buddha to develop mindfulness which, together with alertness, is the main cause of developing shamatha. They are mindfulness of body, feeling, effort, and mind.

Grasped-grasping, Tib. gzung 'dzin: When mind is turned outwardly as it is in the normal operation of dualistic mind, it has developed two faces that appear simultaneously. Special names are given to these two faces: mind appearing in the form of the external object being referenced is called "that which is grasped at" and mind appearing in the form of the consciousness that is registering it is called the "grasper" or "grasping" of it. Thus, there is the term "grasped-grasper" or "grasped-grasping" which is a convenient abbreviation for the mode of operation of dualistic mind. Moreover, when these two terms are used, it alerts one to the fact that a Mind Only style of presentation is being discussed. This pair of terms pervades Mind Only, Middle Way, and tantric writings and is exceptionally important in all of them.

Note that one could substitute the word "apprehended" for "grasped" and "apprehender" for "grasper" or "grasping" and that would reflect one connotation of the original Sanskrit terminology. The solidified duality of grasped and grasper is nothing but an invention of dualistic thought; it has that kind of character.

Great Vehicle, Skt. mahāyāna, Tib. theg pa chen po: The Buddha's teachings as a whole can be summed up into three vehicles where a vehicle is defined as that which can carry a person to a certain destination. The first vehicle, called the Lesser Vehicle, contains the teachings designed to get an individual moving on the spiritual path through showing the unsatisfactory state of cyclic existence and an emancipation from that. However, that path is only concerned with personal emancipation and fails to take account of all of the beings that there are in existence. There used to be eighteen schools of Lesser Vehicle in India but the only one surviving nowadays is the Theravāda of south-east Asia. The Greater Vehicle is a step up from that. The Buddha explained that it was great in comparison to the Lesser Vehicle for seven reasons. The first of those is that it is concerned with attaining the true complete enlightenment of a true complete buddha for the sake of every sentient being where the Lesser Vehicle is concerned only with a personal liberation that is not true complete enlightenment and which is achieved only for the sake of that practitioner. The Great Vehicle has two divisions: a conventional form in which the path is taught in a logical, conventional way, and an unconventional form in which the path is taught in a very direct way. This latter vehicle is called the

Vajra Vehicle because it takes the innermost, indestructible (vajra) fact of reality of one's own mind as the vehicle to enlightenment.

Guardian, Skt. nātha, Tib. mgon po: This name is a respectful title reserved for the buddhas. It means that they both protect and nurture sentient beings who they oversee, like a child who, having no parents has been given or has found a guardian. It is often translated as "protector" but that correctly translates another Sanskrit term to start with and on top of that is insufficient because it does not include the aspect of nurturing. It is also given to other beings such as bodhisatvas who have a similar quality, for example, Guardian Nāgārjuna and Guardian Maitreya.

Intentional conduct, Tib. mos spyod: A name in the Great Vehicle for the path activities done at levels of both accumulation and connection. At this level, one is still intending to directly realize emptiness. Note that intention is the name of one of the fifty-one mental events. Thus this name implies that it is conduct still at the level of dualistic being, though it is a good mind because it intends to reach non-dualistic being. Also, by definition there is no real accomplishment until the path of seeing is reached, so there is no real accomplishment at the level of intentional conduct. Intentional conduct as non-accomplishment followed by the three paths which are levels of accomplishment is a general presentation contained in the common vehicle.

Kaya, Skt. kāya, Tib. sku: The Sanskrit term means a functional or coherent collection of parts, similar to the French "corps", and hence also comes to mean "a body". It is used in Tibetan Buddhist texts specifically to distinguish bodies belonging to the enlightened side from ones belonging to the samsaric side.

The most common description of enlightened being is that it is comprised of three kāyas: dharma, saṃbhoga, and nirmāṇakāyas. Briefly stated, the dharmakāya is the body of truth, the saṃbhogakāya is the body replete with the good qualities of enlightenment, and the nirmāṇa kāya is the body manifested into the worlds of saṃsāra and nirvana to benefit beings.

Latency, Skt. vāsanā, Tib. bag chags: The original Sanskrit has the meaning exactly of "latency". The Tibetan term translates that inexactly with "something sitting there (Tib. chags) within the environment of mind

(Tib. bag)". Although it has become popular to translate this term into English with "habitual pattern", that is not its meaning. The term refers to a karmic seed that has been imprinted on the mindstream and is present there as a latency, ready and waiting to come into manifestation.

Lay aside, Tib. bshags pa: This term is usually translated as "confession" but that is not the meaning. The term literally means to cut something away and remove it from oneself. In Buddhism, it is used in the context of ridding oneself of the karmic seeds sown by bad karmic actions.

Buddhism is a totally non-theistic religion, so it is very important to understand that one is not confessing wrongdoings to anyone, including oneself. There is no granting of absolution in this system. As the Buddha himself said, he has no ability to purify the karmic stains of sentient beings, he can only teach them how to do so. The practice that he taught for ridding oneself of karmic wrongdoings is the practice of realizing for oneself that they hold the seed of future suffering, rousing regret, and distancing oneself from them. In doing so, one lays them aside.

There is a longer phrase that indicates the full practice of laying aside. The Tibetan phrase "mthol zhing shags pa" literally means "admitting and laying aside". Note that "admitting" also does not entail confession; it refers to the fact that one first has to admit or acknowledge to oneself that one has done something wrong, karmically speaking, and that it will have undesirable consequences. Without this, one cannot effectively take the second step of distancing oneself from the actions. Therefore, it is explained that the process of "laying aside" has to be understood to include the practice of "admission" because, without that acknowledgement, the laying aside cannot be done.

Lesser Vehicle, Skt. hīnayāna, Tib. theg pa dman pa: See under Great Vehicle.

Mara, Skt. māra, Tib. bdud: The Sanskrit term is closely related to the word "death". Buddha spoke of four classes of extremely negative influences that have the capacity to drag a sentient being deep into saṃsāra. They are the "māras" or "kiss of death" of: having a samsaric set of five skandhas; having afflictions; death itself; and the son of gods, which means being seduced and taken in totally by sensuality.

Migrator, Tib. 'gro ba: Migrator is one of several terms that were commonly used by the Buddha to mean "sentient being". It shows sentient beings from the perspective of their constantly being forced to go here and there from one rebirth to another by the power of karma. They are like flies caught in a jar, constantly buzzing back and forth. The term is often translated using "beings" which is another general term for sentient beings but doing so loses the meaning entirely. Buddhist authors who know the tradition do not use the word loosely but use it specifically to give the sense of beings who are constantly and helplessly going from one birth to another, and that is how the term should be read. The term "six migrators" refers to the six types of migrators within samsaric existence—hell-beings, pretas, animals, humans, demi-gods, and gods.

Noble one, Skt. ārya, Tib. 'phags pa: In Buddhism, a noble one is a being who has become spiritually advanced to the point that he has passed beyond cyclic existence. According to the Buddha, the beings in cyclic existence were ordinary beings, spiritual commoners, and the beings who had passed beyond it were special, the nobility.

Ordinary being, Skt. pratigha, Tib. so sor skye ba: This term refers to an ordinary being, someone who dwells in samsara. An ordinary being compares with a Noble One, someone who is out of samsara.

Outflow, Skt. āsrāva, Tib. zag pa: The Sanskrit term means a bad discharge, like pus coming out of a wound. Outflows occur when wisdom loses its footing and falls into the elaborations of dualistic mind. Therefore, anything with duality also has outflows. This is sometimes translated as "defiled" or "conditioned" but these fail to capture the meaning. The idea is that wisdom can remain self-contained in its own unique sphere but, when it loses its ability to stay within itself, it starts to have leakages into dualism that are defilements on the wisdom.

Prajna, Skt. prajñā, Tib. shes rab: The Sanskrit term, literally meaning "best type of mind" is defined as that which makes correct distinctions between this and that and hence which arrives at correct understanding. It has been translated as "wisdom" but that is not correct because it is, generally speaking, a mental event belonging to dualistic mind where "wisdom" is used to refer to the non-dualistic knower of a buddha. Moreover, the main feature of prajñā is its ability to distinguish correctly between one thing and another and hence to arrive at a correct understanding.

Rational mind, Skt. mati, Tib. blo: Rational mind is one of several terms for mind in Buddhist terminology. It specifically refers to a mind that judges this against that. It is mainly used to refer to samsaric mind, given that samsaric mind only works in the dualistic mode of comparing this versus that. Because of this, the term is mainly used in a pejorative sense to point out samsaric mind as opposed to a non-dualistic enlightened type of mind. However, it is occasionally used to refer to the discriminating wisdom aspect of non-dualistic mind, for example, in the case of a buddha. In that case it is a mind making distinctions between this and that but within the context of non-dualistic wisdom.

Realization, Tib. rtogs pa: Realization has a very specific meaning: it refers to correct knowledge that has been gained in such a way that the knowledge does not abate. There are two important points here. Firstly, realization is not absolute. It refers to the removal of obscurations, one at a time. Each time that a practitioner removes an obscuration, he gains a realization because of it. Therefore, there are as many levels of realization as there are obscurations. Maitreya, in the *Ornament of Manifest Realizations*, shows how the removal of the various obscurations that go with each of the three realms of samsaric existence produces realization.

Reference and Referencing, Tib. dmigs pa: Referencing is the name for the process in which dualistic mind references an actual object by using a conceptual label instead of the actual object. Whatever is referenced is then called a reference. Note that these terms imply the presence of dualistic mind and their opposites, non-referencing and being without reference imply the presence of non-dualistic wisdom.

Refuge, Skt. śharaṇam, Tib. bskyab pa: The Sanskrit term means "shelter", "protection from harm". Everyone seeks a refuge from the unsatisfactoriness of life, even if it is a simple act like brushing the teeth to prevent the body from decaying un-necessarily. Buddhists, after having thought carefully about their situation and who could provide a refuge from it which would be thoroughly reliable, find that three things—buddha, dharma, and saṅgha—are the only things that could provide that kind of refuge. Therefore, Buddhists take refuge in those Three Jewels of Refuge as they are called. Taking refuge in the Three Jewels is clearly laid out as the one doorway to all Buddhist practice and realization.

Rishi, Skt. ṛishi, Tib. drang srong: A rishi is a holy man. The Sanskrit itself means one who has a sufficient level of spiritual accomplishment and knowledge to bring others along the path of spirituality properly. It was a common appellation in ancient India where there were many rishis. The Buddha was often referred to as "the rishi" meaning the rishi of all rishis or as the "great ṛishi" meaning the greatest of all ṛishis.

Samsara, Skt. saṃsāra, Tib. 'khor ba: This is the most general name for the type of existence in which sentient beings live. It refers to the fact that they continue on from one existence to another, always within the enclosure of births that are produced by ignorance and experienced as unsatisfactory. The original Sanskrit means to be constantly going about, here and there. The Tibetan term literally means "cycling", because of which it is frequently translated into English with "cyclic existence" though that is not quite the meaning of the term.

Satva and sattva: According to the Tibetan tradition established at the time of the great translation work done at Samye under the watch of Padmasambhava not to mention one hundred and sixty-three of the greatest Buddhist scholars of Sanskrit-speaking India, there is a difference of meaning between the Sanskrit terms "satva" and "sattva", with satva meaning "an heroic kind of being" and "sattva" meaning simply "a being". According to the Tibetan tradition established under the advice of the Indian scholars mentioned above, satva is correct for the words Vajrasatva and bodhisatva, whereas sattva is correct for the words samayasattva, samādhisattva, and jñānasattva, and is also used alone to refer to any or all of these three sattvas.

All Tibetan texts produced since the time of the great translations conform to this system and all Tibetan experts agree that this is correct, but Western translators of Tibetan texts have for the last few hundred years claimed that they know better and have changed "satva" to "sattva" in every case, causing confusion amongst Westerners confronted by the correct spellings. Recently, publications by Western Sanskrit scholars have been appearing in which these great experts finally admit that they were wrong and that the Tibetan system is and always has been correct!

Sugata, Tib. bde bar gshegs pa: This term is one of many names for a buddha. It has the twofold meaning of someone who has gone on a good, pleasant, easy journey and who has arrived at a place which is good, pleasant, and full of ease. The meaning in relation to buddhahood is explained at length in *Unending Auspiciousness, the Sutra of the Recollection of the Noble Three Jewels* by Tony Duff, published by Padma Karpo Translation Committee, 2010, ISBN: 978-9937-8386-1-0.

Superfice, superficies, Tib. rnam pa: In discussions of mind, a distinction is made between the entity of mind which is a mere knower and the superficial things that appear on its surface and which are known by it. In other words, the superficies are the various things which pass over the surface of mind but which are not mind. Superficies are all the specifics that constitute appearance—for example, the colour white within a moment of visual consciousness, the sound heard within an ear consciousness, and so on.

Superior fact, Skt. paramārtha, Tib. don dam: This term is paired with the term "fiction" *q.v.* In the past, the terms have been translated as "relative" and "absolute" respectively, but those translations are nothing like the original terms. These terms are extremely important in the Buddhist teaching, so it is very important that their translations be corrected but, more than that, if the actual meaning of these terms is not presented, the teaching connected with them cannot be understood. The Sanskrit term literally means "the superior fact which is above all others".

Tirthika, Skt. tīrthika, Tib. mu stegs pa: This is a very kind name adopted by the Buddha for those who did not follow him but who, because they followed some other spiritual path, had at least started on the path to enlightenment. The Sanskrit name means "those who have arrived at the steps at the edge of the pool". A lengthy explanation is given in the *Illuminator Tibetan-English Dictionary* by Tony Duff and published by Padma Karpo Translation Committee.

Unsatisfactoriness, Skt. duḥkha, Tib. sdug bngal: This term is usually translated into English with "suffering" but there are many problems with that. When the Buddha talked about the nature of samsaric existence, he said that it was unsatisfactory. He used the term "duḥkha", which includes actual suffering but means much more than that. Duḥkha is one of a pair of terms, the other being "sukha", which is usually translated as, but does not only mean, bliss. The real meaning of duḥkha is "everything on the side of bad"—not good, uncomfortable, unpleasant, not nice, and so on. Thus, it means "unsatisfactory in every possible way". The real meaning of its opposite, sukha, is "everything on the side of good"—not bad, comfortable, pleasant, nice, and so on.

Valid cognizer, valid cognition, Skt. pramāṇa, Tib. tshad ma: The Sanskrit term "pramāṇa" literally means "best type of mentality" and comes to mean "a valid cognizer". Its value is that is can be used to validate anything that can be known. The Tibetans translated this term with "tshad ma" meaning an "evaluator"—something which can be used to evaluate the truth or not of whatever it is given to know. It is the term used in logic to indicate a mind which is knowing validly and which therefore can be used to validate the object it is knowing.

Valid cognizers are named according to the kind of test they are employed to do. A valid cognizer of the conventional or a valid cognizer of the fictional tests within conventions, within the realm of rational, dualistic mind. A valid cognizer of the ultimate or valid cognizer of superfact tests for the superfactual level, beyond dualistic mind.

Vipashyana, Skt. vipaśyanā, Tib. lhag mthong: This is the Sanskrit name for one of the two main practices of meditation needed in the Buddhist system for gaining insight into reality. The other one, śhamatha, keeps the mind focussed while this one looks piercingly into the nature of things.

Wisdom, Skt. jñāna, Tib. ye shes: This is a fruition term that refers to the kind of mind—the kind of knower—possessed by a buddha. Sentient beings do have this kind of knower but it is covered over by a very complex apparatus for knowing, that is, dualistic mind. If they practise the path to buddhahood, they will leave behind their obscuration and return to having this kind of knower.

The Sanskrit term has the sense of knowing in the most simple and immediate way. This sort of knowing is present at the core of every being's mind. Therefore, the Tibetans called it "the particular type of awareness which is there primordially". Because of the Tibetan wording it has often been called "primordial wisdom" in English translations, but that goes too far; it is just "wisdom" in the sense of the most fundamental knowing possible.

Wisdom does not operate in the same way as samsaric mind; it comes about in and of itself without depending on cause and effect. Therefore it is frequently referred to as "self-arising wisdom" *q.v.*

INDEX

abhidharma 149, 194, 318, 343
Abhisamayālaṅkara xviii
accumulation of merit 115, 233, 379
accumulation of wisdom .. 233, 379
admiring faith 140
affliction 26, 65, 144, 199, 200, 223, 235, 240, 274-276, 281, 391, 395
afflictions to be destroyed 200
Ākāśhagarbha 14, 38, 172, 228
alchemist's liquid 4, 143
alertness ... iii, iv, 27, 29-31, 37, 39, 191, 203, 207, 209-215, 219, 226, 229, 273, 278, 391, 397
all will become nothing 13, 170
All-Knowing ... xiv, 15, 21, 38, 98, 128, 140, 144, 145, 149, 174, 192, 226, 227, 319, 345, 381
all-knowing one 21, 144, 192
all-knowing physicians 15, 174
Andreas Kretschmar ..... xiii, xxi
antidotes . 32, 35, 88, 173, 217, 264, 266, 269, 276, 278, 283, 313
añjali 152
arhat xvii, 97, 139, 192, 339, 342, 394
arousing the enlightenment mind
. 117, 121, 136, 142, 171, 381, 386
arousing the mind ... 17, 121, 136, 149, 178, 182, 185, 186, 386, 392

Asaṅga .... xviii, 228, 341
Atisha 133, 141, 185, 278
attribute analysis ... 101, 103, 106, 109, 111, 114, 352, 357, 362, 369, 372, 373, 377, 392
austerities 28, 166, 206, 267
authoritative statement 339
avagamana xv
Avalokiteśhvara 14, 172
avarice 229, 255, 256
Avataṃsaka 148
ayatanas 321, 327, 328, 352
bad migrations .. 17, 20, 22, 30, 36, 66, 70, 83, 85, 142, 168, 177, 188, 193, 195, 210, 211, 223, 251, 275, 286, 305, 309
bases of enlightenment mind .. 12
battlefield 25, 198
beautiful umbrellas 11, 162
beginner .. 142, 184, 224, 229, 336
beginningless samsara 23, 196
benefit sentient beings .. 10, 17, 160
bhagavat 23, 63, 143, 154, 178, 196, 270, 341, 365
bliss 3, 4, 7, 132, 133, 143, 154, 320, 379, 393, 405
boat, ship, and bridge 19, 181
bodhi . vi, vii, xv-xx, 147, 184, 393, 394

Bodhicharyāvatāra vi
bodhichitta ... vii, xv-xix, 147, 184, 393, 394
bodhisatva trainings ... 19, 37, 157, 158, 182, 184, 225
Bodhisatvacharyāvatāra .. v, 3, 129
bodhisatva's conduct .. vi, xx, 117, 125, 129, 147, 381
bodied beings ... 18, 19, 22, 45, 49, 82, 117, 121, 180, 181, 193, 244, 249, 303, 382, 386
born into the family 19, 187
Brahmā 6, 137, 138, 151, 178
brahmācharya 137, 138
buddha dharmas 158
buddha essence 138, 309
buddha family 187
buddha in the dharmakāya ... 186
buddha nature ... 56, 141, 260, 364
buddha sons .. 9, 121, 157, 386, 387
Buddha Śhākyamuni 129, 172
buddhahood for the sake of others
.... 149
buddhas gone in the three times 12
buddhas of the ten directions .. 158
bundles 131
byang chub sems . 3, 129, 393, 394, 396
calm abiding . 69, 283, 284, 290, 336
Capable One . 7, 27, 54, 64, 87, 91, 154, 204, 229, 257, 271, 311, 317, 319, 393
capable ones ... 4, 9-11, 34, 55, 84, 143, 159, 161, 162, 220, 259, 306
causal refuge 163, 164
causes and conditions 108, 112, 241, 332, 367, 373
Chandrabhasa 192
Chandrakirti ... 320, 321, 323, 337
chapter one 3, 131

Charvakas 107, 364, 365
Charyāvatāra .... v, vi, 3, 129
Chittamatrins 93, 94, 323, 324, 330, 331, 334, 335
clinging 15, 26, 59, 73, 79, 100, 103, 174, 199, 200, 263, 266, 269, 285, 287, 291, 299, 300, 334-336, 345, 351, 357, 373, 393
clothing 34, 109-111, 119, 219, 339, 369-371, 384
commitment 21, 149, 178, 180, 184, 185, 191, 194, 199, 231, 252
compassion ... 9, 11, 12, 14, 36, 43, 45, 55, 56, 62, 79, 81, 82, 85, 90, 101, 114, 119, 121, 146, 155, 159, 162, 165, 167, 172, 206, 217, 222, 224, 236, 239, 245, 259, 260, 269, 300, 301, 303, 304, 309, 315, 345, 347, 351, 352, 378, 383, 387, 393, 396
compassionate activity ... 9, 11, 12, 14, 36, 159, 162, 167, 172, 222, 393
Compendium of Abhidharma .. 194
Compendium of Trainings 38, 157, 158, 194, 222, 226, 229
complete emancipation 23, 196, 361
complete enlightenment v-viii, xv, 4, 142, 147, 149, 167, 168, 178, 396, 398
concentration ... iii, iv, vii, 31, 69, 103, 173, 182, 206, 214, 218, 232-234, 281-284, 317, 357, 391
Condensed .. 39, 158, 169, 193, 229, 231, 268, 318, 321
conducive side .. 59, 136, 194, 195, 197, 263, 303, 305
confusion .... xii, 12, 35, 103, 168, 183, 220, 354-356, 374, 393, 394, 403
conquerors and their sons . 10, 160

conquerors having the supreme of all good qualities 158
conquerors' sons ... 7, 17, 38, 141, 155, 172, 178, 227
consciousness .. 75, 93, 94, 98-100, 104-108, 147, 149, 242, 294, 331-333, 346-351, 357, 358, 360, 363, 364, 366, 367, 398, 404
contact .... ii, 18, 60, 104, 180, 181, 242, 266, 293, 356, 357, 359
craving . 24, 46, 59, 69, 97, 104, 113, 197, 246, 264, 282, 283, 285, 293, 328, 343, 359, 376
Crushing Hell ... 29, 118, 208, 382
cultivation of virtue 3, 134
cyclic existence .. 57, 92, 138, 261, 267, 285, 286, 304, 330, 334, 335, 394, 398, 401
daughter of the family ... 150, 154, 155, 193
declaration of composition ... 131, 133, 135
dedication ... iii, iv, viii, 117, 149, 163, 179, 227, 381, 388
degrading companions 168
delusion, desire, and anger . 13, 170
demi-gods ... 20, 24, 188, 197, 401
Descent into Laṅka Sutra 184
despicable acts 33, 217
dharmakāya .. 3, 133, 186, 338, 394, 397, 399
Dharmakīrti 132
dharmas with outflows 194
dharmatā 136, 186, 394
dhatus 321, 327, 328, 352
diligence .. 26, 29, 61, 63, 195, 200, 210, 267, 270
direct perception 91, 184, 325, 327
discipline .. vii, 28, 36, 85, 122, 139, 168, 173, 183, 204, 205, 210, 214, 218, 221, 223, 226, 227, 232-234, 252, 256, 281, 282, 309, 312, 317, 387, 388
distraction .. 69, 114, 122, 204, 206, 281, 282, 287, 307, 311, 377, 387, 391
divisions of enlightenment mind 142, 147
downfalls . 22, 29, 38, 174, 193, 210, 222, 223, 226-229, 387
downfalls for a bodhisatva . 22, 193
Drukpa Kagyu school xiv
drunken elephant of mind . 31, 214
dualistic mind .. 147, 379, 391, 393-395, 398, 401, 402, 405
duḥkha ... 104, 223, 240, 244, 349, 359, 405
eight extremes of elaboration . 184
eight states of non-freedom 137, 138
elaboration 184, 394
emancipation ... 17, 21, 23, 38, 42, 64, 65, 81, 173, 177, 178, 183, 192, 195, 196, 214, 228, 235, 238, 240, 271, 274, 302, 361, 382, 386, 398
empty of nature 301, 375
enemy of the afflictions ... 26, 194, 197, 199, 200
enlightened one .. xvi, xvii, xix, xx
enlightenment conduct .... vi, xx, xxii, 53, 92, 95, 256, 326, 330, 339
enlightenment hero .. xvi, xvii, xix
enlightenment mind iii, iv, vii, xii, xvi-xx, 3-5, 12, 17, 19-22, 35, 51, 54, 62, 79, 117, 118, 121, 131, 133, 136, 140-150, 152, 153, 155, 157, 171, 172, 177, 182-185, 187, 191, 193, 209, 221, 231, 233, 235, 252, 258, 269, 284, 299, 303, 309, 315, 376, 378, 381, 383, 386, 392-394, 396, 397

Enlightenment Mind Commentary 184, 376, 378
enlightenment mind's merit .. 152
Entering Enlightenment Conduct vi
Entering the Conduct ... i, iii, v, vi, xiii, xx, xxii, 1, 7, 16, 20, 26, 39, 57, 68, 90, 115, 117, 124, 127, 156, 175, 189, 201, 230, 261, 279, 316, 379, 381, 389
Entering the Conduct of a Bodhisatva .... iii, v, xx, xxii, 1, 7, 16, 20, 26, 39, 57, 68, 90, 115, 117, 124, 127, 156, 175, 189, 201, 230, 261, 279, 316, 379, 381, 389
epidemics 179
equipoise 69, 73, 90, 278, 282, 285, 290, 316, 337
Īshvara 107, 108, 238, 365-367
evil . iii-5, 7, 9, 10, 12-15, 18, 22, 23, 27, 41, 43, 44, 48, 62, 64, 65, 92, 118, 121, 122, 142, 145, 154-157, 160, 167-175, 180, 181, 193, 195-197, 204, 212, 226, 235, 236, 240, 241, 248, 249, 269, 271-273, 286, 326, 329, 367, 378, 383, 386-388, 395
evil deed 18, 175, 180, 193, 395
evil deeds .. iii, iv, 9, 10, 12, 13, 15, 23, 48, 62, 142, 157, 160, 167-175, 181, 195, 196, 226, 248, 269
evil karmas 367
exchange of self and other . 82, 304, 305
expression of worship 131
external things ... 28, 154, 206, 268
Extreme Heating Hell 60, 266
extremes of elaboration 184
faith .. 3, 18, 22, 29, 42, 48, 51, 54, 120, 134, 140, 141, 154, 156, 165, 181, 195, 210, 223, 238, 248, 252, 257, 258, 345, 383, 385
False Aspectarians 330, 334
family line 86, 136, 141, 310
famine 18, 179, 180
farmers 25, 199
fear in my heart 26, 201
feeling .. 97, 103-105, 309, 343, 356, 357, 359, 360, 375, 397
fiction 91-93, 96, 101, 105, 146-148, 185, 232, 319, 321, 323-325, 328, 330, 338, 340, 352, 353, 361, 362, 392, 396, 405
fictional . 91-93, 101, 105, 146-148, 185, 319, 321, 323-325, 328, 330, 338, 352, 353, 361, 362, 392, 396, 405
fictional arousing 146, 185
fictional side 147
fictional truth 319, 361, 396
field realms 163, 182
fine Kashika cotton cloth 160
fire of the end of time 5, 145
first bundle 131
first chapter 7, 156, 183
fishermen 25, 199
five aggregates 184, 346, 397
five external endowments 139
five paths 185
five personal endowments 139
five unsurpassed offerings 158
flowers .. 9, 11, 107, 118, 119, 139, 144, 159, 162, 163, 339, 365, 382, 383
foods of the gods 11, 162
forbearance 234
force of complete rejection ... 169
force of thorough application of the antidote 169, 172
forests 9, 72, 78, 159, 288, 298
form kāyas 186

INDEX   411

formatives 177, 244, 343, 397
former sugatas 184
formless realm 138, 284
fortitude 41, 53, 236, 238, 255, 266, 377
four great elements 182
four perversions 153
four truths of the noble ones . 340, 343
fourth chapter 26, 201
fragrances 9, 10, 159, 161
friends and foes ... 13, 15, 170, 174
frightened by an ordinary illness
.... 14, 173
fruition refuge 163, 166
fully adopting the enlightenment mind .... iii, iv, 17, 177, 233
full-ripening ... 64, 67, 81, 156, 196, 217, 271-273, 277, 302
fundamental ignorance .. xvi, 244, 343, 381, 393
garlands 10, 74, 144, 162, 292
Garuḍa 95, 274, 339
generosity . vii, 28, 36, 41, 53, 204, 205, 221, 224, 232-234, 236, 256, 318
gods and ṛishis 6, 151
going for refuge . 157, 163, 165, 171
gone for refuge to the buddha . 166, 171
gone for refuge to the dharma . 166, 167
gone for refuge to the saṅgha . 167
good human existence 19, 187
good qualities . 6, 9, 11, 35, 43, 50-52, 54, 55, 63, 79, 85-87, 128, 136, 140, 141, 147-151, 157, 158, 163, 166, 167, 171, 187, 208, 220, 221, 223, 239, 250-252, 254, 257, 258, 270, 271, 273, 282, 299, 307-313,

347, 386, 399
grasping a self ... 80, 84, 132, 200, 300, 303, 305, 307, 335, 336, 346
great being 129
great elements 182, 368
great evil deed 193
great fear .. 13, 14, 76, 83, 171, 173, 295, 305
great medicine 19, 181
Great Vehicle .. xvi, 37, 38, 96, 97, 133, 142, 149, 154, 155, 165, 192, 193, 224-226, 228, 229, 327, 335, 338, 340-342, 344, 345, 381, 394-396, 398-400
Great Vehicle saṅgha 133
greatest level of mastery of composition 129
Guardian Maitreya ... 5, 146, 147, 316, 399
guardians of migrators 14, 171
guarding alertness ... iii, iv, 27, 39, 203, 209, 213, 229
guarding the mind 29, 203, 207, 209
guru . 15, 30, 38, 128, 138, 157, 158, 174, 209, 211, 228, 235
Gyalwang Je 186
hands in añjali 152
hangings made of pearls and precious ornaments 11, 162
happiness of gods and men ... 174
heart of enlightenment 12, 164
Heart Prajñāparamita Sutra ... 184
Heaven of the Thirty-Three .. 138
heedfulness .. iii, iv, 21, 68, 88, 90, 191, 194, 279, 313, 315
heedless behaviour 195
hell beings 46, 246, 383
hell fires 23, 196
heroic type of person .... viii, xix
higher training .. 233, 234, 281, 282,

412   INDEX

holy dharma .. 9, 11, 20, 36, 48, 54, 61, 129, 139, 157, 163, 165, 166, 188, 224, 229, 249, 256, 257, 266, 317

human body .. 22, 34, 60, 136, 138, 195, 219, 266, 267

human existence .. 19, 23, 187, 196

ignorance .. xvi, 140, 178, 195, 215, 244, 330, 343, 381, 393, 396, 397, 403

Illuminator Tibetan-English Dictionary 135, 404, 420

illusion-like .. 91, 92, 94, 104, 115, 185, 323, 325, 326, 328-330, 334-336, 340, 359, 379

imagery of lightning 140

images of Vairochana 146

immeasurable palaces 11, 162

incense .. 9, 11, 118, 144, 159, 160, 162, 383

incomparable cloth 10, 160

inexhaustible treasure 20, 188

intellect .... xii, 242, 376

intelligence 19, 142, 187

intentional conduct . 183, 184, 399

interdependent origination ... 184, 329, 353, 364, 391

intermediate aeon of famine .. 18, 179, 180

iron into gold 144

island 19, 181

jewel of that holy mind 7, 155

jewel trees 9, 159

jewelled lamps 11, 162

journey to enlightenment xvii, 148

Kagyu school xiv

Kapila . 100, 104, 241, 347, 351, 359

Kāśhyapa 207

Kauśhika 211, 318

kāya ... 3, 133, 164, 185, 186, 338, 394, 397, 399

kāya for one's own sake .. 185, 186

kāya for others' sake 185

Khenpo Kunpal's commentary   xiii

killers 25, 198

Kṣhitigarbha 14, 172

lakes and ponds 9, 159

lay aside 56, 169, 259, 400

laying aside . iii, iv, 9, 142, 157, 167-169, 175, 177, 226-228, 400

laying aside evil deeds ... iii, iv, 9, 157, 226

laziness ... 32, 59, 60, 216, 263-265

leisure and endowment .. 3, 24, 78, 136, 137, 139, 197, 224, 297, 388

Lesser Vehicle 37, 96, 193, 224, 225, 227, 325, 327, 339, 345, 398, 400

levels of the conquerors' sons . 178

lifespan is ten years 179

lifespan is thirty years 179

lifespan is twenty years 179

like a field 147

like a stupa 147

like a synopsis 147

like the ground 147

living tree 5, 20, 145, 188

Lokeśhvara 10, 161

long-life god 138

Lord Gampopa xiv

lord of death 12, 20, 34, 59, 60, 115, 169, 188, 219, 264, 265, 378

Lotus ... 10, 64, 75, 107, 119, 129, 139, 162, 272, 294, 332, 364, 365, 383

loving kindness .. 35, 49, 155, 221, 249, 257, 271

Madhyamaka .... x, 321, 322, 324, 335-337, 340, 344, 353, 356, 364

Madhyamika 93-100, 107, 111,

324, 330-335, 339-341, 343, 345, 347, 348, 350, 357, 365, 372
mahāsattva 154, 161, 168
main minds 149
Mandāravā 10, 162
manifest clinging 103, 357
manifest realizations 185, 402
manifested field realms 182
many types of evil deeds . . . 13, 170
Mañjughoṣha . . 10, 11, 14, 119, 123, 161, 163, 172, 383, 388, 389
Mañjuśhrī . 128, 146, 155, 193, 234
marks of a warrior 199
master Vīra 138
masters . . . . v, viii, 12, 84, 164, 306
material gains . . 47, 48, 51, 53, 71, 86, 247, 248, 252, 255, 287, 310
meaningless conduct 211, 212
medicine . . . 9, 14, 19, 20, 123, 173, 181, 188, 224, 228, 240, 389
medicines 18, 26, 121, 159, 179, 201, 339, 387
meditative concentration . . . iii, iv, vii, 69, 103, 206, 214, 232, 234, 281-284, 317, 357
melodious praises 11, 158, 162, 163
mental events 149, 347, 399
mental mind 105, 360, 368
merit . . viii, 5, 6, 10, 13, 22, 35, 45, 49, 51, 53, 54, 59, 62, 64, 67, 92, 115, 128, 144, 149-152, 155, 157, 159, 170, 177, 193, 220, 233, 235, 244, 248, 250, 253, 255, 256, 258, 263, 269, 271, 277, 328, 329, 345, 379
meritorious . 4, 7, 51, 140, 153, 155, 252
messengers of death 13, 14, 170-172
Middle Way . . . x, xi, xiii, 184, 185, 284, 319, 322, 324, 353, 398

migrator . xxii, 20, 21, 65, 188, 192, 275, 331, 401
migrators . 4, 6, 7, 14, 17-21, 25, 26, 28, 34, 50, 51, 56, 65, 66, 79, 81, 82, 85, 86, 90, 107, 108, 117-119, 121-123, 133, 144, 147, 152, 153, 171, 178, 188, 192, 199, 201, 205, 219, 251, 252, 259, 260, 274, 276, 299, 301, 303, 304, 309, 310, 315, 349, 365, 366, 368, 381, 383, 384, 387-389, 401
mind for enlightenment . . . 19, 50, 121, 136, 231, 251, 386
mind of engagement 5, 149, 150, 152
mind of enlightenment 21, 185
Mind Only . 94, 185, 324, 330, 335, 398, 402
mind that aspires to enlightenment 5, 147, 149
mindfulness of body 353, 397
mindfulness of feeling 103, 357
mindfulness of mind 353, 360
mindfulness of phenomena . . . 361
minute fraction of the time . 4, 139
modes of karma 21, 192
mountains 9, 29, 118, 159, 208, 245, 273, 368, 382
muni . . 129, 172, 178, 211, 384, 393
Nāgārjuna . . 39, 184, 185, 229, 320, 321, 337, 341, 375, 376, 399
Nāgārjuna's ritual 184
Nālandā v
nature of compassionate activity 11, 162
necessities of life 19, 181
need to obsess over transgressions 157
Ngawang Chokyi Gyalpo 128
Ngog Lotsāwa 141
nihilism 337, 345

414   INDEX

ninth chapter . viii-xi, 115, 241, 379
nirmāṇakāya's Vajra Seat 164
nirvana . xxiii, 17-19, 37, 73, 92, 96,
   97, 105, 106, 113, 165, 177, 178,
   180-182, 192, 223, 226, 232, 236,
   238, 285, 291, 330, 334, 335, 339,
   340, 342, 343, 345, 360-362, 375,
   397, 399
no opportunity for emancipation
   196
noble one 147, 396, 401
non-affirming negation 321
non-conducive side ... 59, 194, 197,
   263, 303, 305
non-distraction 204, 206
non-existence 101, 111, 321, 353, 372
non-existent things 94, 95, 334,
   336, 337
non-freedom 137, 138
non-referencing 343, 402
non-self of phenomena ... 346, 353
obtaining a human body .. 22, 195
oceans of good qualities .. 9, 11, 54,
   157, 163, 258
of the enlightenment mind . xix, 4,
   5, 141, 143, 145, 183
offering of the body 158, 160
offering of unowned things ... 158
offering to the buddhas 6, 152
one hundred and ten spiritual friends
   146
one thousand śhlokas 130
one-pointed mind 283
one's own sake ... 6, 151, 185, 186
ordination . 53, 123, 138, 205, 222,
   256, 388, 420
Ornament of Manifested Realizations
   xviii
Ornament of Precious Emancipation
   183

Ornament of The Sutra Section . 141
ornaments   9, 11, 25, 149, 159, 162,
   199
others' sake 81, 185, 186, 302
outflow 145, 401
Padma Karpo ... i-iii, v, vi, viii, ix,
   xii, xiv, xv, 24, 125, 128, 129, 132,
   135, 138, 167, 197, 290, 323, 359,
   404, 420
Padma Karpo's Collected Works   xxi
palanquin 20, 188
paramita .. vii-ix, xxiii, 28, 36, 115,
   136, 163, 169, 183, 184, 205-207,
   210, 221, 222, 227, 231-233, 315,
   318, 338, 340, 379
path of accumulation 183
path of becoming 20, 188
path of connection 183
path of fearlessness 165
path of meditation 284, 340
path of seeing .. 146, 178, 183, 184,
   284, 340, 399
path to enlightenment ... viii, xvii,
   148, 318, 345, 379, 391, 404
patience .. iii, iv, vii, 24, 41-43, 47,
   53, 54, 57, 155, 197, 205, 231, 232,
   234-240, 243, 246, 250, 255-257,
   261, 265, 317
peace 41, 67, 95, 128, 129, 165,
   184, 193, 223, 236, 277, 320, 337,
   338, 345
perfect body support 136
perseverance .. iii, iv, vii, 59, 63, 69,
   194, 204, 206, 232-234, 263, 264,
   266, 270, 282, 317
Phagmo Drupa xiv
Plantain tree . 5, 101, 113, 145, 352,
   374
powerful vidyamantra 19, 181
praises ... 11, 50, 89, 119, 158, 162,

INDEX 415

... 163, 251, 315, 339, 383
praiseworthiness of the bodhisatva
.... 7, 153
prajna 91, 317, 401
prajñā .. iii, iv, vii, ix-xi, 21, 26, 33, 86, 91, 114, 120, 127, 169, 173, 183, 184, 192, 200, 201, 204, 206, 210, 214, 218, 231-234, 281-283, 310, 317, 318, 320, 322, 336, 338, 340, 355, 364, 376-379, 385, 401, 402
Prajñāparamita .. ix, 169, 184, 210, 231, 318, 338, 340
pratyekabuddhas 145, 341
preceptors 12, 164, 222, 256
precipice 15, 174
preta 401
priceless jewel of a conqueror's body
.... 4, 143
primal substance 109, 240-242, 347, 349, 365, 368-370
prison of samsara ... 4, 25, 143, 198
procrastination 59, 61, 263, 266, 267
profound view 185
prostration 3, 4, 143
protectors 17, 20, 28, 178, 188
pure waters 9, 159
raiments 10, 161
rain of food and drink 18, 179
realization ... xv, 97, 132, 133, 146, 150, 164, 173, 238, 320, 325, 343, 402, 403
reference ... 93, 214, 299, 315, 330, 338, 402
referencing .. viii, 97, 115, 148, 232, 316, 331, 337, 340, 342, 343, 376, 379, 402
refuge .. xii, 7, 12, 14, 133, 141, 149, 151, 155, 157, 163-167, 171-173, 402, 403
refuge of the Great Vehicle ... 149
regret .. 23, 169, 170, 196, 226, 246, 400
rejoicing 177, 226, 251
rejoicing in virtue 177
renunciation . 42, 76, 122, 238, 296, 388, 392
rising moon of mind 20, 188
ritual .. 144, 157, 177, 182, 184-187
roots of merit 144, 150, 151
roots of virtue .. 119, 136, 145, 150, 193, 234, 235, 383
Sa Og brocade 161
Sāṃkhya ... 98, 102, 108, 241, 346, 347, 354, 368, 370, 372
samādhi 164, 173, 183
Samantabhadra .... vi, 10, 14, 119, 161, 172, 384
Samantabhadra's Prayer and Commentaries vi
samsara .. xxiii, 4, 5, 12, 14, 17, 22, 23, 25, 52, 59, 62, 70, 84, 86, 94, 97, 114, 132, 137, 138, 143, 146, 148, 149, 151, 153, 156, 168, 171, 178, 184, 193, 196, 198, 217, 219, 232, 244, 254, 264, 267, 269, 271, 274, 302, 306, 311, 329, 334, 336, 345, 359, 377-379, 381, 392-394, 396, 401, 403
sandalwood .. 74, 76, 160, 292, 295
sands of the Ganges 152, 154
Sanskrit .. v, vii, ix, xi, xii, xv-xxiii, 3, 129-134, 138, 140, 181, 208, 263, 275, 276, 281, 283, 292, 323, 324, 347, 387, 391, 393, 395, 396, 398-406
Sarasvati 129
sattva .. 99, 109, 154, 161, 168, 242, 273, 347, 349, 369, 370, 393, 403
satva 274, 393, 403
Sautrantikas 323-325
second chapter 16, 175

sense faculty 103, 104, 357, 358
sentient being . 6, 17, 136, 150, 151, 154, 179, 329, 398, 400
separated from enlightenment by one life 147
servant . 10, 19, 55, 56, 66, 83, 160, 181, 194, 259, 260, 275, 306
seven limbs 177, 179
seven precious things 152
shamatha 229, 391
sick migrators 18
six paramitas . vii, viii, 36, 221, 222, 232, 233
size of the text 129
skandhas . . . 321, 327, 328, 352, 401
softened glory 128
someone having the vows 157
son of the buddhas 19, 187
son of the conquerors 7, 154
son of the family . . . 144, 147-150, 154, 155, 193, 228
source of happiness . . 50, 155, 251
source of unsatisfactoriness 15, 174
special kind of compassion . . . 155
spiritual friend 7, 38, 153, 158, 227, 228
state of enlightenment 140
state of non-freedom 137
stupidity . 23, 24, 29, 49, 71, 76, 77, 97, 101, 102, 196, 197, 210, 249, 287, 295, 296, 343, 345, 353, 355
Subāhu 5, 150, 151, 267
substantial things . . . 91, 92, 94, 95, 98, 106, 107, 109, 110, 269, 325-327, 334, 336, 337, 346, 363, 364, 369, 371
suffering of samsara 17, 59, 178, 264
suffering of sentient beings . 6, 152
sugata . . . 3, 4, 7, 19, 20, 32, 41, 64, 118, 131-134, 143, 154, 182, 184, 188, 215, 234, 272, 341, 382, 404
sugatas 7, 19, 41, 64, 118, 132, 133, 154, 182, 184, 234, 272, 382
superior fact . 91, 92, 101, 111, 146, 232, 318-321, 324, 326, 328, 330, 334, 342, 349, 352, 362, 372, 396, 404
superior seeing 69, 283, 284
supreme physician 62, 268
supreme qualities 10, 161
Sutra of Authentic Discipline . 139
Sutra of Gayagauri 191
Sutra of Golden Light 167
Sutra of Individual Emancipation 173
Sutra of the Great Nirvana 165
Sutra of the Householder Uncouth 166
Sutra of the King of Concentrations 194
Sutra of the Lamp of the Jewels . . 140
Sutra of the Miracle of Doubtless Utter Peace 193
Sutra of the Recollection of the Noble Three Jewels . . . . vi, xvi, 290, 404
Sutra of the Ten Dharmas 140
Sutra on Certain and Not Certain 155
Sutra On Creating Strength of Faith 154
Sutra Petitioned by Maitreya . . . 168
Sutra Petitioned by Matisāgara 192, 373
Sutra Petitioned by Nārāyaṇa . . 154
Sutra Petitioned by Subāhu . . 5, 150, 267
Sutra Petitioned by Śhrī Dāna . . 152
system of vast conduct 185
taking the vows . . vii, viii, 150, 183
tathāgata . . xvii, 5, 9-11, 22, 56, 61, 71, 94, 133, 137, 139, 150, 157, 160, 163, 195, 260, 267, 288, 309, 322, 335, 339

ten chapters . . . . vi, viii, 130
Tīrthika 97, 166, 174, 244, 288, 323, 342, 365, 404
the conquerors . . 7, 10, 11, 14, 17, 38, 54, 64, 90, 141, 144, 145, 154, 158, 160, 163, 171, 178, 227, 231, 257, 272, 315, 327
The Highest Continuum . . . 133, 185
The Precious Garland 140
The Sutra of Akṣhyamati 182
third-order world 10, 161
thorough application of mindfulness 353, 356, 360, 361, 368
three higher trainings . . . 173, 183, 231, 233, 234, 263, 281
Three Jewels . . vi, xvi, 12, 83, 133, 140, 141, 163-166, 169, 204, 221, 290, 305, 403, 404
three trainings 183
three vehicles 166, 398
time of death . 48, 71, 169, 170, 247, 248, 266, 287, 391, 392
topics of the bodhisatva trainings 157
transgressions of the trainings . 157
Treatise on Designation 179
True Aspectarians 330
true complete buddha . . xvii, xviii, 139, 180, 320, 339, 393-395, 398
Two Truths 105, 133, 317-320, 322, 323, 361
Śhāntideva . . . 1, iii, v-xiv, xx-xxiii, 113, 124, 127, 129, 132, 134, 140, 141, 155, 205, 213, 233, 310, 324, 343, 370, 376, 389
Śhāntipa 146, 235
Śharawa 160
Śhariputra 192
śhīla 173
śhrāvakas . . . 62, 123, 145, 149, 161, 167, 205, 222, 269, 326, 340, 341, 388
unbearable regret 23, 196
Unending Auspiciousness . . . vi, xvi, 290, 404
unfluctuating virtue 177
unfree states 136, 137
unmentionable acts 15, 175
Unremitting Torment . . 23, 24, 27, 55, 81, 83, 196, 197, 204, 259, 302, 305, 379
unsatisfactoriness . . . 6, 15, 17, 151, 165, 174, 175, 179, 402, 405
unsurpassed bliss of the sugatas . . 7, 154
unsurpassed enlightenment . xx, 61, 135, 141, 164, 182, 185, 192, 232, 267
unsurpassed happiness 21, 117, 192, 381
unsurpassed offering 163
Utpala 10, 162, 332
Utter Joy . . 118, 123, 193, 232, 235, 383, 388
Vaibhāṣhikas 324, 340
Vairochana 127, 146, 344
Vajrapāṇi 14, 172
Vajra-Like Samādhi 164
valid cognition . . 92, 325, 327, 363, 372, 405
virtuous dharmas . . . 183, 194, 210, 227, 270
vows of a bodhisatva . . viii, xx, 164
vows of enlightenment vii, 150, 183
wheel of dharma 133, 177, 178, 185
wheel-turning emperor 57, 261
White Lotus of the Holy Dharma 139
wisdom . . . 144, 185, 207, 227, 232, 233, 263, 273, 282, 319, 335, 338, 379, 381, 392, 393, 395, 396, 401,

wish-fulfilling tree 19, 181
wish-fulfilling trees . 9, 95, 117, 121, 159, 338, 382, 386, 402, 405, 406, 420
yogic activity 12, 29, 164, 207
youthful Good Wealth 146

www.ingramcontent.com/pod-product-compliance
Lightning Source LLC
Chambersburg PA
CBHW021814300426
44114CB00009BA/167